The Pubs of Ross-on-Wye & South Herefordshire

The Pubs of
Ross-on-Wye
&
South Herefordshire

by

Heather Hurley

Logaston Press

LOGASTON PRESS
Little Logaston Woonton Almeley
Herefordshire HR3 6QH

First published by Logaston Press 2001
Copyright © Heather Hurley 2001

ISBN 1 873827 52 0

Set in Times New Roman by Logaston Press
and printed in Great Britain by
Bell & Bain Ltd., Glasgow

*This book is dedicated to the memory of my father, Gregory Chilcott,
who always enjoyed a drink in a pub, inn or tavern*

Sources of Illustrations

t- top; b-bottom; m-middle; r-right; l-left

Ross Gazette:
    23, 59, 67t, 73, 81t, 98l, 104t, 110t, 172, 200, 206b, 208b

Ross Heritage Centre:
    22, 38t, 43, 45b, 49t, 52t, 60, 63b, 65t, 83, 104b, 132b, 145t, 187b

Hereford Record Office:
    33(t), 62t, 88, 116, 118b, 12r, 124, 133t, 136, 153, 154t, 158, 162, 163, 190, 199, 203b, 222t, 226b, 247t, 264, 267

Gloucester Record Office:
    40l, 62b, 102b, 107t, 173t, 178, 180, 187t, 196t

Hereford County Library:
    19, 31, 33, 48t, 50t, 51, 53, 61, 64m, 66t, 72t, 79t, 84t, 97t, 99l, 102m, 104m, 149l, 217t, 218, 223, 240, 246t, 249, 252b, 255t, 256t

Ross-on-Wye Library:
    48m, 80, 120r, 271

Hereford Times:
    46t & b, 69t, 165t, 192t

D. Coleman & D. Ruck:
    254t & m, 255m & b, 256m & b, 257, 258

Ross Town Council:
    92

Hereford City Museum:
    69l

I Wraight & M. Dyer
    181

Fred Druce:
    112, 113, 217m

Derek Foxton:
    35. 126m

Roz Lowe:
    229

Gill Barker:
    254b

Alice Hurley:
    99r, 115t

Chase Hotel:
    95

Martin Morris:
    155

John Soulsby:
    155

Paul Davies
    268

Royal Hotel:
    32l

J. Sant:
    144

P. Hughes
    32t

Contents

Acknowledgments

This is the third volume in a series on the Inns and Taverns of Herefordshire and covers Ross and the south of the county. The preparation of this volume would not have been possible without the cooperation of many people who spent time and effort in providing information and illustrations. Thanks to David Bishop, Pontrilas Inn; David Campion, brewery deeds; David Clarke, The Horn; Peggy Clay, Bell Inn; Fred Druce, Yew Tree, Vine Tree and Crown inns; John Eisel, *Hereford Journal* references; Joan Flemming-Yates, Garway inns; Tony Gardiner, Symonds Yat inns; David Gilbert, Fownhope inns; Alex Gohan, Darren Inn, Geoff Gwatkin, maps and the Lamb Inn, Jon Hurley, newspaper articles and wine knowledge; Roz Lowe, Goodrich inns; Owen Meredith, word processing; Margot Miller and Sarah Skelton, prehistory details; Owen Morgan, Half Way House; Virginia Morgan & Sheila Walshaw, Walford inns; Shirley Preece, Game Cock Inn; Doreen Ruck, Orcop inns; John Soulsby, Anchor Inn; Mark Cunningham, Alton Court Brewery; Malcolm & Jan Hall, Lough Pool Inn; and other individual publicans.

Most of the research was carried out at the Hereford Record Office, Gloucester Record Office and the Hereford and Ross libraries and my grateful thanks are due to the friendly staff who were always ready to assist. Other information was provided by the Guildhall Library, Shawcross & Co., Ross Town Council, the *Hereford Times,* and the generous facilities of the *Ross Gazette* and the Ross Market House Heritage Centre. Not forgetting the support and help from Andy Johnson and Ron Shoesmith of Logaston Press.

The sources of many of the illustrations used in this book are listed on page vi. Others are from the collections of Ron Shoesmith and the author.

Heather Hurley, August 2001

Introduction

Preparing the introduction for a book such as this is the final task following the hours of researching, investigating and writing, and the only desire is to see the finished product in print. Time has been well spent in revealing the history of roadside inns, old-established taverns, street corner public houses, country house hotels and the modest beer and cider houses.

It includes all the available information about the past and present pubs of Ross and south Herefordshire, and with the publisher's help there has been a degree of organisation to ensure that the record is as complete as possible.

Here are the stories of the people and places associated with the old coaching inns, which provided food and shelter to travellers; the ancient alehouses, where only beer and ale were served; the town taverns, where wine was also sold; and the numerous beer and cider houses that sprung up during the 19th century.

The contents of this book have been planned to describe the inns and pubs along the routes of former 18th- and 19th- century turnpike roads—roads that led from Ross in all directions like the spokes of a wheel. But it has also been necessary to wander along lanes and footpaths to search for sites of old hostelries.

The first two chapters cover the origin and development of inns, taverns and public houses, and the effects of varying legislation throughout the centuries. The importance of cider-making, brewing, malting and the expansion of the wine and spirit trade in the Ross area is covered from early times to the present day.

Pubs have been altered and changed, opened and closed, built and rebuilt through the ages, and apart from serving as important social centres, when there were few alternatives, many were used as magistrates' courts, sale rooms, doctors' surgeries, meeting places for friendly societies, and are still used as venues for auction sales, dart matches and quiz nights. In the 21st century pubs are closing at an alarming rate, so use them instead of losing them, and the traditional English pub will continue.

Heather Hurley, Hoarwithy

August 2001

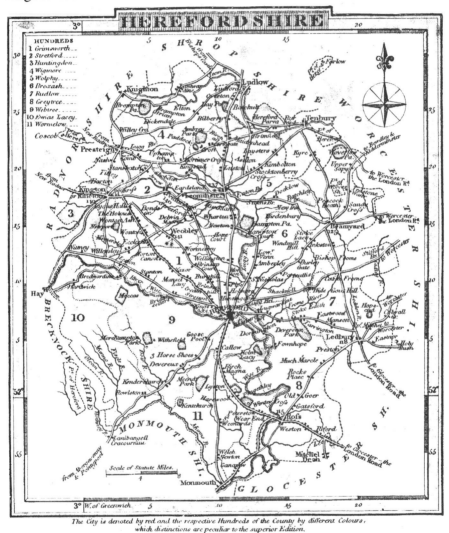

Map of Herefordshire from an 1805 Road Book used by travellers in the county some 200 years ago

CHAPTER ONE

Inns, Taverns & Beer Houses

From the earliest times there have been inns all along country roads, havens where weary travellers sought and found rest and security during the hours of darkness, as well as the food and drink they stood in need of. In the towns, however, taverns were chiefly meeting places for men of the same opinions or occupations, and the inn or tavern signs, in days when those who could read and write were in a minority, were intended to serve not merely as means of identification but also to convey some indication of the company one would be likely to find in the house.

André Simon, 1948

Ever since man realised that fermented grain, fruit and honey produced alcoholic beverages, communal drinking places were established in settlements and along the highways. In the Bronze Age mead was made from hemp and honey, and from fermented lime and honey flavoured with meadowsweet. It is thought that a strong cocktail was produced from hemp and cannabis mixed with alcohol. In the Iron Age a brew was made from emmer wheat, a type of cider produced from crab apples and wine was imported from the Roman world in amphoræ, two-handled storage jars.

At Dinedor hillfort, 2½ miles south of Hereford, the Iron Age population ate a diet of wheat and barley. Surplus grain was stored in underground pits, or above ground in granaries, and some of this would have been used to produce a type of beer doubtless drunk communally during festivals. Nearer to Ross a similar diet of food and drink was enjoyed by the Chase Hill tribe who probably controlled the land where the Roman settlement of *Ariconium* was founded, late in the 1st century A.D., as a modest administrative centre and iron-

1

working site for the 10th Legion. At this date Dioscorides, a Greek physician wrote of a drink which was 'made from barley and often drunk instead of wine, produces headaches, is a compound of bad juices, and does harm to the muscles. A similar drink may be produced from wheat, as in western Spain and in Britain'.

At *Ariconium*, in Weston-under-Penyard, and at Huntsham, in Goodrich, fragments of amphoræ were associated with olive oil and not wine. At Huntsham villa there is evidence from an archaeological excavation, carried out between 1959 and 1970, to suggest that a brewery operated in an aisled barn, where beer, improved with wild hops, may have become a popular drink. Huntsham was a site associated with agriculture, with the produce probably transported along the river Wye. It was unlike the Roman temple at Lydney in the Forest of Dean, where a *mansio*, a guesthouse, was constructed in the 4th-century temple complex dedicated to Nodens. The guesthouse consisted of a large multi-storeyed building set around a courtyard, where pilgrims visiting the temple could stay and drink locally produced alcoholic cordials.

When the Romans arrived in Herefordshire they discovered a region criss-crossed by ancient paths and tracks, but by 100 A.D. they had developed their own road system, which still forms the basic pattern of our present layout, although many roads fell into disuse after the Roman departure. A glance at an Ordnance Survey map indicates the main Roman centres by the direct course of the roads that converge on *Ariconium* and Roman settlements at Monmouth, Gloucester, Kenchester and Newent. Along these routes the predecessors of the inns were established for the benefit of travellers and traders.

The break-up of the Roman Empire in England took place following the withdrawal of the Roman troops, shortly after 410 A.D., and the country descended into the Dark Ages. Although some towns doubtless kept going for a short while, it was to be several hundred years before there were any recognisable new settlements in Herefordshire. The earliest ones recorded are religious establishments such as St. Guthlac's, which was founded on the area now known as Castle Green in Hereford, and the minster at Leominster, founded by King Merewalh of the Magonsæte about 660. Shortly afterwards, the foundation of the Hereford diocese would have encouraged the building of simple churches and the gradual provision of permanent settlements of more than a few houses. Once a cathedral had been built in Hereford on the gravel terrace overlooking the ford across the river, a small settlement would have developed outside the religious precinct. The city's first inns, little more than simple drinking houses, probably date to this period. Indeed, as early as 750, the then Archbishop of York issued a Canon 'That no priest go to eat or drink in taverns', and there were so many inns by the time of King Edgar (959-75) that he issued a decree limiting their number to one per village.

It is not known exactly when Ross became a settlement, though it had obtained the status of a village by the time of the Domesday Survey in 1086. Since there is no reference to Ross, or any settlement there, during the Roman occupation, it is reasonable to assume that the area either around St. Mary's church or further down at Brookend began being settled at some point during the Saxon period. The lack of any major archaeological data concerning the town means it is impossible to say which part of the town was settled first. As the Domesday entry mentions a priest, it may be that the area around the present church was first chosen, though there is no evidence of a church of this date on the site of St. Mary's. This site would have been naturally defensible in a period threatened by Danish and Viking raids, though, again, no evidence has been found for any defences on the sides not protected by the bluff.

When Archbishop Baldwin and Gerald of Wales made their journey through the Welsh borders in 1188 the 'single meal of the day' was served 'with unhopped ale or cider'. When Bishop Swinfield visited his Ross palace in 1289 he was lavishly entertained with 'wine and beer in abundance'. For the townspeople a chantry connected with the fraternity of St. Thomas the Martyr ran a hospice in Ross, and in Hereford, Adam Seys had granted to the monks of Dore 'a piece of land in Hereford that they may have a hostel there'.

During the 13th century there was a gradual increase in the sale of wine, and a separation came into being between 'taverns', which sold both ale and wine, and 'alehouses' which sold only ale. In addition to these there were the wayside inns or 'hostels' that provided accommodation for travellers as well as food and drink. At that time,

Ross, with a population of around 500, supported a brewer and several taverns which blossomed into inns in the following century. According to Duncumb, during the reign of Henry VI:

> It would seem that complaints of the irregularities of inn-keepers, tavern-keepers, and others, had become sufficiently numerous that Bishop Spofford considered it necessary, in A.D. 1441, to appoint John Abrahall, steward of his treasury; Uriah Delahay, bailiff of the liberties of the cathedral; Richard Wystaston, receiver-general of the diocese; John Dewsall, John Wellington and Hugh Carew, commissioners to inquire as to the sale of bread and ale, the use of proper weights and measures, and other regulations in force within the manor of Ross, and to punish all bakers, brewers, tavern-keepers, victuallers, regraters, forestallers, and other offenders who were found acting illegally in their several vocations.

It was during the 14th and 15th centuries that the influence of the church started to wane and merchants began to travel. Wayside inns and alehouses became features of the countryside in villages, at crossroads and beside ferry crossings. A.E. Richardson in *The Old Inns of England* came to the conclusion that:

> The accommodation would be rough and limited, often consisting of no more than a common dormitory. The buildings were generally infested, rats and mice ran wild among the rushes of the floor, and the bedding, in which the travellers slept naked in the fashion of the time, was as likely as not verminous, as indeed it often continued to be in the smaller out-of-the-way inns until after Pepys' day. Ale was the national beverage, and this was universally provided at meals, and could be obtained at roadside houses which displayed the sign of an evergreen bush attached to a projecting pole.

An evergreen bush indicating an inn, from a 14th-century manuscript

In the towns a higher standard was expected, as described by Geoffrey Chaucer in *The Canterbury Tales*:

> The chambres and the stables weren wyde
> And wel we weren lodged at the beste.

Although there had been previous attempts at curtailing the number of drinking houses, the first formal licensing law came at the end of the 15th century. It empowered Justices of the Peace to obtain sureties for good behaviour from the landlords and, if necessary, to close alehouses. Some 50 years later the Justices obtained the power, which they still retain, to both licence and suppress alehouses—hence 'licensed premises'.

Legislation continued and 1553 saw an Act of Parliament that curtailed the number of 'taverns', and thus limited the sale of wine. Indeed, the Act also prohibited the sale of French wines. The limits on taverns provide an indication of the size and importance of the towns at that time—London was allowed 40; York, nine; and Bristol, six. Hereford was limited to three, the same as Lincoln, Worcester, Southampton and Oxford. This did not mean that the population of the country was being deprived of places in which to drink—there were approximately 44 alehouses for every tavern in the latter part of the 16th century! This was equivalent to more than one drinking establishment for every 200 persons, a far higher ratio than exists today. These early alehouses were probably little different to the timber-framed and thatched houses that surrounded them. The larger ones would have had sheds at the rear where brewing was carried out and possibly cellars in which to protect their brew from temperature variations.

Taverns, being of a higher status, were probably of a superior construction. This may well be the reason why the more important towns and cities in the country tend to be well-endowed with substantial stone cellars of a late medieval date. They were obviously designed for public use and usually had well-constructed vaulted roofs and entries leading directly from the streets.

By Elizabethan times, Ross had emerged as a busy market town, with four quarterly fairs, on a 'very great thoroughfare' leading from Hereford, Monmouth, Brecon and South Wales to London and other parts of England. During this settled time the 'inn first enters its great days' in town and country, and as A.E. Richardson wrote:

5

The inn now began to fulfil a definite function in social life, half public and half domestic; and the passage of the century witnessed an astonishing increase in its numbers. This may have been partly due to the suppression of the monasteries and consequent disappearance of their guest-houses, but there is no doubt that the new type of hostelry throve chiefly because it accorded so perfectly with the changing social system. In 1577 an Order in Council was made for a return of the exact number of inns, alehouses and taverns throughout England, with a view to levying a tax on them towards the cost of repairing Dover Harbour. From this we learn that in Norfolk (a teeming wool county) there were 480 houses, while in Staffordshire only 105. In the thinly populated eastern and middle marches of the Scottish Borders there were 238, while in Middlesex there were no less than 876, made up of 132 inns, 24 taverns and 720 alehouses.

During the greater part of Elizabeth's reign, wine was abundant and inexpensive. When a pullet cost 2s., a quart of wine sold from the cask was purchased for 4d. There are numerous references to wines in Shakespeare's works, such as 'A man cannot make him laugh;—but that's no marvel; he drinks no wine' *(Henry 1V Part 2)*. The brewers were busy producing two sorts of beer the 'double' selling at 4s. a barrel and 'the other sort of beare of the best kynde at 7s. 6d'.

Although there is little or no documentation of inns in Herefordshire during the 16th century, it is probable that some of the still so named New Inns were established at that date due to 'Elizabeth's complaints about the lack of suitable places to stay'. Some centuries later it became fashionable to change the commonplace New Inn name, but the ones at Ross, Goodrich and Walford could have commenced trading during her reign. The existing **New Inn** in Hentland replaced the 'New Inne at Crosse Owen' of 1540.

Various attempts were made during the Civil War to levy duty on both the manufacture and the sale of beer and ale—attempts which were consolidated following that war and still apply to this day. This was when beer was brewed in three different qualities: strong, table, and small, and each variety attracted a different rate of duty. It was not until the late 19th century that the duty levied became based on the original gravity of the beer. The specific gravity (density) of the liquor before fermentation gives an indication of the amount of sugars present and therefore the likely alcoholic content of the final brew. Prior to the

6

use of a hydrometer other methods were used to judge the strength of the beer, one of which was for the examining officer to don a pair of leather breeches, pour some of the beer to be tested upon a stone step and then to sit on it. If, at the end of a specified time, he found that he was stuck to the step, then the beer was deemed to be strong!

After the turmoil of the Civil War a revolution in road travel began, so town and wayside inns played a more important role, as Richardson describes:

> The large houses flourished on the influx of new custom and on their new-found importance as stages in a regular coaching system; and the amenities they offered must have been a substantial comfort to the shaken passenger deposited there after an arduous day's journeying. From the mass of contemporary evidence available, it would seem that landlords were now genuinely eager to do their best for travellers. The rooms were well furnished at the larger inns, which catered for regular as well as chance custom, the supply of food and drink was generous, the stables were roomy, and the ostlers, waiters and serving-maids generally civil and obliging.

By the late 17th century there were already a number of well established inns in Ross, and others along the roads to Hereford, Gloucester, Ledbury, Monmouth and Abergavenny. Inns displaying a Crown sign often indicated an establishment dating from the Restoration. As such signs showed loyalty to the reigning monarch they disappeared during Cromwell's period of power, but were later revived.

Inn signs had developed from the Middle Ages when the tavern, inn or alehouse needed to identify themselves in a visual manner to a population which was mainly illiterate. The earlier signs chosen usually represented an association with a religious house, a local family, a trade, a place, or a traditional story, but became more varied.

At the turn of the 18th century even more pack horses, cumbersome wagons, traders' carts, carriages, and droves of livestock, were using the badly neglected and narrow roads of Herefordshire. It is not surprising that the method adopted to cope with this problem was the setting up of Turnpike Trusts. The system was established in 1663 to improve the New Great North Road in the counties of Cambridge, Hertford and Huntington, but it was not till the 1750s that it had spread throughout the country.

With an increase in travel and transport along the mail and coach routes, modest ale-houses blossomed into larger coaching inns and post-houses, offering rest and refreshment to the weary traveller. The stable yard presented a busy scene, with impatient horses waiting to be changed and harnessed. These facilities were available at inns at Ross, Monmouth, Ledbury, Hereford and Gloucester as well as at smaller establishments in the countryside.

However, in 1781 the Hon. John Byng was not impressed with the Beaufort Arms at Monmouth, 'I arriv'd here this evening, rather tired, and am now sitting in a mean room at this bad inn; which may be the best here. The stables are new and good, that's a comfort; for if my horse does not fare and sleep well, well there wou'd be an end of my travel'.

Arriving at Gloucester on an 'intolerable bad' road, Byng wrote 'the first person met in Picadilly cou'd tell more of the country, than I cou'd learn in the Bell Inn'. However he was delighted with the road back to Monmouth 'mounted upon such a clever horse, that if at the end of 40 miles, I do but shake my whip, or close my legs, he instantly curvets from playfullness, distaining to trip on any stone' and he found the landlord 'tolerably intelligent'. In Ross he 'put up at the Swan and Falcon' and dined on 'salmon every day'. At Ledbury in 1787 he dined 'in haste, on some tough mutton chops; a sad inn; and well that I had not made it my night stop'.

Typical 'Rules of this Tavern' such as the following probably date from the 18th century:

> Four pence a night for Bed, Six pence with Supper,
> No more than five to sleep in one bed,
> No boots to be worn in bed,
> Organ Grinders to sleep in the Wash house,
> No dogs allowed upstairs,
> No Beer allowed in the kitchen,
> No Razor Grinders or Tinkers taken in.

A vivid impression of 18th-century travellers arriving at an inn is supplied by Richardson:

The tired traveller arriving at one of the large solid inns of the later eighteenth century would generally have been justified in expecting the highest degree of 'comfort and elegance'. If the coach was timed to stop for half an hour to change horses and enable the passengers to dine, the waiters would be standing at the door in readiness to assist him with his hat, shawl and coat. The landlord and landlady would be waiting in the hall, where there would be a good display of cold meats, game pies, cheeses and pastries on view in a special glazed cupboard. The coffee-room or dining parlour would reveal an immense central table, round or rectangular, laid in readiness for the meal, with good plated cutlery and spotless table-linen. Some inns could boast a special dining-room for coach passengers, while the upstairs bedrooms, each with its curtained four-poster and good plain furniture, often of mahogany, including a mirror, a washing-table and a wig-stand, were still generally known by individual names such as the Moon, Star, Crescent or Paragon.

Although there was a duty on beer, spirits were exempt and towards the end of the 17th century, and well into the 18th, there was what Monckton, in his *History of the English Public House*, described as 'one of the biggest orgies of over-indulgence our island history has ever seen'. Every small alehouse in the country was in a position to sell cheap brandy and, in particular, gin. The result was that consumption of spirits, sold in taverns, inns, alehouses, brandy shops, dram shops, and by street hawkers, increased from half-a-million gallons in 1684 to over eight million gallons in 1743—an increase of well over one gallon per person per year! This was the 'Gin Era' a period of drunkenness, misery and wretchedness so well depicted by Hogarth. The various 'Gin Acts' that followed, together with increased duties and a strengthening of the powers of the Justices, rapidly changed this trend. But it was not until 1751 that the sale of spirits was successfully brought under the control of the Justices with licences issued to those already possessing an alehouse licence, and by 1758 excise duty was paid on less than two million gallons per year.

From the end of the 18th century and into the early years of the next, came the great coaching era. Apart from the traditional stage-coachmen, fashionable men drove their own lavish vehicles, drawn by quality horses. A breakfast was often served to private parties in a separate parlour of the inn, such as that taken by Lord Nelson and his companions at the **Swan and Falcon** at Ross in 1802. When William Cobbett rode through Ross in 1821, he would have mixed with the locals when he stopped at the **King's Head** for refreshments. He found

16  **99**

Whereas by the Laws and Statutes of This Realm

NOTICE

IS HEREBY GIVEN TO ALL

INN KEEPERS, ALEHOUSE KEEPERS, SUTLERS, VICTUALLERS

and other Retailers of

ALE and BEER

AND EVERY OTHER PERSON or PERSONS KEEPING A PUBLIC HOUSE
IN ANY
CITY, TOWN CORPORATE, BOROUGH, MARKET TOWN, VILLAGE, HAMLET, PARISH,
PART or PLACE IN THE *Kingdom of England*

That, as from the **24**th *day of* **JUNE. 1700**

THEY SHALL BE REQUIRED TO RETAIL and SELL THEIR ALE & BEER

by the **FULL ALE QUART** or **PINT**

According to the Laid Standard

IN VESSELS DULY MARKED *with* **W.R** *and* **CROWN**

be they made of

WOOD. GLASS, HORN. LEATHER or **PEWTER** etc.

Any Person Retailing Ale or Beer to a **TRAVELLER** or **WAYFARER** *in Vessels not
signed and marked as aforesaid will be liable to a* **PENALTY** *not exceeding*

FORTY SHILLINGS

FOR EVERY SUCH OFFENCE

By Act of Parliament ~ at WESTMINSTER
In the Reign of Our Sovereign ~ WILLIAM III by the Grace of God, King,
Defender of the Faith &c

Ross 'an old fashioned town' with a 'very dull' market, and found it contemptible, in a 'country of cider and perry', that 'the owners and cultivators of the soil, not content with these, shall for mere fashion's sake, waste their substance on wine and spirits'.

A few years later the *Ross Guide* recorded:

> The principal Inns in Ross are - the Swan, which keeps Post Chaises, and Horses for hire, and from which the London and South-Wales Coaches set out. The King's Head, at which Post Chaises and Horses are also let out. The George, at which is held the Excise Office. Parties making the excursion down the Wye, may be provided with pleasure boats at each of the above-mentioned houses; cold collation, the best wines, and every other necessary refreshment for the voyage. Besides the above, there are many Inns in Ross, where travellers are civilly and satisfactorily treated.

Ross had now become a popular tourist centre with inns and hotels offering 'well aired beds', 'superior post horses', 'Pleasure Boats', 'homebrewed beers', 'excellent stabling' and an 'Omnibus to meet every train'. By 1876, 34 hotels, inns and taverns were listed in the town including the **Castle Inn**, the **Pheasant**, and the **Nag's Head** which were later taken over by the Stroud Brewery Company. The **Crown and Sceptre**, the **Plough**, the **Barrel** and the **King's Head** are the only inns that have survived from the 17th- and 18th-centuries without altering their names.

By the mid-19th century the Friendly Societies were well established in Ross and in many South Herefordshire villages including Fownhope, Hoarwithy, Llangarron, Goodrich and Much Marcle. All meetings were held in pubs except the Linton Provident Friendly Society which 'Contrary to custom, the rule appears that meetings were not to be held at a public house, but were to take place in a room hired for that purpose, or in one lent at a private residence; no liquor was to be drunk'.

Friendly Societies date from 1778, when they were founded to provide a payment in sickness, injury, or old age, to members who paid a regular subscription. In Ross, during the 1850s, the Ross Friendly Society held their meetings at the **New Inn** before moving to the National School in the churchyard. The Loyal Man of Ross Lodge also met at the **New Inn**, and the John Kyrle or Man of Ross Lodge at the

Nag's Head. At a later date the **Barrel Inn** Friendly Society was formed and probably held their meetings in the large decorated room above the pub.

Another occurrence during the 19th century was the rise of the Temperance Movement to encourage less drunkenness, due to the fact that many criminal offences were found to be drink related. The movement started in England around 1820, from American influences. In 1831 the British and Foreign Temperance Society was formed, and the church took up the cause in 1862. In 1868 'A Grand Temperance Fête and Monster Meeting' was held on the banks of the Wye in Hereford, and in 1880 a 'Temperance Gathering at Fownhope' was reported as 'a fête which was a great success'.

By 1891 there were two temperance hotels at Symonds Yat, and the Harp Temperance Hotel at Hoarwithy. The 1902 licensee of the Ross **New Inn** obviously took the pledge as, by 1914, he had opened the **Gwalia Temperance Hotel**. From this date the temperance movement lost impetus and influence, due to the First World War, but was reactivated in the 1920s, when the subject occupied many pages in the *Hereford Times*, including an account of a meeting held by the British Woman's Temperance Movement and addressed by the Rev. Bannister.

The Temperance Movement had little or no effect on the number of licences renewed and granted. At Harewood End, in 1870, a special sessions was held for renewing alehouse licences and granting certificates to keepers of beerhouses. Eleven beerhouse certificates were granted, and 28 licences were renewed, in one day.

Apart from earlier attempts to regulate the marking of drinking vessels to show the capacity, it was during the 19th century that most of the legislation that affects the present-day consumption and sale of alcoholic drink was enacted. The Alehouse Act of 1828 meant that the licensee no longer had to find sureties for his behaviour. However, he was bound to use the legal, stamped measures, not to adulterate his drinks, and not to permit drunkenness on his premises. The Beerhouse Acts of 1830, 1834 and 1840 followed—the first allowed premises to open for the sale of beer, but not spirits, on payment of a simple excise licence; the second differentiated between 'on' and 'off' licences and made 'on' licences more difficult to obtain; whilst the third ensured

*The one-time Gwalia Temperance Hotel now presents
an interesting façade in Ross-on-Wye*

that licences were issued only to the occupier of the premises. Throughout the country as a whole there was a proliferation of beer-houses following the first Act, many in the country areas.

At that time there were few restrictions on licensing hours. As a whole, the only non-permitted hours were during Divine Services on Sundays, Christmas Day and Good Friday. Beer houses could only open between 4 a.m. and 10 p.m. The 1872 Licensing Act tidied up and tightened the complex legislation, but at the beginning of the 20th century public houses were, in general, still allowed to open for some 20 hours each day.

When the railways rapidly took over from coach travel, many coaching inns closed due to lack of business, but changes in licensing laws led to the opening of small town and village beer houses, which often doubled up as other trades or businesses, such as a shop, forge or post office.

Towards the end of the 19th century and in the early years of the following one, considerable efforts were made to close down inns and public houses by refusing to renew licences, even though this resulted in the payment of compensation to the owners and landlords. This was more common in the towns than in the countryside and in Hereford, by 1919, the Compensation Authority had approved the closure of no less than 35 public houses at a cost of some £16,000.

After the Second World War there were several minor Acts, which culminated in the 1961 Act that provided for 'restaurant' and 'residential' licences. It also gave the customers' grace—the ten minutes of 'drinking-up time'. A late 20th century Act restored the situation to more or less what it was at the beginning of the century by allowing inns to stay open throughout the day if they so wished, most commonly any times between 11 a.m. and 11 p.m., with a somewhat shorter 'window of opportunity' on Sundays. A new millennium has brought new thought and it is most probable that restrictions upon public houses will be further reduced leading to the possibility of 24-hour opening once again.

If these latest proposals become law, the *Daily Telegraph* reports that 'we are unlikely to see a nationwide outburst of drinking at dawn. But, cautiously, we can raise a glass to the aim of treating people as responsible adults capable of making their own decisions about when to drink'.

> When you have lost your inns drown your empty selves,
> For you will have lost the last of England.
>
> Hilaire Belloc

CHAPTER TWO

Brewers, Cider Makers & Wine Merchants

In 1607 Camden noted that 'Ross maintains its reputation for iron works and drives a considerable trade in cyder and wool' and in 1682 Thomas Baskerville wrote that at:

> Hom-lacy, where my honoured uncle, the Lord Scudamore, now defunct, did live, a person to which the whole country is obliged for his worth, he being the man that brought the now so much famed redstreak cyder to perfection, called by the Prince of Florence or Tuscany, when he came to see Oxford, and had drunk of it, vin de Scudamore.

By improving the quality of cider, Lord Scudamore made it a fashionable drink in demand in the cities of London, Oxford and Bristol. From the 17th century, considerable literature began to appear on the subject of cider, including the following taken from *Cider*, issued by the National Association of Cider Makers in 1980:

> *Sylva* by John Evelyn for the Royal Society in 1664
> *Vinetum Britannicum* by John Worlidge in 1676
> *The most Easie Method of Making the Best Cyder* by John
>   Worlidge in 1687
> *Cider, A Poem* by John Philips in 1708

Cider became accepted by people in all walks of life, and was even sent to the tables of the gentry. They, however, scorned the traditional two-handled pottery mug and drank from ornately engraved cider glasses.

Cider was also renowned for its medicinal powers. In 1664, John Evelyn wrote 'Generally all strong and pleasant cider excites and cleanses the Stomach, strengthens Digestion, and infallibly frees the Kidnies and Bladder from breeding the Gravel Stone'. Remarkable properties indeed!

Defoe wrote in 1726 'so very good, so fine and so cheap ... great quantities of this cider are sent to London, even by lane carriage tho' so very remote, which is an evidence of the goodness of it beyond contradiction'.

Captain James Cook also carried cider on his ships, as a scurvy preventive, during his second voyage of exploration from New Zealand to Tahiti. By 1800, cider was considered to be a 'cure for a wide range of ills, including vomiting, gout, ailments of the urinary tract and rheumatic diseases, and to be an effective and cleansing surgical dressing'.

Until relatively recently cider was made on almost every farm in Herefordshire. It was sometimes produced as a cash crop, but was usually made to be used by the farmer's family and labourers. Cider is made from bitter-sweet apples, which are richer in sugar but rather unpleasant to the taste as they contain a lot of tannin. After crushing the apples and pressing to extract the juice, farm cider was produced without the addition of cultured yeast, fermentation relying upon the natural yeasts in the apples to produce a still, cloudy, acidic, invigorating and thirst-quenching drink. This was much appreciated during the heat of the next summer when the farmer would provide bread, cheese, and cider for those helping with the hay-making, a practice that continued into the 20th century. These delights of making hay, along with others, are described by Laurie Lee in his best-selling book *Cider with Rosie*.

During the late 18th century cider was still being produced in the traditional method on farms and private estates. Advertisements in the *Hereford Journal* show the importance of this trade, with 'Four Hogshead of Cyder' to be sold at the Meend in 1787; 'Small Pony Bay Horse about 12hh. with hair rubbed off his side by the cord from Cyder-making' in 1789; and 'A ten-foot cider mill and runner, little worse than new, with the Apparatus complete' for sale at Lugwardine in 1801. In Hereford, James and Smyth were selling 'Twenty

Hogsheads of Cider of superior quality, some of which is exceedingly fine and rich, and fit for Bottling' in 1836, and, two years later, a dwelling house at Mordiford was for sale along with 'Cider House with Mill, Two Gardens, Fold and Two Orchards well stocked with choice Fruit Trees'.

From the late 19th century, cider started to be produced commercially by several Herefordshire companies. H.P. Bulmer & Co., W. Evans & Co., and H. Godwin & Son were established in Hereford. In South Herefordshire, there was H. Weston & Sons at Much Marcle, the Golden Valley Cider Works at Pontrilas, and Thomas A. Powell at Upton Court in Upton Bishop, but no commercial cider works were established in Ross. More recently, there has been a revival in traditional cider making at Broome Farm, Peterstow, and at Lyne Down Farm in Much Marcle.

Despite its earlier reputation for cider drinking, Ross had developed a taste for beer by the 18th century. The 1811 *Book of Trades* states:

THE BREWER

The art of brewing is of very high antiquity, but in no country has it been carried to greater perfection than in our own. The different counties are, many of them, celebrated for their peculiar ales, and London porter is famous in almost all parts of the civilized world. Different as these several sorts of liquor are, they are nevertheless composed of the same materials variously prepared.

Malt liquor, in general, is composed of water, malt, hops, and a little yeast: and the great art is to find out the proper proportions of each ingredients, to what degree of heat the water must be raised before it is poured on the malt and how best to work it afterwards.

There are two kinds of malt, distinguished by the colour; these are called brown and pale malt, and they depend on the degree of heat that is used in drying. The malt which is dried by a very gentle heat differs in its colour but little from the barley; but if exposed to a higher temperature, it acquires a deeper hue, till at length it becomes of a dark brown.

When the malt is made, it must be coarsely ground in a mill, or, what seems to be still better, bruised between rollers; it is then fit for the brewer, in whose hands the process of making beer is completed.

At this time, in large city breweries, the process of mashing no longer used human labour—the machinery was kept moving by means of steam engines, but the method used in the small brew houses in Herefordshire would doubtless have been as follows:

Boil twelve gallons of water, put it into a tub with about two gallons of cold water, let it stand until the steam is sufficiently off to reflect your face with ease to yourself: put in the malt, stir it well up, and let it stand three hours. This will produce about seven gallons: after this, mash again with about twelve gallons of water more, and let it stand about two hours, stirring it well, and frequently, boil the first gently in the mean time, after being run off from the grains for nearly three quarters of an hour with three quarters of a pound of hops, strain it, boil the other in the same manner: mix it with the first, let it now stand till it is about blood warm or as warm as new milk then put in a quarter of a pint of yeast, work the whole if possible in one vessel let it stand till next afternoon, then run it in perfectly clean barrels: it ought to work after tunning, a week or ten days: in a few weeks it will be fit for use.

In the late 18th century, Ross had, for its size, numerous brewhouses and malthouses, including Mrs. Bellamy's 'Malt-house, Stable, Ware-house' together with a 'Cider-mill and Cider-vaults'; Thomas Hardwick's malt houses, barley lofts and brew house, probably situated near the river Wye in Dock Pitch (Wye Street); and William Llewellyn's business as a maltster and dealer in spiritous liquors. William Gammon, a currier, was also a maltster in the town, and in the Brookend there was a brewhouse, and a malthouse that by 1813 was 'not used as such' by Thomas Jones.

The *Book of Trades* continues:

Malt is used also for distilling spirituous liquors. For this purpose it is ground, and the wort taken as in common breweries: this is fermented, and then it is called wash, which is put into a still about three parts full. A brisk fire is made under it till the wash is nearly boiling, when the head of the still is fixed on and luted to the worm in the worm-tub. The fire is allowed to decrease till the spirit begins to run. The first produce is called low wine, which is distilled a second time, and then it is pure malt spirit.

Compound distillers mix with malt spirits, juniper-berries, aniseeds, &c. and distil the whole over again, the produce of which is gin, spirit of aniseed, &c. which, though useful in certain medical cases, never fail to injure and debilitate the constitution when drunk as a common beverage.

Distillers obtain a great quantity of spirit from sugar, treacle, and molasses, in the same way as they do from malt; to these they are always obliged to have recourse in those years in which there has been a scanty crop of corn. The revenue of the state is greatly enriched by distilleries, but the morals and health of the people are unquestionably injured by them.

Rum is distilled from sugar, and the sugar cane, in the West Indies; that sold in Europe is generally very much cooper'd, that is, adulterated, before it comes into the consumer's possession. Brandy is extracted from wine by distillation. French brandy is esteemed the best, on account of the superior quality of the wines made in France. The brandy made in Cogniac, Bourdeaux, and Rochelle, bears the highest price. Brandy distilled a second time is called spirit of wine; and this, after another rectification, is called pure alcohol, or rectified spirits.

Brandy in its pure state is colourless, and it obtains its yellow tint by extracting the colouring matter from the new casks in which it is kept. But if it should not have acquired the usual tinge in this way, it is coloured artificially, to give it the appearance of having been kept some time; it also undergoes as much coopering as rum, if not more, as its increased price is a greater temptation.

Before the turn of the 18th century, the long established Brookend Tanyard, run by the Freres, was also malting and brewing beer on a larger scale. Outside Ross, a brewhouse and hopkiln is recorded at Much Birch, and an extensive brewery at Fownhope was operated by Nathanial Purchas & Co. who also sold 'neat French Brandy, Jamaica Rum and other Spiritous Liquors'. It was in 1799 that G. Lipscomb went from Hereford to Fownhope and wrote in his *Journey into South Wales:*

Brandy, Rum, &c.

TO be fold Wholefale, at the Brew-Houfe, at Fownhope, near Hereford, neat French Brandy, Jamaica Rum, and other Spirituous Liquors, by
NATHANIEL PURCHAS and Co.

MAY 11, 1771.

N. B. A Labouring-Man, and his Wife, of good Character, not too far advanced in Years, without any Children; efpecially fuch as are not gone out, or are able to go to fervice. The Man to have fome little Tafte for Gardening; and the Woman a good fpinner of Flax, may hear of a comfortable Being gratis, and conftant Employ for the Man, by applying to Mr. Whittlefey, at Fownhope, near Hereford.

Nathaniel Purchas was a little parsimonious with his 1771 advertisement for staff, using it as a means of selling his wares

We arrived at Mr. Purchas's brewery, the spot to which we had been directed. It is built on the east side of the Wye, and sheltered by a wall rock which rises boldly behind it.

Mr. Purchas has cut steps up the hill, planted it with juniper bushes, and other shrubs, thrown a screen of firs along a field on the right, and built a castellated prospect house on the brow of the steep. Our request to be permitted to examine this agreeable place was readily granted; and the proprietor himself conducted us through every part of the premises.

From the summit is a most interesting view of a rich and highly cultivated country.

By 1827 Thomas Purchas had already opened his wine and spirit merchants in Ross, at the former **Black Lion** in Broad Street, but from the following advertisement in the *Hereford Journal*, he obviously kept a business interest in the Fownhope concern with Messrs. Reynolds:

Messrs. Reynolds, Purchas, and Reynolds, beg to inform the Public, that they are now-prepared to supply strong BEER, PORTER, (fully equal to London), and TABLE BEER, in any quantities, and of such qualities as they trust upon trial, will ensure them a large portion of the trade in the County and City of Hereford, and the neighbouring districts.

Reynolds, Purchas, and Reynolds, further beg to inform the Public, that their Vaults and Cellars are now largely stocked with WINES and SPIRITS of the most superior qualities that the London markets could supply, or ready cash procure; and in inviting the public attention to their Establishment Reynolds, Purchas, and Reynolds, beg to state, that they take their ground in the different branches of their concern principally upon the superior qualities of their articles; and to guard as such as in their power against any other Wines being substituted for theirs, every bottle delivered from their Premises will be sealed on the cork: 'Reynolds, Purchas, and Reynolds Fownhope'.

Messrs. Reynolds, Purchas, and Reynolds, cannot conclude this announcement with out expressing their warmest acknowledgements for the promises of patronage and support (far beyond their most sanguine expectations) which they have already received. They confidently hope that the system upon which they propose to conduct their business will fully show to be worthy of the continuance of this patronage, and of the strong interest in flavour of the Fownhope Concern which is already excited.

All articles ordered from them will be delivered at Hereford, Ross, and Ledbury, free of expense.

From a modest start in Ross—Purchas originally only occupied part of the premises in Broad Street—he soon acquired the whole building, and was probably responsible for the rebuilding, which now houses the **King Charles II**, above the old cellars. T.W. Purchas & Sons traded for well over 100 years in Ross, selling wines, spirits, ales, stout and mineral water to appreciative customers. After the First World War, the business was taken over by Charles Edwards Ltd., from Worcestershire, and in 1921 they were selling half-pints of Old Cognac Brandy for 6s., Irish and Scotch Whiskey for 5s., Finest London Gin for 4s. 7d., Superior Golden Sherry and Old Port for 1s. 11d., and British Fruit Wines for 10¹/₂d. Charles Edwards continued there, but in the late 1930s opened the **King Charles Bar**, which became the **King Charles II**.

The earliest known vintner in Ross was John Farne, an innkeeper probably at the **Saracen's Head** in the Market Place. Until his death, in 1658, he was dealing in rum, brandy and wine. In the early years of the 18th century there was a wine merchant recorded at Fownhope by the name of William Phillips, the vicar's son, who married Anne Gwatkin. From the late 18th century there was a marked increase of wine and spirit merchants in Ross, with four listed in 1822 including T.W. Purchas. It was due to the Alehouse Act of 1828 and the Beerhouse Act of 1830, both designed to discourage the sale of spirits, that the number of merchants in Ross dipped during the mid-19th century, although some innkeepers were also wine and spirit merchants. However, by the 1870s the regulations were changed so wine merchants now faced competition from grocers such as Barnwells and Brandons, and hotels who were able to sell wines and spirits. According to the *Ross Gazette* of 15 September 1870:

> Ross Royal Hotel Company, wine merchants. The company having imported a large stock of wines from the Continent, are prepared to vend them on terms favourable to the public. Also spirits, bottled ales, perry, etc. Notice is particularly requested to a superior St Emilion claret at 16s. per dozen, and a really good dinner sherry at 24s. per dozen.

W. Pulling & Co. were running the wine shop at the **Swan**. This company, from Hereford, was acquired by Tanners of Shrewsbury in 1978 'together with the bonded warehouse and the old Hereford Distillery. William Pulling was a cider maker from Totnes in Devon, who first leased warehouses in Ledbury in 1760. As wine merchants and distillers in Hereford, Pullings dates from 1813'.

J.C. Reynolds was not so successful when he moved from Fownhope to Hereford and established himself as a brewer, maltster and wine and spirit merchant in 1834. The brewery ceased to operate, and was closed for a number of years before being purchased by Charles Watkins in 1845. He changed the name from the Hereford Brewery to the Imperial Brewery.

In Ross, brewing on a commercial basis appears to have been started in the early 1820s by John Hill at his 'House, Malthouse, Stable etc.' in Brookend Street. About two decades later this was taken over by former grocers Joseph and Benjamin Turnock as the Ross Ale and Porter Brewery. The Turnocks moved the business to Station Street and, in 1865, it became a limited company called the Alton Court Brewery. In 1893 the brewery underwent 'complete renovation', and in 1897 the company was licensed to 'carry on a wines and spirits business in connection with the brewery'. At this time the premises of the 'Brewers, Maltsters and Aerated Water Manufacturers' extended from Brookend Street along Station Street, to Henry Street. Harvest Ale, Mild Ale, and Bitter were

An advertisement showing the Alton Court Brewery Buildings

22

brewed on site, together with Golden Crown and Golden Hop 'Brewed especially for Private Families'. Stout and Porter were 'carefully brewed on a new and improved principle' and were 'strongly recommended - more especially for invalids'. During the 1950s the Alton Court Brewery ran into financial difficulties. The company was taken over by the Stroud Brewery in 1956 and the premises in Ross were closed down.

A well observed account of the workings of the Alton Court Brewery, in between the two World Wars, was recalled by Jessie Stonham in *Daughter of Wyedean*:

> The only other industry I remember was at Alton Court Brewery, then a flourishing business and occupying most of both sides of the Station Road between the bottom of Broad Street and Henry Street. Its malt house also continued up Henry Street and the entrance to the cooperage went from here, eventually coming out on to the Broad Street. It was a very busy place when I was a child and we loved to

The now demolished Alton Court Brewery as sketched by local artist Mark Cunningham

23

The Alton Court Brewery Co., Ltd.,

Established nearly a
Century.

ROSS.

Brewers, Maltsters, & Mineral Water Manufacturers.

Bottlers of
Bass' & Worthington's Pale Ales,
Guinness' Stout, and
Lager Beer.

Speciality   -   -   -   Family Pale Ales.

Malt and Hops in large or small quantities,
and at market prices.

Price List on application.

Telephone No. 50.
Telegraphic Address: "Brewery, Ross."

A mid-20th century advertisement

walk past the windows through which we could see the men treading over and working on the malt. The smell was strong but quite attractive. The cooperage was, of course, the place in which the wooden barrels for the beer were made. This was a real craftsman's job and as children we were occasionally taken to see the men at work. We enjoyed scuffling our feet through the chippings after the wood had been trimmed ready and watching the hammering of the metal bands on to the casks.

The beer made there was delivered by large drays drawn by shire horses. These lovely creatures were in evidence at the town Carnivals, which commenced when I was much older. They were beautifully groomed and had their manes and tails plaited with coloured ribbons. With their leather harness shining and their brasses highly polished they made a lovely sight.

It was interesting to see them delivering the great wooden barrels to the local public houses and hotels. There were grids, usually square, which would open up upon the pavement and reveal one end of a cellar below. A contraption somewhat like a ladder would be let down and fastened in position and then the barrels, held back by a man holding the rope to which they were attached, would be slowly lowered into the cellar. There they were either stored till needed or connected to the hose through which the beer would be pumped to the 'beer engine' in the bar above.

Recent information reveals that the extensive brewery and massive maltings, situated along Station Street, were closed and sold to businesses in Ross in the late 1950s. Some other brewery properties were also sold at this date, but it was not until 1962 that Alton Court Brewery's 112 inns and hotels were conveyed to West Country Breweries Ltd. Out of the 37 listed in the Ross and South Herefordshire area only 18 remain open in 2001.

The Ross malting house at the turn of the last century

The only other brewery established in Ross was the one at the **Barrel Inn** started by W.H. Goulding in the late 19th century. In 1895 he was described as a 'brewer and wine and spirit merchant. Barrel Inn, Brookend Street. Families supplied with casks of genuine

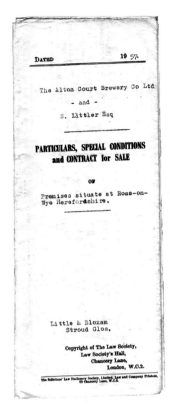

The 1957 sale contract for Alton Court Brewery

home-brewed beer, with malt and hops from: 10d. to 1s. 4d. per gallon. Well-aired beds'.

The **Barrel Inn** brewery was acquired by Herbert Mew some time before 1905. There he brewed a selection of 'Brilliant Ales' and Nourishing Stouts', with a 'delicious flavour and aroma of selected hops being very noticeable'. Mew also sold home-brewed Ginger Beer and Lemonade. In the 1920s he was bottling Bass and Worthington's Ales and Guinness's Stout. After Ernest Rennie took over in the 1930s, the brewery appears to have ceased, and the **Barrel Inn** was taken over by the Alton Court brewery from across the road. Pipes linked the two premises, so that Alton Court Brewery's beers could be bottled at the former Barrel Brewery. In 1962 when the 'Barrel Inn with the brewhouse outbuildings yard and garden' were taken over by West Country Breweries, half of the building was demolished to make way for a car park, but the **Barrel Inn** was re-opened in August 2001 after years of closure.

Although pubs in the area covered by this book were involved with other breweries, including Arnold Perrett & Co., Hereford & Tredegar Brewery Ltd., and Allsopp & Sons, it was the Forest Steam Brewery at Mitcheldean that made the most impact. The Forest Brewery was acquired by the Cheltenham Original Brewery Co., in 1937, and, like the above mentioned breweries, were all eventually taken over by Whitbread during the 1960s. In March 2001 the *Guardian* reported 'The chief executive of Whitbread, David Thomas, was signing a £1.625bn deal to sell the company's chain of 2,998 pubs to the venture capital firm Morgan Grenfell of Private Equity'.

He who drinks Strong Ale, goes to bed mellow,
Lives as he ought to live, and dies a jolly good fellow.

(Old Song)

CHAPTER THREE

Ross-on-Wye
PALACE POUND, RIVERSIDE & THE WEST END OF HIGH ST.

Ross is scenically situated between the river Wye and the wooded hills of Chase and Penyard, and its name is derived from the Welsh meaning 'promontory'. For over 2,000 years man has been associated with the immediate area—an Iron Age hillfort was constructed on Chase Hill, and the Romans established an iron-working centre at *Ariconium* below Penyard. In Saxon times a settlement developed at Ross, which, at the time of the Domesday Survey, was a village and manor of the Bishop of Hereford. In the 12th century King Stephen granted the right to hold a market and, during the reign of Edward I, the Bishop's Red Book records a rich variety of tradesmen, shops, mills, and forges.

By the time of Elizabeth's reign, Ross had become an important market town on the main thoroughfares from Hereford, Monmouth and South Wales to London, and the ancient ford and ferry river crossing at Wilton was replaced by a splendid stone bridge after the Bridge Act of 1597. In 1637 the horrors of the plague hit Ross, followed by plunder and damage caused by the Civil War. From the 17th century communications by river and road were improved. Serious efforts were made to establish the Wye as a commercial waterway whilst the Ross Turnpike Trust, formed in 1749, improved the road network.

In the 18th century the natural and untamed beauty of the Wye attracted artists, poets, writers, and those seeking the Picturesque

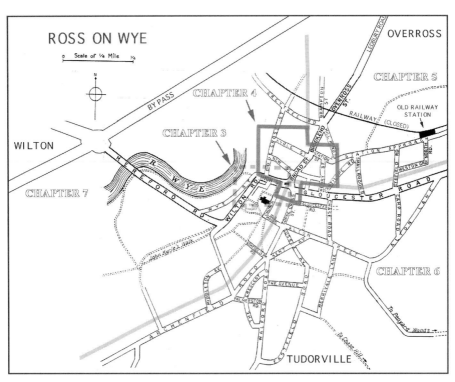

ROSS ON WYE

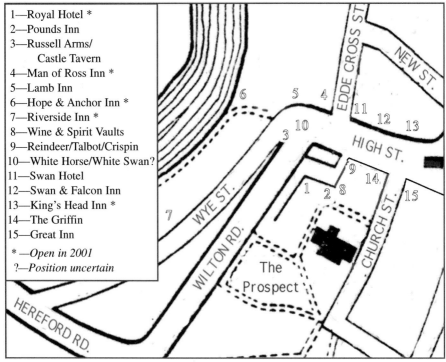

1—Royal Hotel *
2—Pounds Inn
3—Russell Arms/
    Castle Tavern
4—Man of Ross Inn *
5—Lamb Inn
6—Hope & Anchor Inn *
7—Riverside Inn *
8—Wine & Spirit Vaults
9—Reindeer/Talbot/Crispin
10—White Horse/White Swan?
11—Swan Hotel
12—Swan & Falcon Inn
13—King's Head Inn *
14—The Griffin
15—Great Inn

* —Open in 2001
?—Position uncertain

who started their trip from Ross. This became known as the Wye Tour, which developed into a commercial enterprise and led to the town becoming a tourist centre. The effects of the Ross Improvement Act of 1830 significantly changed the appearance of the town and transformed it into a much more pleasant and attractive place.

The 19th century saw new roads, buildings and industries established. Brewing became a major industry joining the earlier ones of agriculture, ironworking, milling, and tanning. After the completion of the Hereford and Gloucester Canal in 1845, and the opening of the Hereford, Ross, Gloucester railway in 1855, the river trade went into total decline. In 1871 the livestock market was moved to be nearer the railway, but the open produce market continued to be held below and around the market house.

Although no national events happened in Ross, it is rumoured that Henry IV and Charles I both stayed in Ross inns. On the other hand it is known that George IV, Lord Nelson, and Lloyd George visited the town. Writers associated with Ross include Charles Dickens, John Byng, Alexander Pope, and Samuel Taylor Coleridge. In the 20th century the talented Mariad Evans and Dennis Potter both lived in Ross. Prominent citizens that shaped Ross and left their mark include John Kyrle, Walter Scott, Nathaniel Morgan, Wallace Hall, Thomas Blake, along with many others from whom the town has benefitted.

From medieval times Ross developed into a prosperous market town served by a good network of roads. By the 16th century it was known as a 'great Market Town ... having in it yeerely foure very great Faires' with a 'considerable trade in cyder'. With this trade, and its position on a direct road from London to South Wales and Ireland, it is not surprising that Ross gained a reputation for 'offering good inn accommodation'. As business and travel increased the inns, taverns and alehouses flourished, they served refreshments, offered accommodation and played an important role as a meeting place for commerce and pleasure.

Most of the early references to Ross inns and taverns don't record their names, but it is safe to assume that the following incidents took place in the town centre. This one, typical of its type, occurred in 1224:

Walter son of Mainard accused Walter de Furno that, as he and his brother Robert were leaving a certain tavern at Ross, Walter de Furno came, and as he was watching, wickedly and feloniously stabbed his brother Richard with a small knife in the stomach on account of which wound he died. And he offered to prove that it was so by combat against him, as the court would give judgement. And Walter de Furno came and defended that death with his body. And therefore Walter de Furno gave security to defend it and Walter son of Mainard gave security to prove it, and they came armed the following day. Walter's pledges were Robert Perk, Simon Preposidus de Adeltone and Hugh Grotte. And Walter de Furno was defeated and hanged.

(courtesy of Geoff Gwatkin)

In 1603 Sir Herbert Croft's men were at Ross and:

being in lodgings in the Inne where there horses were, the founder and his company comminge to the same place for to buy provisions, one Anthony Gaunt being overtaken with drinke went into the stable and there made water where the sadles were and then cam to ... on of the gromes [stable lads] and pushed this grome underfeete in the stable and by that meanes fell together by the eares. And as the founder and Gaunt and their company were going home on[e] of Sir Herbert's men with a pyke sett upon them and by means thereof the founder let off a Birdinge peece by Chance which did hurte on[e] of Sir Herbert's men and one or two more Butt noe hurte or damage to the Infant by any shott as we whose names are underwritten will corporallt depose.

(courtesy of Pat Hughes)

The 'outrage' was committed by 'some of the workmen in yor hnors iron works at your ffurnace of Billemene [Bill Mills]'. Towards the end of the 17th century John Harbutt was charged twice for keeping a 'disorderly alehouse'.

During the 18th century many inns were closed, replaced or renamed, whilst new ones appeared. This was the start of the coaching era when modest establishments blossomed into busy coaching inns. Despite the advent of the 'Flying Coach' service of the 1720s, this form of travel was slow to catch on, but with improved roads at the end of the century Thomas Pruen was running a coach service from Hereford to London, followed by Phillpott's 'New and Elegant Mail Coach' which called at Ross every Sunday, Wednesday and Friday on its way to London from South Wales.

Ross inns changed with the times, many coaching inns eventually giving way to hotels, then being closed or redeveloped, while, due to the Licensing Acts made between 1828 and 1840, a proliferation of beer houses opened during the mid-19th century. With a growth in the population and an expansion of the town, public houses also sprung up in the new residential areas.

Despite the number of licensed premises in Ross, there was only one case of drunkenness in 1920, but in 1936 when Richard Owen of a 'tramp fraternity' was charged with being drunk and disorderly, the chairman of the bench clearly thought there had been an increase in the number of such cases, so warned Owen to tell his friends to keep away from Ross if 'they couldn't keep off the drink'. By 1952 the Licensed Victuallers Association reported the 'worst trade in Ross inns for years', and hoped that the extensions made to the car parks would increase the number of day trippers and boost the takings. The Ross licensees were still complaining in 1960 that television and and high prices were 'reducing consumption of alcohol in the town'. Since then many inns and pubs have closed, and in 2000 the remaining publicans objected to the opening of a Wetherspoon pub in the old post office, which could put the smaller establishments out of business.

On a superb site, chosen by the bishops of Hereford to build their palace in the 12th century, stands the **Royal Hotel** in Palace Pound. Part of the hotel's conference facilities stand on the site of the **Pounds Inn**. In 1696 this inn was kept by William Fisher and remained in the family for a number of years. By 1816 Widow Thomas had taken over as landlady when the **Pounds** was advertised 'to be Let—now in full business, capable of accommodating 16 or 17 Lodgers with Excellent Yard, Stable, Garden, Outhouses and numerous Pens and Standings

---

ROSS TO CHEPSTOW,
ALONG THE VALLEY OF THE WYE.

A SUPERIOR FOUR-HORSE COACH,
"THE TOURIST,"

in connection with the Great Western Railway, leaves the Station and Barrett's Royal Hotel, Ross, on the arrival of the first trains from Cheltenham, Gloucester, Hereford and Shrewsbury, for Monmouth, Tintern Abbey and Chepstow, reaching the latter place in time for trains to all parts of South Wales. Returning from the Railway Station and principal Hotels, Chepstow, after the arrival of the express trains from London and South Wales, passing through St. Arvans, Tintern Abbey, Landogo and Redbrook, arriving at the King's Head Hotel, Monmouth, at 4.30 P.M., and Barrett's Royal Hotel, and the Railway Station, Ross, in time for trains to the North and West of England and mail to London.

Passengers are allowed time to view the ruins of Tintern Abbey going and returning.

JAMES BARRETT, JOHN WEBB, WILLIAM SNOWDEN,
June, 1856.   *Proprietors.*

Coach tour of the Wye Valley, 1856

together with Pasture Ground called the Prospect'. Adjoining the inn was the 'Parish Pound' where stray animals were kept until ownership was established.

Due to its elevated position the **Pounds Inn** and the Prospect provided an ideal site in the 1830s for 'erecting a Mansion, which would command the

The remaining wall of the Pounds Inn, now part of the outbuildings of the Royal Hotel

most pleasing, extensive and picturesque views', or 'a very desirable spot for the erection of villas'. This was an opportunity seized by James Barrett who purchased the **Pounds Inn**, Beast Market and Prospect. He demolished the old inn to provide space for the **Royal Taps** for his adjoining grand hotel, retaining a single wall that still survives on the west side of the Buckingham Suite. When the foundations of the **Royal**, which was built by Barrett in 1837 at a cost of £15,000, were being laid, the contractor came across a dungeon, belonging to the bishop's palace. 'It was entered through the roof, along its sides were stone benches, and fixed in the walls, which were hewn out of the rock, were half a dozen massive iron rings to which the chains of prisoners could be attached'.

Barrett's Royal Hotel became a successful coaching inn,

The Royal Hotel in 1838

32

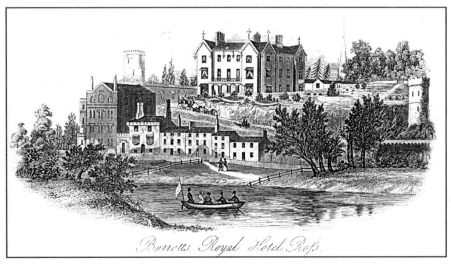

Barretts Royal Hotel Ross.

1855 coach from Barrett's Hotel to Monmouth

posting house and a 'favourite starting point of summer parties who make the celebrated tour of the river Wye'. After Barrett died in 1859 the 'Family and Posting House' was purchased by Thomas Blake, a notable businessman and bene-factor to the town during the latter part of the 19th century. Blake was born in Ross and rose from being a post office clerk to become a highly respected non-conformist and Liberal Member of Parliament. He served on various committees and charities including the Ross Savings Bank, the Ross Dispensary, the Cottage Hospital, and acted as a Town Commissioner and a Turnpike Trustee. In 1873 he presented the town with the Ross Free Library in Broad Street, a new Baptist Chapel in 1881, and a fresh water supply in 1887. After purchasing the **Royal Hotel** in 1860 Blake managed to resolve the controversy over the townspeople's access to the Prospect, which he 'secured to them by deed for their enjoyment for ever' in 1870.

Thomas Blake's Company was formed:

for the purpose of purchasing the Royal Hotel ... so successfully conducted for the last twenty-five years ... The Royal Hotel is a first

33

class establishment ... There is everything about the noble hotel to tempt parties ... to prolong their stay ... its coaches run daily to and from Monmouth and Chepstow ... The late Mr. Barrett, who built this hotel, and carried it on so admirably for nineteen years, retired therefrom with a large fortune. Its popularity is now even greater than in Mr. Barrett's time, the Royal Hotel at Ross having not only an English but a European notoriety. It contains spacious Entrance Hall, Coffee-room, Ball-room, Commercial-room, Bar, Nine drawing rooms, linen-room, Thirty-three Bed-rooms (making up nearly fifty beds), Dressing-rooms, Three water-closets, Grand and Back Staircases. ... Stabling for Forty Horses ... extensive Pleasure Grounds and Gardens, planted with choice Shrubs and Flowers, the whole being most tastefully laid out with Ornamental Walks, Alcoves, etc.

In 1869 the *Ross Gazette* reported:

ANNUAL BALL AT THE ROYAL HOTEL

The annual ball at the Royal Hotel, Ross, took place on Friday last, when all the resources of this extensive and well-managed establishment were fully brought to bear. The decorations of the ballroom were very appropriate and profuse, and the way in which the supper-room was set out gave rise to numerous expressions of admiration on the part of the visitors. Although there was, necessarily, an absence of the personal supervision of Mrs. [Elizabeth] Gordon, the esteemed manager of the hotel, yet there was full proof of her instructions being carried out to the letter by Miss Roberts and an able staff of assistants — not omitting the important functionary, the *chef de cisene*, who performed his duties, as he always does, in a highly satisfactory manner. The company was not quite so large as it was last year, but was quite as fashionable. Captain Power and Mrs. Power were unable to be present in consequence of a domestic affliction; but, as a whole, we may say that the *réunion* was of an elegant and pleasant character.

Since then the **Royal** has remained the most prominent hotel in Ross, where such famous visitors as Charles Dickens, the Duke and Duchess of Teck and Lloyd George have stayed. The Duke and Duchess's visit in 1891 was prominently reported in the *Ross Gazette*:

Visit of the Duke and Duchess of Teck, then staying with Lady Henry Somerset at Eastnor Castle near Ledbury. The royal party drove into the decorated town of Ross at 12.45 on Wednesday 23rd September

1904 letter cover from the Royal Hotel
(Derek Foxton collection)

THE ROYAL HOTEL

ROSS - ON - WYE

Family and Residential.

BEST HOTEL IN THE WYE VALLEY.

*Stands in Private Grounds overlooking the
"Horseshoe" Bend of the River Wye.*

Every Comfort.   Electric Light throughout.

POSTING.   GARAGE.   PETROL.

Send for Illustrated Tariff.

Telegrams: "Royal Hotel, Ross."   'Phone 40.

1891 advertisement for the Royal Hotel

1891. The horses and postillions were supplied by the Royal Hotel Company. After a rousing welcome the party embarked on the Wye for Goodrich Court, and, after luncheon with Mr. and Mrs. Moffett, continued to Symonds Yat by water, and then drove back to Ross.

On arrival of the party at the Royal Hotel, they were received by vociferous cheers from an immense concourse of spectators, and the volunteers fired three volleys from the hotel steps. On alighting from the carriages, a deputation was waiting in the entrance hall of the hotel, in order to present Her Royal Highness, on behalf of the inhabitants of Ross, an elaborate album, containing views of Ross and neighbourhood. ... As Her Royal Highness approached the deputation, she appeared in the best of spirits, and bowed gracefully to all present.

... the Royal party left amidst the heartiest cheering, being again escorted by the Yeomanry, Volunteers, and Fire Brigade with lighted torches; the band playing 'The girl I left behind me'. The procession was followed to the outskirts of the town by a big crowd.

To commemorate Dickens' visit of 1867, an event took place on 12 June 1915 'in the presence of a large gathering of members of the Gloucester Branch of Dickens Fellowship—who were on their annual excursion—and a number of Ross friends, the Mayor of Gloucester unveiled a very artistic tablet, which the Directors have caused to be affixed in the entrance hall of the hotel' where it has remained. Today this hotel continues to occupy the finest site in Ross overlooking the famous horseshoe bend of the river Wye, but it has lost its coaching inn character and for some time has lacked some of the charm and atmosphere that it once possessed. It is hoped that this may be recaptured as the ownership changes in the new millennium.

In 1830 the Ross Improvement Act enabled the Town Commissioners

A Royal Visit.

The above signatures are reproduced from the Royal Hotel Visitors Book, in which they were written on the occasion of the visit of Queen Mary to Ross, in 1891. They comprise the Duchess of Teck, Queen Mary (then Princess Mary of Teck), her father the Duke of Teck, and her brother Prince Alexander George of Teck. The royal party took boat from Ross to Symonds' Yat, landing at Goodrich Court for luncheon.

37

Charles Dickens plaque at the Royal

ROSS-ON-WYE

Family and Residential   Best Hotel in the Wye Valley

Stands in Private Grounds overlooking
"Horseshoe Bend" of the River Wye

Every Comfort   **Electric Light**   **Garage**

Hot and Cold Water and Gas Fires in Bedrooms

Proprietors : TRUST HOUSES, LTD.

Telegrams : "Royal Hotel," Ross   'Phone 40

*An advertisement for the
Royal Hotel in the mid-1900s*

to pave, drain, clean, light and improve the town's facilities. The western end of Ross was transformed during the 1830s by the Commissioners and the Turnpike Trustees. Wilton Road was cut through the cliff to replace the steep ascent of Dock Pitch (Wye Street), buildings were demolished and the top of the High Street was dramatically lowered to provide an easier gradient for horse-drawn vehicles. This tremendous task of lowering a street is apparent in the frontage of 53/54 High Street and the former coach entrance beside 4 High Street. Surplus sandstone from these works were used to build mock gothic walls and towers on the edge of the escarpment which helped to give the town a completely new and almost Continental character.

Once the Ross Turnpike Trustees and Improvement Commissioners had completed their work, they were left with an awkward corner piece between the new Wilton Road and the old Dock Pitch. It is difficult to ascertain whether

An 1867 advertisement for the Castle Wine and Spirit Vaults

an existing building was modified from the **Russell Arms**—run by John Landers in 1832—or a completely new one was built in 1838 to form the **Castle Tavern,** a building which displayed fancy barge boards and gables so as to harmonize with the **Royal** above. The tavern was called the **Castle** because it opened at the completion of the towers and walls, which were built to suggest a castle site. John Landers appears to have been the first landlord of the **Castle,** which offered billiards and 'Pleasure Boat trips' to residents and visitors. By 1867 the tavern had been taken over by Edwards and Co. as the **Castle Wine and Spirit Vaults,** before it passed to the Alton Court Brewery in the early 20th century,

Walter Townsend became the brewery's tenant at the **Castle Vaults,** but after his death in 1916 his widow, Charlotte felt 'unable to carry on the business which did not appear profitable'. Although Walter had left savings and stock valued at £200, together with a 'motor

The Castle Hotel in 1943

1920s advertisement for the Castle Hotel

car parked at the Alton Court Brewery' worth £228, and property in Wye Street, her financial affairs were put in the hands of a 'competent accountant' and Charlotte had to leave. From the 1940s the tavern was called the **Castle Hotel**, and after the brewery sold the premises in 1961 it closed and was converted into flats called Malvern House.

In Wye Street another inn emerged following the 1830s development. This was the **Man of Ross Inn**, housed in a building that dates from the 17th century, but which has been largely rebuilt and refaced. It also displays the then fashionable barge boards, and has a single-storied extension that houses the bar under a high curved gable. The inn sign depicts John Kyrle, who is known as 'The Man of Ross'. He was born in 1637 and from childhood lived in his parents' house in the High Street. His many charitable works and deeds were celebrated by the poet, Alexander Pope, in 1732, eight years after Kyrle's death.

The Man of Ross. Left : in the mid-20th century; right : in 2000

It was around 1847 that James Watkins, probably the corn and flour dealer listed in the market place, opened the **Man of Ross Inn**. In 1851 Watkins was also an 'eating-house keeper' in the Wye Terrace. Other publicans followed at the inn, including John William Millington 'a sign painter, heraldic and scenic artist' who romantically named the inn **Ye Man of Ross Inn** around 1914. In 1920 he was fined £10 with £2 2s. costs for illegally charging more for bottled beer and stout. During Millington's long tenancy the inn became part of West Country Brewers, and was later taken over by Whitbreads. At the turn of the 21st century the two cosy bars were still open.

Further down Wye Street on the river side is the site of the **Lamb** inn, an 18th-century hostelry which was open when this street was called Dock Pitch —the only road into the town from Wilton Bridge. Waggons and carts piled high with essential commodities were skilfully but slowly driven up the steep rutted pitch, so a refreshment stop at the **Lamb** must have made a

Pope's Eulogium on the "Man of Ross."

ALL our praises why should lords engross?
　Rise, honest Muse, and sing the Man of Ross:
　Pleased Vaga echoes through her winding bounds,
　And rapid Severn hoarse applause resounds.
Who hung with woods yon mountain's sultry brow?
From the dry rock who bade the waters flow?
Not to the skies in useless columns tost,
Or in proud falls magnificently lost,
But clear and artless, pouring through the plain,
Health to the sick and solace to the swain.
Whose causeway parts the vale with shady rows?
Whose seats the weary traveller repose?
Who taught that heav'n-directed spire to rise?
The "Man of Ross," each lisping babe replies.
　Behold the Market-place with poor o'erspread!
The Man of Ross divides the weekly bread:
He feeds yon almshouse—neat, but void of state,—
Where age and want sit smiling at the gate:
Him portion'd maids, apprentic'd orphans blest,
The young who labour, and the old who rest.
Is any sick? The Man of Ross relieves,
Prescribes, attends, the med'cine makes and gives.
Is there a variance? Enter but his door,
Balk'd are the courts, and contest is no more.
Despairing quacks with curses fled the place,
And vile attorneys, now a useless race.
Thrice happy man! enabled to pursue
What all so wish, but want the power to do!
Oh! say, what sums that generous hand supply?
What mines, to swell that boundless charity!
Of debts and taxes, wife and children clear,
This man possess'd—five hundred pounds a year.
Blush, Grandeur, blush—proud courts, withdraw your blaze;
Ye little stars! hide your diminished rays!
　And what! no monument, inscription, stone!
His race, his form, his name almost unknown!
Who builds a church to God, and not to fame,
Will never mark the marble with his name;
Go, search it there, where to be born and die,
Of rich and poor makes all the history;
Enough, that virtue fill'd the space between;
Prov'd by the ends of being to have been.

In front of the Man of Ross is a sculpture of leaping salmon by Walenty Pytel

41

welcome break. It was 'a coaching inn and well-known to travellers', with evidence suggesting that Richard Townsend was the innkeeper in 1782 when the inn, stables, coach house and stock were valued at £300 for insurance purposes. In 1829 the **Lamb** was for sale, and was advertised as 'All that Old-established and well-accustomed Inn' containing a 'Bar, Parlour, capacious Dining-room, six bedchambers, two kitchens, three cellars and Brewhouse — Also Garden Ground with Stables and Yard'. The inn then passed for a short time to John Morgan, an auctioneer and land agent, presumably as a speculative buy, for it was totally redeveloped during the mid-1830s.

Below the site of the **Lamb** is the **Riverside Inn** converted from a café and restaurant into a pub in 1999, and on the riverside is the busy and popular **Hope and Anchor Inn**. Its enviable position on the banks of the Wye was recognised in the late 18th century by Stephen Lane, a modest victualler in 1782, who shared the premises with a basket maker, a glazier and a flax dresser. He would have served both the thirsty bargees and the inquisitive Wye tourists of the 18th century. In Christian symbolism the anchor is a symbol of hope; thus 'Hope we have as an anchor of the soul'(*Hebrews*, 6.19).

The Wye had always been a means of communication, but it was not until 1662 that a serious effort was made to make the river navigable. Barges loaded with cider, hops, wheat, oak-bark and timber were hauled by teams of men downstream for trans-shipping into larger sea-going vessels at Brockweir, and coal, slate, deals and other

The Riverside Inn in 2001

heavy commodities were hauled upstream to Hereford, Hay and along the Lugg to Leominster. From 1809, after the construction of a proper towing path, horses pulled the barges making an easier life for the bargemen still working on the barges and tending and looking after the horses.

From the mid-18th century excursions down the Wye became fashionable by those poets, writers and artists seeking the Picturesque. From a boat hired at Ross the untamed beauty of the river from Ross to Chepstow was praised and captured in prose, picture and verse. The journey became known as the Wye Tour and was soon commercialised by innkeepers and boat proprietors, and remained popular until the early 20th century, although later travellers tended to make use of the Wye Valley railway.

Stephen Lane's trade to the bargemen was obviously boosted by hiring boats and serving refreshments to the Wye tourists, and the property blossomed into the **Hope and Anchor Inn**. By 1835 the Newtons' were retailing beer and cider, and various members of the family were employed in ropemaking, basketmaking and hiring pleasure boats. At the end of the 19th century George Hobbs ran the inn followed by the boatbuilder, Henry Dowell, in the early 1900s. More recently John Gardner turned the pub into a huge success, but after nearly 30 years sold the premises to Banks Brewery in the 1990s.

Boats, baskets and sieves at the Hope & Anchor in 1851

The prices of boats on hire on the Wye in the early 1900s

The Hope and Anchor in 2001

A little way up High Street on the right is St. Mary's Street and at the end of a passageway leading from the east side of St. Mary's Street was the site chosen by Richard Watkins to open a wine and spirit merchants in the 1840s. It became known as the **Wine and Spirit Vaults**, and although listed under inns and taverns it appears to have been more of an off-licence, and at the beginning of the 20th century was taken over by the wine merchant T.W. Purchas and Sons. It was really Harry Morris who established the premises as a public house in the 1930s, but after he 'died suddenly behind his bar' in 1942 his 'grief-stricken' widow left the interior as a 'mausoleum to the man she loved'. She continued as landlady, but as the bar was left undisturbed it became covered with dust and draped with cobwebs. The locals nicknamed it the **Hole in the Wall**, and it became an attraction

RICHARD TAYLOR,
WINE, SPIRIT,
ALE AND PORTER
VAULTS,
ST. MARY'S STREET,
ROSS.

EAST INDIA PALE AND BURTON ALES;
DUBLIN PORTER, IN CASKS & BOTTLES;
CIDER AND PERRY.
CHOICEST WINES, SPIRITS, & CORDIALS,
&c., &c.,
ON THE MOST REASONABLE TERMS.

1851 advertisement for the
Wine & Spirit Vaults

45

visited by customers and their friends for a quick drink and gaze at the curious scene. Florence Morris was always dressed in black and sat silently in a corner while her son served a limited selection of drinks and, as his main occupation was in insurance, the hours of opening were very irregular. The pub closed in the 1970s, and after Florence's death the property with its 1930s contents and fittings were auctioned in 1983. It is not clear what the premises behind locked doors are now used for.

Also on the east side of St. Mary's Street was the site of a much earlier hostelry, which, in 1645 towards the end of the Civil War, was called the **Reindeer**. Throughout the centuries there has been a habit of changing the names of inns which can make

The Wine and Spirit Vaults in the 1970s

'Johnny Walker' strides across the bar and the Lemon Hart man rolls his barrel—just as they did the day Harry Morris died

46

for difficulties in location and identification. The **Reindeer** serves as a prime example. Although the documentation is confusing, it appears that by 1675 this inn had become the **Old Falcon**, and was known at the end of the 17th century 'by the sign of **Marlborough's Head**'. The **Talbot** of 1768 and the **Crispin** of 1803 could have occupied the same site.

Most of these signs are significant—the **Reindeer** is derived from the reins used in drawing a sledge. The **Old Falcon** was a reminder that falconry was a royal sport, but the known dates for the **Marlborough's Head** in Ross are too early to be named after the first Duke of Marborough, so may be it was named after some local personality. The **Talbot** was a popular inn name representing a type of hound used for hunting, and the **Crispin** commemorates the patron saint of cobblers and shoemakers, a justified name for Ross was renowned for its trade in boots and shoemaking. St Crispin's day is 25 October which was also the day of the battle of Agincourt in 1415.

An ancient inn known in 1652 as the **White Horse** stood at the western end of the High Street possibly the same building where Matthew Young ran the **White Swan** in 1768, for this inn had no connection with the later **Swan Hotel**. The latter was erected in the 1860s as part of another wave of development in Ross after the passing of the second Improvement Act. The **Swan Hotel** occupied the corner of High Street and Edde Cross Street on the former site of Price's land agency business and other premises. It was built in 1867 by the Swan Hotel Co. Ltd. as a 'Family, Commercial and Posting House' and was managed by Mrs. Reece and Mrs. Price, but in 1914 the hotel was for sale. The copious sale particulars describe and illustrate the hotel's facilities, which included 14 bedrooms, a billiard room, smoking room, dining room, lounge bar and assembly room.

In 1914 the **Swan Hotel** offered the additional attraction of a 'well-arranged wine shop having two entrances from the street' which was run by William Pulling, the wine merchant from Hereford who was responsible for the manufacture of the still popular 'Hereford Gin'. The extensive stabling accommodated 80 horses in a yard that included a coach house, and a garage had been installed for the occasional motorist. The yard was let to Mr. Baynham who operated a horse omnibus service to and from the railway station. By the 1920s the **Swan** had been taken over by Trust House Ltd. and continued as a hotel until the 1980s when it finally closed. The large building was gradually redeveloped by a local builder to provide offices for South Herefordshire District Council and is now used by Herefordshire Council and the Ross-on-Wye Tourist Information Centre, with flats above.

The **Swan Hotel** had replaced the fading **Swan and Falcon** which in the 18th century had been Ross's most prominent coaching inn, situated on the north side of the High Street. In the deeds of 1749 Philip Hodges is named as the innkeeper. Over the years the inn was variously recorded as the **Swan and Old Falcon**, **The Swan**, **Swan and King's Arms** and the **Swan Hotel**. It was under the tenancy of Daniel Pearce in 1787 that the Hon. John Byng 'put up at the Swan and Falcon' while touring South Wales. In his *Torrington Diaries* he wrote 'Before

SWAN HOTEL

(SITUATE NEAR THE RIVER WYE),

FOR FAMILIES AND COMMERCIAL GENTLEMEN,

AND

KING'S HEAD: COMMERCIAL & AGRICULTURAL HOTEL,

In the Centre of the Town, ROSS.

THERE IS A BILLIARD ROOM AT EACH HOTEL.

Posting in all its branches. Loose Boxes and Lock-up Coach Houses.

FLYS AND OMNIBUSES MEET ALL TRAINS.

M. E. REESE & M. PRICE, Proprietors.

DISTRICT HEAD-QUARTERS OF THE CYCLISTS' TOURING CLUB.

THE SWAN HOTEL,

(Facing the River Wye).

ROSS, HEREFORDSHIRE.

Tourists, Cyclists, Families and Commercial Gentlemen visiting the West of England will find superior accommodation, combined with domestic comforts and moderate charges at the above Hotel. The Hotel commands extensive views of the River Wye, with its enchanting scenery, and is conveniently situated for visiting Goodrich Castle, Symonds Yat, Tintern Abbey, Raglan Castle. The Forest of Dean, etc., and is within a short distance of Hereford, Monmouth and Gloucester, by rail. Club and Billiard rooms. Posting in all its branches. Loose Boxes and Lock-up Coach Houses.

Flys and Omnibuses meet all Trains.

Miss PRICE, - : - - Manageress.

ROSS.

The Swan Hotel

(OVERLOOKING THE RIVER).

FIRST-CLASS, with MODERATE CHARGES.

LADIES' COFFEE ROOM.

BILLIARDS.

The HOTEL OMNIBUS meets all Trains.

POSTING.

Swan advertisements. Top : 1874;
middle : 1895; lower : c.1900

48

The Swan in 1910

Nearest
Hotel
to the
River.

SWAN HOTEL,

ROSS.

FOR FAMILIES
and GENTLEMEN.

Excellent Cuisine.   Moderate Tariff.

POSTING.
GARAGE.

Telephone 44.

For Tariff, apply to the Manageress.

The Swan in the 1920s

dinner, walk'd round the churchyard, and much admired the prospect walk' and 'after our dinner (salmon every day) we enquired for a boat'. The next day Byng 'was early up after sleeping well in a large good bed, better than the looks of the inn promised'.

In its heyday the **Swan and Falcon** consisted of a dwelling-house with out-houses, stables, outbuildings, courtyards and a garden formerly used as a bowling green. In 1793 it was purchased by James Yearley, a former butler to Sir Hungerford Hoskyns from Harewood House. With his former experience, he was obviously very capable of attending to the every needs of Lord Nelson and his guests, when they breakfasted at the **Swan and Falcon** in 1802, before continuing their journey down the Wye on their way towards Monmouth. The Yearsleys remained at the inn until 1818 when John Green became the landlord. From the late 1820s the ambitious James Barrett took over

The nobility and gentry were important customers of the Swan in 1793

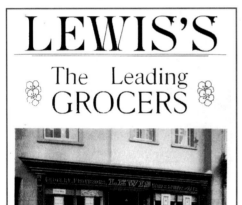

The Swan & Falcon, after its conversion to a shop

the busy inn with its regular coach services to London and Milford on the 'Royal Mail', to Carmarthan on the 'Regulator', and to Gloucester on the 'Rising Sun'.

Having learnt the trade it was this ambitious James Barrett who left the **Swan and Falcon** in the 1830s to build and run his own grand **Royal Hotel**. He took the coaching trade with him and from thereon the **Swan and Falcon** rapidly declined and shrank in size as parts of the premises were sold off for other uses. The last landlord was Thomas Sivell who offered 'Good Accommodation' and 'Excellent Stabling' until about 1860. The old inn was then closed and converted into shops, which did include a wine and spirit merchant. The inn was remembered as late as 1943 when a conveyance described the property as 'formerly **Old Swan Inn** and Yard' with a 'large room known as the Assembly Room, workshops, stables, Coach House and Brew House'.

On the same side of the High Street stands the impressive **King's Head**, one of the only two inns in Ross that have been in continuous use from at least the 17th century without changing its name. The owners claim that the **King's Head** dates from the 14th century, but it certainly enjoys a documented history from the Civil War, when William Nicholls, the innkeeper, who may have suffered 'losses and damages' during that uncertain period. The present building is of three storeys with an early 19th-century front, but its beamed and panelled interior reveal earlier features including a 50 ft. well and extensive cellarage. From the early 18th century the **King's Head** also emerged as a coaching inn when the 'London and Oxford Flying Coach' carried passengers to Oxford for 17s. or London for £1 7s. It was also the inn chosen by the newly established Ross Turnpike Trust to hold their first meeting in June 1749.

> **KING's - HEAD INN,**
> *ROSS, HEREFORDSHIRE.*
>
> WILLIAM THOMAS, late fervant to Philip Westfaling, of Rudhall, Efq. has taken and entered upon the above INN, which he is fitting up in the moft neat and commodious manner.——He, therefore, takes this opportunity of informing the Nobility, Gentry, Travellers and others, who may honor him with their encouragement, that he has laid in an affortment of the beft *Wines, Spirituous* and other *Liquors*; and they may depend upon his utmoft exertion, and moft ftudious endeavours to merit every favor conferred upon him, and alfo his unremitted attempts to render the accommodations of his houfe comfortable and convenient.
> ☞ Neat poft-chaifes and able horfes.

A new landlord at the King's Head in 1788

The **King's Head** was sold in 1780 as 'that old and well accustomed Inn', and the business passed to the Howells family until 1814 when the ageing Mary Howells was 'replaced' by a Mr. Collins. He took over the 'large and commodious House' with 'Wines and Liquors of the finest quality, well aired beds, and a good Larder. All set up for the Posting Business, for families making expeditions and Pleasure Boats for Parties with cold Collations'.

During the mid-19th century James Maddy served

> **KING'S HEAD**
> **HOTEL & POSTING-HOUSE,**
> ROSS.
>
> IN confequence of the ftatements made by interefted individuals, to the difcredit of the above long-eftablished Houfe, and to his injury as Landlord,
> **JOSEPH GARDNER,**
> begs moft refpectfully to inform the Public, that he has newly Painted, Papered, and in fact, well fitted up the KING's HEAD HOTEL, and rendered it in every refpect fuitable for the accommodation of Families of the firft refpectability.
> Amongft other falfe ftatements it has been faid, that the above Hotel is not a Pofting-houfe; in contradiction to fuch affertion, Joseph Gardner begs to fay that it has been eftablished as a Pofting-houfe for upwards of fifty years.
> Jofeph Gardner has entered upon the above Eftablifhment with a firm determination to afford the public the convenience of a SECOND POSTING-HOUSE & HOTEL in Rofs, and thereby prevent *Monopoly*; and fince attempts have been made to give the King's Head a defcription to which it is not entitled, and thereby ferioufly injure him, he earneftly trufts the Nobility, Gentry, Commercial Gentlemen, and the Public generally, will do him the favour to patronife him, and judge for themfelves. And he begs to add, that for their further accommodation, he has made fuch arrangements as will enable him to Poft them at our shilling per mile, with excellent and faft Horfes, in conjunction with the George Hotel, Chepftow; King's Head Hotel, Monmouth; Royal Hotel and George Hotel, Cheltenham; Crofs Keys, Tewkefbury; and Marlborough Arms, Marlborough.
> **Steam Packet Office.**
> Carriages of every defcription; and fuperior Pleafure Bpats for the excurfion down the Wye.

Putting the record straight in 1836

James Maddy's long stay at the King's Head.
Upper : 1851; lower : 1867

as landlord for many years, and in 1866 he purchased extra stables and another coachhouse, which enabled him to accommodate 100 horses in 'first-class stables'. Horses are extremely labour intensive to look after, so this large yard would have presented a noisy and colourful scene with bustling stable lads, grooms, ostlers and coachmen busy with their individual tasks, while a blacksmith rapidly replaced shoes and repaired coaches. By the mid-1870s Mrs. Reese and Mrs. Price from the **Swan Hotel** were also the proprietors of the **King's Head**. They were followed by a succession of inn-keepers before the inn was taken over by Trust Houses in the 1920s. A decade later they were offering 'Comfortable accommod-ation' for £3 13s. 6d. a week. In 1984 the old inn was completely renovated and now includes a 'Royalist Bar'.

The south side of the High Street was the site of two ancient inns, both associated with traditional stories that probably contain some grain of truth. The **Griffin**, later known as the **Rose and Crown**, stood on the corner of Church Street opposite the **King's Head**. The **Griffin** was said to have been visited by the future King Henry IV in 1399, and by King Charles I in 1645, but the 'sleeping place' of Charles I was also claimed by Gabriel Hill's **Great Inn** which stood on the opposite

KING'S HEAD

Family & Commercial Hotel,

HIGH STREET,

E. KNIBBS,
PROPRIETOR.

GOOD STABLING.   *POSTING.*

BILLIARDS.

GOOD STOCK ROOMS.

'BUS MEETS ALL TRAINS.

The King's Head in 1896

corner of Church Street. There is no evidence to support either of these royal visits, but traditions are hard to ignore. One visit was commemorated on 29 May 1813, when scholars from the Walter Scott School, each wearing a 'slip of oak' were marched to the 'old chamber on the East side of Church Lane, where, according to credible tradition, King Charles the Martyr slept on his journey from this place during his troubles in 1645'. The chamber visited was in a building 'formerly called Gabriel Hills **Gt. Inn**'.

The **Griffin** was named after a mythical animal, supposedly the offspring of a lion and an eagle. As it represented the noblest of

The King's Head in 2000

creatures, it was much used on coats of arms. The change of name from the **Griffin** to the **Rose and Crown** doubtless indicated loyalty to the monarch after the Civil War.

CHAPTER FOUR

Ross-on-Wye
THE MARKET PLACE &
ADJOINING STREETS

The spacious market place forms the heart of Ross, the traditional meeting place where colourful stalls present a lively scene. The sandstone market house was built in 1650, and its upper chamber has been used for various purposes including a school, a magistrates' court, a council chamber and a public library, but since 1997 houses the Ross Market House Heritage Centre.

In 1799 Thomas Bonner wrote:

> The mouldering quality of the stone is unfavourable to its long duration. 24 pillars in three rows of eight. The pillars sustain a range of chambers, in them the lord of the manor's court is held, the other parts are mostly used as deposits for grain etc. At its west end is a bust in bad preservation of King Charles the second. The steps up to the market house were built where the messuage or tenement called the Boothall formerly stood.

The life of a town such as Ross evolves around its market place, where in the past a number of inns provided a cheerful place to gossip, carry out business deals and enjoy a tankard of ale. On the south side the 'Man of Ross House' opposite the market became a coaching inn for a short period during the 18th century. It was after the death of John Kyrle in 1724 that his property passed to his relative Vandervort Kyrle. Then it came into the hands of Walter Kyrle, who let the house to a saddler, James Prosser, who converted it into the **King's Arms Inn**, which, according to Charles Heath, had been 'the best inn in the town'.

55

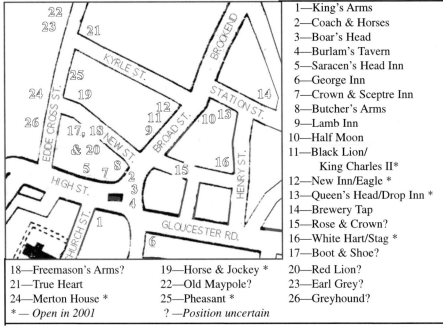

	1—King's Arms
	2—Coach & Horses
	3—Boar's Head
	4—Burlam's Tavern
	5—Saracen's Head Inn
	6—George Inn
	7—Crown & Sceptre Inn
	8—Butcher's Arms
	9—Lamb Inn
	10—Half Moon
	11—Black Lion/ King Charles II*
	12—New Inn/Eagle *
	13—Queen's Head/Drop Inn *
	14—Brewery Tap
	15—Rose & Crown?
	16—White Hart/Stag *
	17—Boot & Shoe?

18—Freemason's Arms?	19—Horse & Jockey *	20—Red Lion?
21—True Heart	22—Old Maypole?	23—Earl Grey?
24—Merton House *	25—Pheasant *	26—Greyhound?
* — Open in 2001	? —Position uncertain	

In 1779 the Kyrle estate was advertised for sale including the 'well accustomed Inn', but it seems unlikely that it was sold, as a descendant of John Kyrle later sold the property to J.S. Collins who closed 'the premises as an inn'. The property was purchased by Samuel Philpot Brookes, a surgeon apothecary and by 1835 the old inn had been divided into two parts.

The right-hand side was taken by Benjamin Powle, a printer, and since the early 20th century has been occupied by the *Ross Gazette*. An interesting link with the former inn was the tradition of drinking beer from a copper flagon 'to celebrate the completion of each week's publication'. The flagon was presented to the paper in 1877 and is inscribed 'The Ross Gazette, established 3rd February 1867' followed by

R O S S, *Herefordſhire*.

TO be Sold, by private Contract, together or in parts, the very valuable Eſtate, formerly belonging to "The Man of Roſs." The greateſt part ſituate within a quarter of a mile of the ſaid town; the reſt at Munſlow, near Ledbury, in the ſaid county; alſo three ſubſtantial houſes in the ſaid town of Roſs, one of which is the well accuſtomed Inn, called The King's Arms, which ſaid eſtates, houſes, &c. are together of the yearly value of 477l. and conſiſt of ſeveral very compact farms; with a great deal of very rich meadow land cloſe adjoining to the river Wye. Great part let to ſubſtantial and punctual tenants (who pay all taxes, land tax excepted, which is at the low rate of 8d per pound) under leaſes for twenty-one years, eleven of which are expired. The whole Eſtates are covered with great quantities of fine timber, and ſome young plantations.

Theſe Eſtates and Houſes are in the beſt repair, ſome of the barns new. They want no recommendation for eligibility of ſituation, being the moſt elegant ſpot in the country for any improvement.

☞ For further particulars apply to William Hutcheſon, Eſq. at Briſtol; Meſſrs. Mynd and Griffiths, Attornies; Roſs; or Mr Jenkins; Attorney; New-Inn, London.

Sale of the King's Arms in 1779

the lines 'Hey, John Barleycorn, Ho, John Barleycorn, Old and young thy praise have sung, John Barleycorn', words presumably inspired from the traditional folk song 'John Barleycorn' in praise of beer, and dating from 1600.

Although the **King's Arms** had closed in 1805, it may be that George Evans attempted to re-open it as the **Mitre**, for an advertisement in the *Hereford Journal* for 1816 records:

> to be let and entered on immediately. The Mitre Hotel or Man of Ross House, situated in the town of Ross, and well calculated for carrying on an extensive Business. The Proprietor being entered upon a larger concern is the sole reason for the House and Business being Disposed of. Apply Mr. G. Evans, Mitre Inn, Ross.

This seems straightforward, but an 1852 reference adds to the mystery and confuses the whereabouts of the **Mitre**. In Nathaniel Morgan's will he left 'two dwelling houses with stables, coach house and garden in Dock Pitch — one formerly called the Mitre'. Could this

John Kyrles' house before modernisation

57

Samuel Coleridge composed the above lines at the King's Arms in 1795

The Ross Gazette offices in the old King's Arms in 2001

have been a forerunner of the **Man of Ross**, in Wye Street, earlier called Dock Pitch?

On the east side of the Market House was a quaint row of tenements known as Underhill which housed a variety of trades and two drinking dens. One, called the **Coach and Horses**, was for sale in 1797 'together with ground whereon the Butcher's Shambles stand situate near the Market House'. At the other end of this dilapidated row was the **Boar's Head**, a former shop 'opened as a public' in the early 19th century. As a result of the Improvement Acts, Underhill was 'pulled down for the purpose of widening and improving the thoroughfare', and both inns were demolished.

The one time **Saracen's Head** faces the Market House, but is no longer an inn. It is easily recognised being the only timber-framed building in the vicinity and sporting 'string courses of oak, carved with Tudor roses, heads with pointed beards and moustaches, and foliage and grapes on the beam beneath the eaves' all of which was revealed in the 1890s after being hidden for many years under layers of plaster.

*The Coach and Horses in Underhill (left) and the Crown and Sceptre in
Broad Street (right) in the early 19th century*

There is a tradition that this inn was occupied by the vintner, John Farne, who, in the middle of the 17th century, 'succoured his aged vicar, Mr. Price, when the latter was evicted, penniless from the living during the Commonwealth and the Anabaptist took his place'. Farne died in 1658 and his monument still survives in the nave of St. Mary's church.

Sometime before 1796 the inn was divided into two parts and the right-hand half became known as the Old Saracen's Head, occupied by Samuel Steale a 'gingerbread baker'. After him this part was always used by a druggist or chemist until recent times. The left-hand side of the building continued to be used as an inn under various publicans until it was acquired by the Alton Court Brewery in the 1890s. They restored the **Saracen's Head** and the bar, parlour, kitchen, sitting room, club room and three bedrooms were repaired and painted, giving the inn a new lease of life. However, it gradually fell onto hard times and closed around 1969. Alongside the former inn is a covered footway, now known as Pig's Alley, but long ago it was called 'the church way' which then led 'through and along the Saracen's Head yard' to the parish garden. Here, it is said, was a dwelling 'occupied by a Florist to the church' whose business 'was to raise flowers and evergreens, to dress the Altar and Aisles on the principal festivals'.

59

The Saracen's Head in the 1960s

Overlooking the market place, at the corner of Gloucester Road and High Street, is a row of rather unattractive modern shops called George Place. The name is a distant reminder that this was the site of the **George Inn**, one of Ross's earliest inns. In 1549, when the building formed part of the endowment of St. Mary's Chantry, the **George** was kept by William Tomes. A hundred years later, during the Commonwealth, a notorious landlord, Stephen Endall, was reprimanded for fighting in the streets, and for keeping a shuffleboard table in his inn. In 1771 the **George** was put up for sale, being advertised as 'a good convenient and well-accustomed House, having a soft and hard Water Pump, five Stables, and good Cellarage', together with a 'Large bake-house and brew-house'. Thomas Green Prichard was the innkeeper during the construction of the new Gloucester Road

82. Ross—The Saracen's Head Inn.

All that messauge or Inn in High. Street Ross known as The Saracen's Head Inn and all that adjoining messuage or shop known as No. 13 High Street Ross aforesaid with the outbuildings and yards thereto adjoining and belonging.

Part of the Alton Court Brewery transfer to West Country Brewery in 1962

60

ROSS, MONMOUTH, RAGLAN, & ABERGAVENNY ROYAL MAIL OMNIBUS.

THE Public are respectfully informed that the above OMNIBUS leaves the GEORGE HOTEL, ROSS, at a Quarter before Eight o'clock every Morning, arriving in MONMOUTH at Ten Minutes past Nine, at RAGLAN about Ten, at PENPERGWM STATION in time for the Third Class Train to Newport, and in ABERGAVENNY at Half-past Eleven ; returning from the ANGEL HOTEL, ABERGAVENNY, at Twelve o'clock, after the arrival of the Mails from Merthyr Tydvil, Brecon, and Crickhowell, calling at Penpergwm Station, after the arrival of the 12.15 Train from Cardiff, Newport, Newport-road, and Little Mill Stations, arriving at Monmouth at 2.5 o'cloc⸱, p.m., and at Ross in time for the Four o'clock Train to Hereford and all parts of the North, Bristol Cheltenham, and London.

NOTICE.—Places secured and Parcels booked at low rates at the George Hotel, Ross, the Beaufort Arms Hotel, Monmouth, the Beaufort Arms and Ship Inns, Raglan, and the Angel Hotel, Abergavenny.

6286]   GEO. HUMPHREYS.

The Royal Mail Omnibus took 1 hr. 25 mins. from Ross to Monmouth in 1855

"THE GEORGE"

FAMILY AND COMMERCIAL HOTEL,

AND POSTING HOUSE,

GLOUCESTER ROAD, ROSS.

JOHN COLE,

PROPRIETOR.

WINES AND SPIRITS OF THE BEST QUALITY.

AN ORDINARY EVERY MARKET DAY.

1867 advertisement for the George

around 1825, which must have altered the inn's design, position and its address, because it appears that during this development part of the old **George** was pulled down and a new front added to face the new Gloucester Road.

According to the *Ross Gazette* of 1827, the Excise Office was held at the inn and from the 1830s the **George** became more of a 'Commercial Hotel' catering for carriers and drivers of market carts with Thomas Roper as landlord in 1851, and by 1874 the landlord and his daughter were also 'licensed to let horses'. In 1891 it was described as a 'commercial and family hotel and posting house', with Mrs. Margaret Denton as licensee. It was during the 1890s that the **George** was taken over by Wintle's Forest Brewery, and was offered for sale by them in 1923 as 'a stone-built premises consisting of seven bedrooms, two sitting rooms, a commercial room, stabling for eleven horses, with a large coach house and cellarage for beers, wines and spirits'. In 1934 a new landlord discovered a stock of 19th-century wines and liquors in the cellars, which provided his regular customers with an entertaining tasting. The **George** was demolished in 1960 and the only remains of this ancient hostelry is its last inn sign which is displayed at the Market House Heritage Centre.

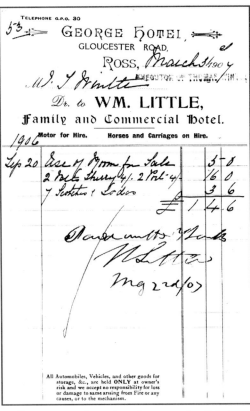

Seven scotch and sodas cost 3s. 6d. in 1907, the equivalent of 17½p. today

THE GEORGE HOTEL, Freehold and Fully Licensed

ROSS, HEREFORDSHIRE

Occupying a Main Corner Position at the junction of Gloucester Road and High Street, in the centre of this busy town. The Premises are Stone-built, and comprise :—

SECOND FLOOR :—Four Bed Rooms, and Store Cupboard.

FIRST FLOOR :—Three Bed Rooms, Sitting Room, Club Room, Ante-Room, Bath Room (h. & c.), W.C.

GROUND FLOOR :—Bar, Smoke Room, Ladies' Room, Sitting Room, Commercial Room, Kitchen, Larder, Closet, Lavatory and W.C.

BASEMENT —Cellarage for Beers, Wines and Spirits.

IN REAR :—Excellent Yard with Brick-built Stabling for 11, Large Coach House with Loft over, Coal House, Ostlers Room, W.C., and Urinal, Two Timber-erected Sheds with Corrugated Iron Roof.

The Property is of Freehold Tenure, and let to Mr. J. J. O'Brien, a tenant of about five years' standing, on Quarterly Tenancy at

Per   £70   Ann.

Land Tax, 20s. 10d. per Annum. Compensation Charge, £7 10s.

The George was for sale as a freehold, fully-licensed hotel in 1923

The George in the mid-20th century

In 1580 Richard Taylor was the innkeeper of **Barlam's Tavern** situated in the market place on the road leading to 'de subter hell'. A similar pub name—**Berew's Inn**—was remembered by Henry Purchas in the late 19th century.

The George inn sign, now in the Ross Heritage centre

The only inn to survive in the Market Place is the **Crown and Sceptre** at the top of Broad Street, another inn that dates back to the 17th century without suffering a change of name. The **Crown and Sceptre** was kept by John Hill in 1687, and its architecture reflects a building of that period, although alterations have since been carried out. Its large swinging sign is depicted in an early 19th-century painting when the Meredith's were the innkeepers. When J.R. Horlick ran the **Crown and Sceptre** in 1855 he advertised the inn with 'Well aired

73. ROSS.—GEORGE HOTEL.

ALL THAT messuage or Inn known as The George Hotel situate at Ross in the County of Hereford and all outbuildings and appurtenances thereunto belonging comprising in the rear a yard with brick built stabling for eleven large coach house with loft over coal house ostlers room W.C. and urinal and two timber erected sheds with corrugated iron roof and all other outbuildings and appurtenances thereunto belonging which said premises are now in the occupation of John Weeds as tenant AND ALSO ALL THAT messuage and shop adjoining being Number 14 High Street Ross aforesaid now in the occupation of J. Metcalfe as tenant and all outbuildings and appurtenances thereunto belonging TOGETHER with the site thereof and the land occupied therewith.

Conveyance from Wintle's to the Cheltenham Original Brewery in 1937

CROWN AND SCEPTRE INN,

ROSS.

J. R. HORLICK,

Wholesale and Retail Dealer in Wines and Spirits,

HOME BREWED BEER, ALE, PORTER, CIDER, &c.

Well-aired Beds.   **Good Stabling and Lock-up Coach-House.**

Mid-19th-century advertisement for the Crown and Sceptre

The Crown and Sceptre at the beginning of the 21st century

Beds, Good Stabling and a Lock-up Coach House'; 'wines and spirits and home-brewed beer, ale, porter, cider etc', were available. The inn was in the capable hands of William Jackson in 1891, but was sold in 1898 before Mrs. Walker took over as landlady. In 1928 the Alton Court Brewery purchased the 'public house and other buildings therein known as the Crown and Sceptre Inn' and Mrs. Clara Harper ran the pub during the Second World War. The Brewery was taken over in 1962 and the **Crown**

A grocery and off-licence of 1920 in the former Saddler's Arms

and Sceptre eventually became a Whitbread pub. In 1985, the 'small central pub' served Whitbread beer and a limited range of bar snacks. In the evenings 'full meals were available in the pretty little dining room that adjoins the bar'.

Within sight of the Market Place was the **Butcher's Arms** later called the **Saddler's Arms**. This establishment occupied the corner of Broad Street and New Street, but by the mid-19th century it had closed as an inn and became E. Hill & Son, a shop selling groceries, 'Bottled Ales and Stout' and 'Wines and Spirits'. The Hill family continued to run the house as an 'off licence' and grocery store until 1926. It is now a newsagents shop.

Further down Broad Street on the west side was the **Lamb**, first listed in 1851 under the management of Richard Davis and in 1891

> 76. ROSS.—LAMB INN.
>
> ALL THAT piece or parcel of land situate in the Urban Parish of Ross in the County of Hereford with the messuage and other buildings thereon now known as "The Lamb Inn" and Numbered 11 Broad Street AND ALSO ALL THAT cottage behind or near to the said premises formerly Numbered 12 Broad Street with stable yard and garden adjoining same now in the occupation of William Davis as tenant All which premises hereinbefore described are delineated on the plan drawn in a Conveyance dated the twenty-third day of January One thousand nine hundred and twenty made between Hannah Edith Purchase of the one part Griffiths Thomas William Purchase and John Raymond Morton Ball of the second part and Emily Louise Nicholls of the third part and therein coloured pink and light pink TOGETHER with the freehold passage on the North East side of the Lamb Inn premises delineated and coloured brown on the said plan.

Transfer from Wintle's to the Cheltenham Original Brewery in 1937

T. W. PURCHAS & SONS,

Wine and Spirit Merchants,

BROAD STREET,

ROSS.

AGENTS FOR

Raggett's Nourishing Stout.

S. ALLSOPP & SONS and BASS & CO.'S

BURTON ALES, IN CASK & BOTTLE.

BURGOYNE'S AUSTRALIAN WINES.

STRETTON HILLS MINERAL WATERS,

&c., &c., &c.

Full PRICE LIST on application.

Wine merchant's advertisement in 1896

T.W. Purchas & Sons on Coronation day, 9 August 1902. Originally the Black Lion

with a landlady having a rather imposing name—Mrs. Urania Dawson. This inn continued to serve its customers until recent times, but has since reverted to becoming an off-licence, trading as a branch of Thresher's.

The **Half Moon** of 1768 was probably in Broad Street, and may have opened out to become the **Full Moon** of 1851. Its site is understood to have been within 'a lot of ramshackle little shops towards the lower end of Broad Street' immediately below the Baptist Chapel. This row of buildings were demolished and long before 1921 were replaced by 'a block of shops'.

The **King Charles II** in Broad Street has enjoyed a chequered history, for it stands on the site of the ancient **Black Lion** recorded in the 14th century. There is a huge gap in the documentation until 1746 when the **Black Lyon** was occupied by Josias Jackson. In 1779 the victualler was Thomas Griffiths who only lived in part of the building. Apart from running the **Black Lion** he

A 1921 price list of wines and spirits

The King Charles' Bar in the 1940s, formerly T.W. Purchas and originally the Black Lion

The King Charles II in 2001

An 1855 advertisement for the New Inn

also worked as a tiler. A few years later, after the inn had closed, Thomas Purchas moved his wine business into the premises. He eventually purchased the whole property and was probably responsible for rebuilding the former inn around the late 18th or early 19th century above the old cellars, which are hewn out of the solid rock. After T.W. Purchas and Son had traded for 100 years in Ross, the wine business was taken over by Charles Edwards Ltd. from Worcester. This company later opened the **King Charles Bar** in the 1930s, which eventually became the **King Charles II**, an inn which offers all the usual services in modernised surroundings. Of particular interest is a collection of photographs depicting old Ross, which are displayed in the pool room.

The **Eagle**, on the corner of Broad Street and Kyrle Street, was originally called the **New Inn**, but the managers in 1969 decided this name was too commonplace so the brewery decided to call the pub after the Eagle, the name of the Lunar Module which had landed on the

New Inn bottle token

Changing pub signs. Left & centre: the 1969 space tribute.
Right: the 1999 eagle

The imposing front of the Eagle in 2001

Moon in that year. A plaque inside the inn claims it was built in 1716, but it was certainly described as being 'newly erected' in 1790 under George Bird. From 1812 to 1867 the Wellington family ran their 'Commercial and Agricultural House' for 'Excursionists and Tourists', and by the mid-19th century the **New Inn** warranted an entry under 'Hotels and Inns' in a Herefordshire directory, but never quite made it as a coaching inn. The landlord in 1891 went under the rather attractive name of Samuel Marriman, later followed by the Best family of publicans from 1914 to 1941. At some period it was acquired by the

The Drop Inn is a typical name of the late 20th century

The Brewery Tap is now a television centre

The Stag in 2001

Alton Court Brewery and was sold to West Country Breweries in 1962. The **Eagle** has recently been extensively modernised and offers accommodation and meals in the refurbished restaurant.

In 1855 the east side of Broad Street was altered following the opening of the railway in 1855. To make the station more accessible from the town centre, a new road was built. Originally it was called Queen Street, but the name was later changed to Station Street. Here, in 1859, William Delahay operated a beer retailers, which by 1876 had become the **Queen's Head**. Changes occurred, including the closure of the railway, and it now goes under the name of the **Drop Inn** serving as the headquarters of the Ross Rugby Football Club.

The Alton Court Brewery, established by Joseph Turnock in 1865, gradually expanded along both sides of Station Street and opened the **Brewery Tap** in Mill Pond Street during the 1890s with Mrs. Elizabeth

The sign of the Stag

Woodman as licensee. This public house closed shortly after the brewery ceased operations in 1960, but the red brick building still survives and is now a television centre.

Running from Broad Street parallel to Station Street is a narrow lane called the Crofts where Ann Pendree ran a beer house called the **Rose and Crown** in 1851. Further east, at the corner of the Crofts and Henry Street, the notable builder and contractor, J.B. Kemp, was also retailing

71

Sale of the Maidenhead at the Swan and Falcon in 1784

beer in 1867. This was probably the forerunner of the **White Hart**, renamed the **Stag** in the mid-20th century. It is now within the Enterprise Inns group, which supports recycling projects, and continues to be a popular drinking establishment.

New Street and Kyrle Street join the western side of Broad Street to Edde Cross Street and Trenchard Street. This is an area where there were several back street inns and beer houses during the last 300 years. New Street, known earlier as Back Lane, was the site of William Mynde's **Boot and Shoe** in the 18th century. Another inn of a similar date was the **Freemasons' Arms** opened by Humphrey Matthews in

The floral display on the front of the Horse and Jockey in 2001

1770. He was not a stonemason, but a plumber and glazier who 'neatly fitted up his dwelling house, facing the back lane, Ross, and has opened the same as an inn'. A few years later in 1781 this 'good accustomed Public House pleasantly and very conveniently situated for business'

72

NOTICE.   NOTICE.

Benjamin Clark,

TRUE HEART INN,

KYRLE-STREET, ROSS,

DESIRES to inform the Public that he has just taken to the above Fully Licensed Premises, where he will supply LIQUORS, &c., of the best Brand, and STOUT, ALES, &c., of the best quality.

THE CELEBRATED

Alton Court Brewery Ales.

B. Clark further wishes to give notice to the Inhabitants of Ross, and Farmers of the Neighbourhood generally, that he has also taken to the

OLD-ESTABLISHED

WHEELWRIGHT'S

BUSINESS,

Which has been carried on for years on the Premises opposite to and adjoining the True Heart Inn, where, by strict attention to Business, combined with Moderate Charges, he hopes to secure a fair share of public Patronage.

ORDERS EXECUTED on the Shortest Notice.

REPAIRS by Practical Workmen, at Reasonable Prices,

*The True Heart in 1892 included a wheelwright's business
as well as a fully-licensed inn*

73

was for sale with an 'exceedingly good malthouse, stables and other convenient outbuildings'. It may have been this establishment that changed its name to the **Maidenhead**—an inn that was advertised for sale in 1784 with a similar description.

It is possible that the existing **Horse and Jockey** in New Street could have replaced either of the inns previously mentioned, as the first known record dates from 1822 when James Bird occupied the building. Later innkeepers included Joseph Cross and John Barrow, a watch and clock maker. From the 1850s Mary Fenner and Ambrose Marshall totalled 70 years between them serving their customers. The skittle alley was removed in the 1990s and interior alterations have taken place, but the early 19th-century bow-fronted brick building still houses the **Horse and Jockey** in the 21st century.

The Merton was a comfortable licensed hotel in the mid-20th century

From 1835 there was a beer house in New Street which became known as the **Red Lion** in 1851, but closed a few years later.

In Kyrle Street a carpenter, wheelwright and beer retailer called Thomas Bubb named his house rather romantically the **True Heart** in 1851, and maybe the inn sign would have shown Cupid shooting an arrow into a heart! James Bubb followed Thomas until 1890 when George Hodges took over. He augmented his income by acting as a carrier and dairyman and lived at Millbrook House. Later publicans kept the tiny public house open well into the mid-20th century.

In Trenchard Street, which is the southern continuation of Edde Cross Street, the **Old Maypole** of 1851 was probably on the same site as the **Maypole** ran by Thomas Jarvis in 1768. This inn name usually indicates that this was the site of an ancient maypole used for May Day celebrations.

The other beer house in Trenchard Street was called the **Earl Grey** and was probably named after the second Earl Grey, Prime Minister from 1830 to 1834, who is renowned for putting through Wilberforce's Act to abolish the African slave trade. The **Earl Grey** in Ross only traded during the first half of the 19th century.

Merton House stands where Trenchard Street runs into Edde Cross Street. It is a gracious mansion built in the early 19th century on gardens belonging to Walter Hill. In 1802, shortly before the present house was built, Lord Nelson and his guests walked through the gardens on their way to the river to continue their journey down the Wye to Monmouth. Throughout most of the 19th century the Hooper family of solicitors lived at Merton House. Eventually, around 1937, Arthur Beard opened the house as a hotel.

Since 1967 the hotel has been run by the Rotary Club who have converted and extended the property to accommodate disabled and frail guests. Of particular interest is the chapel and an upper room, which display heraldic shields representing the ancestry of Elizabeth I and James I.

In Edde Cross Street a beer retailer called James Burgess named his premises the **Pheasant** in 1851. The inn passed to the Griffiths family in 1882 with Robert Griffiths as licensee in 1891. As with many pubs in Ross, in 1940 the freehold was conveyed to the Stroud Brewery and it continued as a brewery inn into the 1960s,

418. Ross—The Pheasant Inn.

First all that messuage or Inn in Edde Cross Street Ross known as The Pheasant Inn with the land and outbuildings thereto adjoining and belonging AND SECONDLY ALL THAT cottage adjoining the property first described known as No. 53 Eddle Cross Street with the garden and outbuildings thereto adjoining and belonging.

Liquidation conveyance of the Pheasant from the Stroud Brewery Co. to West Country Breweries in 1962

The Pheasant sign, as an inn in the 1950s, and as a restaurant in 2001

when it was sold. It is now a licensed restaurant called the Golden Pheasant, but still has a traditional sign hanging out from the dense cover of ivy.

Also in Edde Cross street was the **Greyhound Inn**, run by a Mrs. Hicks in 1832.

CHAPTER FIVE

ROSS-ON-WYE
BROOKEND TO OVERROSS & BEYOND

The Brookend, the continuation of Broad Street to the north, is named after the Rudhall Brook and its tributaries. These streams provided the power needed in the past for milling, tanning, malting, and brewing industries all of which were established at this end of Ross. In 1824, Mr. Harris was working the Town Mill, Mr. Frere was at the tanyard, and Thomas Jones, John Griffiths, Mr. Woodall, Sam Trotter and John Hill were the maltsters, all in Brookend.

Beer had been brewed on the premises of inns or at the tanyard until John Hill started the first brewery in Ross during the 1830s from his 'House, Malthouse, Stable' in Brookend. The industry was continued by Joseph Turnock who moved the business to Station Street and expanded the Ross Brewery to form the Alton Court Brewing empire by 1865.

Two women writers of the 20th century referred to the Brookend and the Brewery. In 1939 Margiad Evans wrote in her *Autobiography:*

> The jasmine is in bloom against the back scullery wall. It's a cold, clammy thaw. Went to the station about my luggage past the Brewery. The building threw the street into grey shadow ... a street which is nearly always empty. It smelt malty, and there was a soft hiss of steam. Men were rolling barrels into the reverberating entries ... M— came to tea. I met him in the road between the Vine Tree and the Vicarage, walking in his sandals.

The lesser-known Jessie M. Stonham in her *Daughter of Wyedean* published in 1978 remembered:

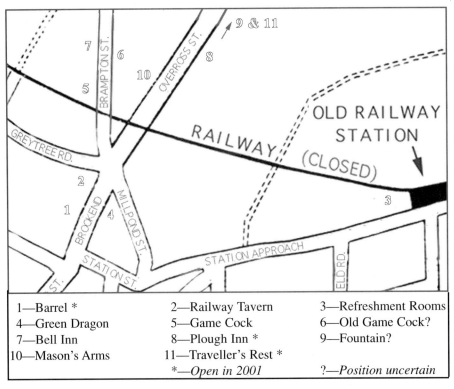

1—Barrel *	2—Railway Tavern	3—Refreshment Rooms
4—Green Dragon	5—Game Cock	6—Old Game Cock?
7—Bell Inn	8—Plough Inn *	9—Fountain?
10—Mason's Arms	11—Traveller's Rest *	
	*—*Open in 2001*	*?—Position uncertain*

The only other industry I remember was at Alton Court Brewery, then a flourishing business and occupying most of both sides of the Station Road between the bottom of Broad Street and Henry Street. Its malt house also continued up Henry Street and the entrance to the cooperage went from here, eventually coming out on to the Broad Street. It was a very busy place when I was a child and we loved to walk past the windows through which we could see the men treading over and working on the malt. The smell was strong but quite attractive. The cooperage was, of course, the place in which the wooden barrels for the beer were made. This was a real craftsman's job and as children we were occasionally taken to see the men at work. We enjoyed scuffling our feet through the chippings after the wood had been trimmed ready and watching the hammering of the metal bands on to the casks.

One pub of the Alton Court Brewery was the **Barrel** in Brookend Street, advertised for sale in 1792 as 'A Freehold Messuage or Public-house called the Barrel' in the possession of Mary Lucy. It became the **Barrel and Woolpack**, described in 1813 as a 'Public-House' with 'a

A forced sale of the Barrel in 1792

71. ROSS—THE BARRELL INN AND COTTAGES.

FIRST ALL THAT messuage or Inn in Brookend Street Ross known as The Barrell Inn with the brewhouse outbuildings yard and garden thereto adjoining and belonging SECONDLY ALL THAT messuage or dwellinghouse with the outbuildings yard and garden thereto belonging on the north side of the property above described AND THIRDLY ALL THOSE two messuages or dwellinghouses with the outbuildings yards and gardens thereto belonging also on the north side of the property first above described and known as Nos. 4 and 5 Brookend Street.

In 1962, the Barrel, together with the adjoining cottages,
was part of the voluntary liquidation of the Alton Court Brewery

kitchen, parlour, large dining-room over the cellar, two good bedrooms attics and other conveniences'. The name reflected an association between brewing and woolstapling, but reverted to the **Barrel**, which was run under the ownership of three long-term publicans, Joseph Brain, George Hall and William Goulding during the 19th century. The latter opened a brewery alongside the inn, which continued under Herbert Mew, but ceased in the 1930s. However, the **Barrel** stayed open as an inn and the premises were rearranged to

1914 prices for beers from the Barrel Brewery

form the **Barrel Bar** with a snooker hall entered by a side door. However, this project was also unsuccessful, and after some years of closure and a complete refurbishment the **Barrel** once again opened its doors in August 2001.

By the end of the First World War prices had escalated—
a dozen pint bottles of pale ale or stout had increased in price
from 2s. 6d. in 1914 to 7s. 6d. in 1921

The Barrel in mid-2001, just before reopening

At the bottom of Brookend, Adam Lewis opened his **Railway Tavern** in 1851. He was obviously anticipating the opening of the Hereford, Ross, and Gloucester Railway. The route had first been surveyed in 1844, but financial crises meant that the prospectus was not issued until 1850 . At that time the capital requirement for the 27 miles was £275,000. The parliamentary bill was agreed in April 1851 and the line opened in June 1855. The tavern was housed in a 17th-century former tanhouse, which already had an existing malt house and brew house. Documents dating from the late 17th century show that the Brookend Tanyard and Malt House were owned by John Merrick the Elder, a tanner of Ross. His son, of the same name, took over the property before it changed hands in 1722 and was subsequently used

ROSS.

NEAT AND CLEAN HOUSEHOLD

FURNITURE,

BREWING AND WASHING UTENSILS,

LIGHT WAGGON & CART,

SPRING CART,

Long and Short Harness, &c. &c.

TO BE SOLD

BY AUCTION,

BY

J. MORGAN & SON,

On *MONDAY*, the 20th day of *JUNE*, 1836,

ON THE PREMISES, IN THE

BROOKEND STREET,

The Property of Mr Charles Frere,

WHO IS DECLINING BUSINESS:

CONSISTING OF Mahogany Four-post and Tent Bedsteads with Furniture, Stump Ditto, Feather Beds, Bolsters, and Pillows, Hair Mattresses, Blankets, Bedquilts, and Counterpanes, Bed and Table Linen, Mahogany Chest of Drawers, Mahogany Night Tables, Mahogany and Painted Wash-hand Stands, Swing and Box Dressing Glasses, Bed Room Chairs and Carpets, Mahogany Dining, Pembroke and Tea Tables, Mahogany Chairs with Horse-hair Seats, Bureau, Mahogany and Oak Writing Desks, Eight-day Time Piece, Mahogany Sideboard, Barometer, Thermometer, Mahogany Sofa with Chintz Cover, Carpets and Rugs, Dinner and Dessert Services of Iron-stone China, China, Glass, and Earthenware, Mahogany Dinner and Supper Trays, Copper Coal Scuttles, Brass Fender and Fire-irons, Kitchen and Culinary Requisites, Brewing and Washing Utensils, Mashing Tub, Skeels, Tunpails, 2 Buckets, 6 Tubs, 3 Hogs-heads, 5 Barrels, Brewing Sieves, Wood Bottles, Water Tub, &c. &c.

ALSO;

3 Ironing Boards and Trestles, Long Table, 3 Counters with Drawers, Flour and Corn Bins, 4 Beams, Scales, 2 Sets of Weights, Grittling and Malt Mills, 2 Sets of Short Harness, 1 Set of Long Harness, 1 Set of Gig Harness, Pad and Straps, Straw Cutter with Three Knives, Box Ditto, 1 Light Waggon, 1 Narrow-wheel Cart, 1 Spring Cart, 4 Wheelbarrows, 2 Dozen Hurdles, Quantity of Poleing, Doors and Shutters, Old Timber, 2 Ladders, Pikes, Iron Bars, and Sundry Tools, Iron Gate, with various other Effects.

☞ *The Sale will commence at Eleven o'Clock in the Forenoon; and the whole will be Sold without reserve.*

Sale of the Brookend Tanyard in 1836

by local tanners, Michael Powles, Thomas Pritchard and Daniel Pearce during the early 19th century.

In 1808 Daniel Pearce sold the Tanyard and Malt House to James Frere, a former currier, who traded as a tanner at the

Brookend till his third son Charles, took over the business in 1827. An Indenture of that date records details of the property and its boundaries:

> All that Messuage Burgage or Tenement with the Malt House and other Buildings Tanyard Garden and Orchard thereto adjoining and belonging situate lying and being in the Town of Ross aforesaid in or near a certain Street there called the Brookend and heretofore in the tenure or occupation of Daniel Pearce his tenant or tenants since the said James Frere and now of the said Charles Frere Also All that Tanhouse (formerly a Bark Mill and Bark Kiln) with the Pits, Yard, Buildings ...

By 1836 Charles Frere ran into financial difficulties so the 'Excellent Tanyard' and its 'Neat and Clean Household Furniture, Brewing and Washing Utensils' were put up for sale. From about this time the tanyard appears to have ceased and been replaced by the New Tanyard at Overross operated by Elles Lee Saunders

In the mid-19th century the Brookend property was probably divided into two—the tanyard being used for other purposes and the tanhouse, brew and malt house converted into an inn. Adam Lewis was followed by a succession of landlords and by the 1940s a Mrs. Harrison was the landlady at what was then

The Railway Inn c.1950

UP TRAINS.	Ex. 1 & 2	1, 2, 3		Ex. 1 & 2	1 & 2	1 & 2
	a.m.	a.m.	a.m.	p.m.	p.m.	p.m.
Hereford Dep.	6 45	9 50	..	1 10	*5 45	8 45
Holme Lacy	6 55	10 0	..	1 20	5 55	8 55
Fawley	7 5	10 10	..	1 30	6 5	9 5
Ross	7 15	10 20	..	1 40	6 15	9 15
Mitcheldean........	7 25	10 30	..	1 55	6 25	9 25
Longhope..........	..	10 38	..	..	6 33	9 33
Grange Court	7 37	10 50	..	2 5	6 45	9 45
Gloucester } Arr...	7 5½	11 5	..	2 20	7 5	10 5
Gloucester { Dep...	8 0	11 30	..	2 45	7 20	12 40
Cheltenham, Arr. ..	8 45	11 30	..	3 0	7 30	10 40
Stroud	8 25	11 57	..	3 10	7 47	1 5
Cirencester	9 5	..	....	3 50	8 35	..
Swindon	9 15	1 10	..	4 5	8 55	2 10
Bath	10 25	2 55	..	5 15	..	..
Oxford	11 0	4 0	..	5 35	10 10	..
PADDINGTON	11 15	3 45	..	6 0	11 0	4 35

Ross station was of considerable importance in 1862 with five trains each day from Hereford to Paddington

rather grandly called the **Railway Hotel,** catering for anglers, cyclists and motorists in her 'Excellent Accommodation'. After the railway closed in 1964 the hotel was converted into retail units, but the building is still easily recognised.

In 1905 John Richards was licensed to run a bar in the **Railway Refreshment Room** at Ross station for Great Western Railways.

On the east side of Brookend there was only one inn. Called the **Green Dragon**, this inn probably dates from the 18th century. The inn was mainly associated with transport and in 1822 was run by William Deeley who 'occasionally supplied wagons to Newham'. The **Green Dragon** with its skittle alley, cart shed and 'stone-built Stabling for four' became one of the 72 public houses owned by Francis Wintle's Forest Brewery at Mitcheldean, which were all sold in 1937. The **Green Dragon** appears to have been de-licensed sometime before 1941, and the premises have since been demolished and replaced with modern shops. In its heyday it was a cider house run by one Duckam Jones and was famous for a local brew called 'Stun'em'.

The lower end of Brookend has always been susceptible to flooding and the floods of 1797 and 1809 were memorable. In 1875 an artist's impression depicts the flood water in the Brookend, showing water girth-high on a horse, a man paddling a boat, and floating barrels

---

74. ROSS.—GREEN DRAGON.

ALL THAT messuage or Inn known as the Green Dragon situate at Brookend Ross in the County of Hereford and all outbuildings and appurtenances thereunto belonging comprising in the rear a small yard with timber erection of skittle alley cart shed urinal W.C. coal store and stone built stabling for four with loft over and all other outbuildings and appurtenances thereunto belonging which said premises are now in the occupation of William James as tenant

Wintle's sale of the Green Dragon in 1937

of beer from the brewery. In early 2001 the street was closed due to severe flooding which caused great damage to property. In 1827 there was a 'Turnpike at the termination of Brookend Street, where the road branches off in two different directions, here is a considerable suburb, called respectively Brampton-street and Over Ross'. This turnpike was removed in 1830 which led to the establishment of a toll-free entry into Ross from How Caple and along Brampton Street. This was much appreciated by the farmers and drovers who mainly used this route.

At the bottom of Brookend, known as Five Ways, is Greytree Road which leads to the former site of the Cattle Market opened in 1871. According to Fred Druce, in *Remembrance of Things Past,* Mrs. Bubb, the landlady at the **True Heart**, in Kyrle Street, wrote to the Ross Town Commissioners asking for permission to rent one end of a shed for a refreshment bar which 'would be of great convenience for farmers and others'. The livestock market was moved to a new site at Overross in 1988, where no licensed facilities are available.

Leading north from the end of Brookend is Brampton Street, once known as the 'poorest and most poverty-stricken street in Ross', although beer retailers were able to establish the **Game Cock** in 1851, and the **Old Game Cock** in 1876 on opposite sides of the street; the names are somewhat confusing. The **Game Cock** was put up for sale in 1868 when it

A well-creased and cut photograph of regulars outside the Game Cock some 100 years ago

*Although breweries sold unprofitable houses in the mid-20th century,
they usually made sure that they could not be reopened as inns, either by
ensuring that they were delicensed, or by including a condition in the sale.
The Game Cock was sold in 1960*

was described as a 'Dwelling House used as a Public House known by
the sign of the **Upper Game Cock**'. It consisted of two sitting-rooms,
a back kitchen, four bedrooms, and a garden, and was occupied by
James Gardner at a rent of £16 a year.

Both Game Cocks, which were named after a breed of cock
formerly used in cock fighting, were in business until the 1880s, but

only one survived into the 1930s under the care of Elizabeth and James Castree. It was then taken over by the Alton Court Brewery and from 1939 to 1951 Tom and Mable Jones were the tenants at the **Gamecock**, and although there was a shortage of beer during the war years it remained a 'busy little pub'. In early 2001, Tom's son recalled life at the **Gamecock** in the *Ross Gazette:*

> The Gamecock was quite a small pub. As you went through the front entrance the public bar was on the left, the Jug and Bottle was in front of you and the Smoke Room was up a few steps and on the right. The public bar was used by men only and only very occasionally did women venture into this area. The Jug and Bottle was used by people taking away bottles of beer and cider and was also used by ladies as a small bar.
>
> In those days large bottles were charged for and the excess charge was refunded when the bottle was returned, something that should be reintroduced today to avoid unnecessary wastage.
>
> The Smoke Room was not used much, people smoked a lot in those days, pipes, cigarettes, and took snuff and 'twist' — and in the public bar, so having a separate smoke room was really unnecessary.
>
> It tended to be used for occasional private parties when people wanted to be separate from the main public bar.

Thomas Jones left in 1951 and George Allen took over the running of the **Gamecock** until the brewery ceased production in 1960. It was sold as a 'detached freehold unlicensed property ideal for use as a private residence' and was purchased by a local builder to be incorporated into a housing scheme.

The **Bell Inn** was another licensed establishment on the west side of Brampton Street. It was opened in 1889 by James Atkins, a church-going man who occupied a pew 'about four away from the statue of Col. Rudhall.

The Bell about 100 years ago

At the turn of the century he was also a keen bell-ringer whose name is engraved in the belfry for having rung over 500 grandsire triple changes'. In 1905 James and his family left the **Bell Inn** when he was presented with a walking stick engraved with 'Jas. Atkins : Ross : From a few Old Pals, 16 / 11 / 05'. The walking stick was a necessary aid to James, who, for some unknown reason, had a wooden leg. The inn closed a few years later during the First World War when many pubs suffered from poor trade.

In 1825 Thomas Vobes occupied a 'House, Garden, Malthouse, Carpenters Workshop, and Cider Mill' in Brampton Street. This may

*The fixtures at the Plough Inn in 1898 were considered
to be worth £28 12s.*

have been the site of the **Angel Inn** that was run by Walter Smith in 1768. No further references have been found to this establishment, and although a number of maltsters and carpenters were listed after 1825 it appears that Thomas Vobes' premises went out of use.

At the bottom of the Brookend, Overross Street leads towards Ledbury. This was an important thoroughfare in medieval times which was improved by the turnpike trusts in the 18th century. This may have led to the establishment of the **Plough Inn** housed in an earlier building with a gabled wing and a projecting upper storey. Thomas Dew was at the **Plough** in 1768 and a succession of innkeepers tended the needs of travellers and the growing population around Overross. Towards the end of the 1800s the **Plough** was purchased by Alfred Wintle who also operated the corn mill at Bill Mills, and had by this time expanded into malting, bottling beer and manufacturing mineral water. In 1886 an agreement was made between the Wintles and George Seabright for renting the **Plough** for £24 a year. This was continued by Miss Annie Elizabeth Seabright, presumably his daughter, who also agreed to purchase from Wintles 'all malt beer and mineral water used and sold at the inn'. At a later date she replaced the 'woodwork of the skittle alley, the Dairy or Pantry, part of the piggery,

---

THE PLOUGH INN, Freehold and Fully Licensed
ROSS, HEREFORDSHIRE

Stone-built Premises, comprising :—

FIRST FLOOR :—Four Bed Rooms.

GROUND FLOOR :—Bar, Tap Room, Smoke Room, Private Ditto, Wash-house, Kitchen and Pantry.

BASEMENT :—Cellarage.

IN REAR :—Good Paved Yard, Brick-built Stabling for two, Brick-built Skittle Alley, with large Loft over, W.C., Timber-built Store Sheds, &c., and Good Garden.

The Property is of Freehold Tenure, and let to Miss A. Seabright, a tenant of about 35 years' standing, on Quarterly Tenancy, at

Per   £40   Ann.

Compensation Charge, £3.

N.B.—Certain Out-buildings are claimed by the tenant.

Sale of the Plough Inn in 1923

ALL THAT messuage or Inn known as the Plough Inn situate at Ross in the County of Hereford and all outbuildings and appurtenances thereunto belonging comprising in the rear a paved yard brick built stabling for two brick built skittle alley with large loft over W.C. timber built store sheds etc. and garden and all other outbuildings and appurtenances thereunto belonging TOGETHER with the site thereof and the land occupied therewith which said premises are now in the occupation of F. G. Llewellyn as tenant.

*The Plough was included in the Wintle's conveyance to
the Cheltenham Original Brewery in 1937*

a 60 Gallon Copper Brewing Furnace and erected a urinal'. Ann was still there in 1923 when the **Plough** was offered for sale, and remained there until 1926. The **Plough** is still open and is well worth a detour from the centre of the town for a quick drink.

The earliest Friendly Societies were established in Ross from 1778. By means of a weekly subscription they provided a form of insurance for the less wealthy against sickness, disability and old age, and were usually associated with public houses. In 1794 'the Members of the Friendly Society' held their meetings at the **Fountain** at Overross but later moved on to the **Nags Head**. By the 1820s John Green was paying rent for a 'Club' at Overross which may have been the site of the **Fountain**, an inn that has since been lost as a result of modern development.

Almost opposite the **Plough** in Overross is 'Mason's Arms Cottage' a reminder of the **Mason's Arms**, one of the many inns, taverns and beer houses that opened in Ross during the mid-19th century. This was partly to cope with a

The Plough, with its old-fashioned front door, in 2001

population which had more than doubled from 2,347 in 1801 to 4,912 in 1901, together with changes in the licensing laws. The **Mason's Arms** was started as a beer house by Edward Gardener in 1847 and stayed in the same family for at least 50 years. The last publican appears to have been Thomas H. Jones who moved to a pub at Walford after the Stroud Brewery had sold part of the premises for 'proposed development'.

Mason's Arms Cottage, once the Mason's Arms Inn

Before the spread of housing, the north side of Ross was open countryside until the sale and development of the common fields of Cawdor, and land belonging to the Over Ross and Springfield estates. In the 1890s both estates came up for sale and the particulars describe the 'Wine and Beer Cellars' and a vinery at Over Ross House, and 'excellent cellarage with Cask Entrance' at Springfield. So the occupiers of these houses could select wine and drink beer and cider from their own stock instead of visiting the local inns.

From Overross the Ledbury Road leads to the Ross parish boundary where the **Travellers' Rest Travel Inn** stands next to the

The Travellers' Rest Travel Inn in 2001

roundabout at the start of the M50. This site was originally known as the Black House where the Ross and Archenfield Friendly Society owned a cottage and garden in 1840. This may have led to the opening of a beer

house called the **Travellers' Rest**. Situated on the main route from Ross to Ledbury, the road has undergone many changes, but it was during the construction of the motorway in 1960 that the Black House, Smithy and **Travellers' Rest** were completely demolished and replaced by the new roadside inn and restaurant, which since then has been extended and had various alterations. The legend associated with the Black House implies that the premises had supplied biers, hired mourners and provided sin eaters at local funerals. This ancient custom was obsolete by 1833 when it was described by Fosbroke:

Two views of the Travellers' Rest junction in 1956, before the M50 was built

In the county of Hereford was an old custom at funerals to hire poor people, who were to take upon them the sinnes of the party deceased. One of them (he was a long, leane, ugly, lamentable poor rascal) I remember lived in a cottage on Rosse highway. The manner was, that when the corpse was brought out of the house, and layed on the bier, a loaf of bread was brought out, and delivered to the sin-eater, over the corpse, as also a mazer bowl of maple, full of beer (which he was to drink up) and sixpence in money, in consideration whereof he took upon him, *ipso facto* all the sinnes of the defunct, and freed him or her from walking after they were dead.

CHAPTER SIX

Ross-on-Wye
THE GLOUCESTER ROADS, COPSE CROSS & TUDORVILLE

The important road from Hereford and South Wales to Gloucester has by-passed the centre of Ross since the construction of a relief road in 1985. This completed the A40 improvements first started in 1960. Previously the main roads from Hereford Monmouth, Ledbury, Gloucester, and the Forest of Dean met in Ross, and established the town as a 'very great thoroughfare' with a reputation for 'good inn accommodation'.

The original way through Ross towards Gloucester was extremely circuitous through Underhill, rows of ancient shops and houses which once stood on the east side of the market place. Coaches, wagons, carts and droves of animals followed a narrow causeway between the buildings and under a low arch before continuing along the High Street and Old Gloucester Road. In 1825, a new Gloucester Road was built leading due east from the Market House, which required the removal of two houses at Underhill.

Underhill remained a hazardous and dirty place until all the buildings had been demolished in 1863. At a later date the *Ross Gazette* considered:

> The effect of the removal of the upper row of seven houses has been to increase the salubrity of the town, to bring the Townhall more in view, to widen the pavement on the lower side of the street, and the erection of a superior class of houses and improvement of others adjoining thereto; in fact, it may be said to be the greatest improvement made in the heart of the town of Ross during the present century.

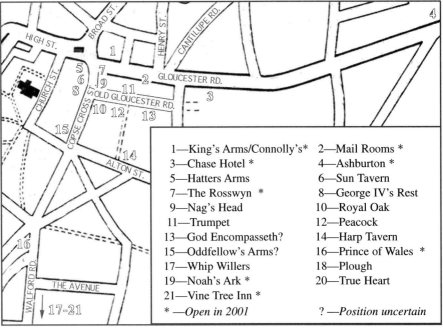

1—King's Arms/Connolly's*   2—Mail Rooms *
3—Chase Hotel *   4—Ashburton *
5—Hatters Arms   6—Sun Tavern
7—The Rosswyn *   8—George IV's Rest
9—Nag's Head   10—Royal Oak
11—Trumpet   12—Peacock
13—God Encompasseth?   14—Harp Tavern
15—Oddfellow's Arms?   16—Prince of Wales *
17—Whip Willers   18—Plough
19—Noah's Ark *   20—True Heart
21—Vine Tree Inn *
* —Open in 2001   ? —Position uncertain

*Connolly's Irish Bar—
one time the King's Arms*

The new Gloucester Road was slow to be developed with a number of gardens, yards and orchards still lining the road in 1840. After the removal of the **Coach and Horses** and the **Boar's Head** at Underhill there was space for another licensed premises which was seized by Emanuel Taylor in the late 1860s. He opened an 'Ale and Porter Stores' called the **Volunteer**, perhaps named after the Ross and Archenfield Rifle Corps which existed at that time. It was probably the forerunner of the **King's Arms** of 1876 run by William Wade. In recent times the **King's Arms** changed its name to **Connolly's Irish Bar**, a typical theme pub of the 1990s.

94

In late 2000 this was the only pub in Gloucester Road, but in May 2001 Wetherspoons opened their new public house, the **Mail Rooms**, in the former post office, built in 1899. The £900.000 project created 25 new full and part time jobs. The premises have been transformed into a spacious seating area, open to the roof, with the walls decorated with paintings, photographs and text relating to the local area.

The old post office, now a Weatherspoon's house called the Mail Rooms

The entrance to the **Chase Hotel** is in Gloucester Road. The Chase, named after the hill where the bishops of Hereford hunted in medieval times, has only been an hotel since the late 1920s. The mansion house was built in 1818 by a Ross attorney, John Cooke, to replace Old Chase and Chest's

The Chase in 2001

95

or Chase mill. Cooke built a Georgian mansion, and in the grounds extended the mill pond to form ornamental pools, and erected a water wheel to pump the 'pure spring water' up to the house.

John Cooke's daughter married Dr. George Strong, a physician in Ross, who took a keen interest in the past and wrote *The Heraldry of Herefordshire* in 1848 and *The Handbook to Ross and Archenfield* in 1863. After Cooke died in 1867 the Strongs continued to live at the Chase prior to its sale in 1878. It was purchased by General Sir James William Fitzmayer before the estate passed to Colonel Oswald Middleton in 1895. After active service he made his home at the Chase for 32 years, and played an important role in the life of Ross.

Around 1927, the **Chase** was acquired by John Brawn who converted the property into a hotel. While under the management of Brawn, during the Second World War, 400 school girls were evacuated there, and narrowly avoided a 500 lb. bomb which fell into the hotel grounds. Since then the hotel has undergone many changes, and has been enlarged and extended to form a 'Rectangular box with 3 by 4 bays with stringcourse and porch' according to the rather unimaginative Listed Building description, and remains a prominent hotel in the town.

The CHASE HOTEL

Ross-on-Wye

PHONE 210

MODERNISED GEORGIAN COUNTRY HOUSE, standing in own grounds of 14 Acres within 2 minutes of Town Post Office. 6 Reception, 60 Bedrooms (h. & c.), 12 Bathrooms. Dining and Ball Room. Garages. Electric and all Public Services. Licensed.

SALMON AND COARSE FISHING AVAILABLE.

Brochure Gratis.   *Resident Owner.*

The Chase Hotel in the 1950s.
A typical advertisement of that date

Also in Gloucester Road is the **Ashburton**, an inn established sometime after 1960. It was possibly named after Lord Ashburton who had owned several large estates in the area. The adjacent industrial estate is also named after him.

From the Market Place the narrow High Street continues in a southerly direction to the Old Gloucester Road, which formed part of

96

The Chase Hotel in 1962

The Ashburton in 2001

the main road through Ross to London. At the top of the High Street on the west side a 'hat man and beer retailer' by the name of William Scudamore opened his miniature **Hatter's Arms** in 1851. It was taken over by Herbert Thomas, then William Harris, also a

97

Left : 1892 advertisement for the Sun Inn.
Above : The Sun fire mark

postman, before closing its doors in the early 1900s. Hatters have acquired their reputation for madness only in relatively modern times, mainly thanks to Lewis Carroll. The expression 'mad as a hatter' was originally American and 'mad' meant 'angry'. In 1851 another hat manufacturer in Ross was William Glover in Broad Street.

A few doors away the **Sun Tavern** was opened in 1867 by a beer retailer called Mr. E. Phipps. He had acquired the premises formerly used by Robert Brown and James Kibble as a 'Grocers, Tallow chandlers and Soap makers', and in addition to all this activity there was also a brewhouse. In 1813 the property and contents were insured for £2,000 by Sun Policy 878314—an insurance number still displayed on the outside wall. The dwelling house 'Brick and Tiled except a small part of Lathe and Plaster' was insured for £350; household goods, clothes, books and plate—£100; stock and utensils—£1,000; melting house—£100; stock and utensils—£200; brewhouse—£50'. Presumably Phipps named his tavern after the fire plate depicting a golden sun with a beaming face that was affixed to the wall. The **Sun Tavern** also served as a refreshment room throughout the 19th century and apparently closed around 1914. Part of the building is now used as a wine bar.

Almost opposite the wine bar, on the east side of the High Street, is the **Rosswyn**, often mistaken for an old established inn because the building dates from the 15th century and features interior carvings of 1608, door panels said to be of an even earlier date, a Jacobean

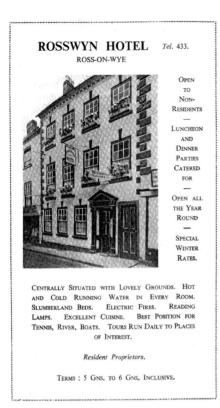

ROSSWYN HOTEL *Tel. 433.*
ROSS-ON-WYE

OPEN
TO
NON-
RESIDENTS
—
LUNCHEON
AND
DINNER
PARTIES
CATERED
FOR
—
OPEN ALL
THE YEAR
ROUND
—
SPECIAL
WINTER
RATES.

CENTRALLY SITUATED WITH LOVELY GROUNDS. HOT
AND COLD RUNNING WATER IN EVERY ROOM.
SLUMBERLAND BEDS. ELECTRIC FIRES. READING
LAMPS. EXCELLENT CUISINE. BEST POSITION FOR
TENNIS, RIVER, BOATS. TOURS RUN DAILY TO PLACES
OF INTEREST.

Resident Proprietors.

TERMS : 5 GNS. TO 6 GNS. INCLUSIVE.

Left : A post-war advertisement for the Rosswyn. Right : The fireplace

staircase, and a carved Elizabethan fireplace. Before becoming a hotel in the 1940s the **Rosswyn** was the home of a doctor, and known as Chepstow House. During the occupancy of the present owner renovations have revealed a fireplace in the public bar which was found behind seven other fireplaces themselves hidden by a brick wall. Also discovered at this time was a small room in the cellar, which is now used as a wine bar.

A few doors away from the former **Sun Tavern** was the **George the Fourth's Rest**. This former beer house was re-named after an event that occurred in 1821, when an unexpected George IV passed through the town on his return from Ireland. His journey continued along the Old Gloucester Road, which was obstructed by horseless wagons that blocked the way. The disgruntled king 'was obliged to wait' at this modest ale house while the traffic jam was cleared, but the town of Ross was later warned that 'unless a better way was made through the town the mail would be taken off the road'. This

The one time King George's Rest

incident led to a major improvement in the town with the construction of the new Gloucester Road in 1825 replacing the narrow and inconvenient Old Gloucester Road. The **George the Fourth's Rest** changed its name for a brief period to the **Butcher's Arms** when run by John Perks a butcher in the 1890s. By 1902 it had returned to a similar name—**King George's Rest**—but this was unsuccessful and it closed shortly after 1926. The building still stands and the royal visit is commemorated by a blue plaque.

Two major inns formerly stood facing one another at the top of Old Gloucester Road, the **Nag's Head** in the High Street and the **Royal Oak** in Copse Cross Street. Both inns are recorded from the 18th century, but their positions on the original main road from Ross to London strongly suggests earlier foundations. The building that housed the **Nag's Head** dates from the 17th century, and is traditionally said to have been frequented by John Kyrle; in 1827 his chair was still at the inn. The name would have indicated that riding horses were for hire at the inn, but during the 19th century the **Nag's Head** catered for the carriers including Robert Jones' wagons from Monmouth, Worcester and 'all parts of the North', and Joseph

```
On the Ground Floor:-

HALL
SMOKE ROOM about 30' long with widths varying from 12'8" to
         10'10".  Two fireplaces.  Power Point.
BAR about 23' x 16'2" with fireplace, 'Appollo' heating
         stove, seats.
LARDER
SCULLERY about 13'9" x 8'6".
STORE ROOM
Side Entrance leading to CELLAR.
LIVING ROOM/BACK KITCHEN  about 14'6" x 14'2" fitted Sink (H&C)
         Brick fireplace with back boiler for hot water supplied.
         Cupboard.

On a Half-Landing is a W.C. and BATHROOM  with panelled Bath and
Washbasin, heated linen cupboard with electric immersion heater.

On the First Floor:-

LANDING
KITCHEN about 15'9" x 12'9" with Sink (H&C)  Power Point.
BEDROOM about 16'6" x 11'6" with gasfire and cupboard. Power Point.
CLUB ROOM  about 24'2" x 18' with fireplace, power point.
STORE ROOM  about 10'10" x 11'3".

On a Half-Landing are two STORE ROOMS
```

The 1960 sale details of the Nag's Head

Troke's wagons from Gloucester and Hereford. Stephen and Elizabeth Butt ran the **Nag's Head** during the 1840s, followed by John Preece, who was still there in 1875 when it was acquired by Wintle's Forest Brewery. In 1878 the licence was transferred from James Wolf to John Enfield, and an extension was granted for a house-warming party. During the 20th century the inn was run by a number of tenants, and it was taken over by the Stroud Brewery who sold it as a de-licensed property in 1960. Since then the former inn has been used as a shop, craft centre and offices, and although a listed building it is in a sorry state of repair. The building is of three storeys above a cellar, and is said to feature some 17th-century doors.

In 1954, Charles Evans knew of the **Nag's Head** association with John Kyrle when he wrote in the *Hereford Citizen and Bulletin:*

> So, in Ross, at the Nag's Head, we find a club named after this now famous man in the 1850s. There was at this inn the Lodge called: 'John Kyrle or Man of Ross Lodge of Loyal and Independent O.F.' At the New Inn ... where the much travelled Goodrich Friendly Society came to rest, we also find this one, the Loyal Man of Ross Lodge, I.O.O.F., Manchester Unity. Both the Lodges came into existence in the same year, 1853. Much is made today, and rightly in many ways, of this renowned and indeed world-famous citizen of Ross-on-Wye.

The **Royal Oak** is a popular pub name dating back to the restoration of the monarchy in 1660 when King Charles II declared that his birthday, the 29th May, should be celebrated as Royal Oak

The Nag's Head in 2001, looking rather down-at-heel

Day. This was still being celebrated in 1813 by the scholars of the Walter Scott School, when after morning service they paraded through Ross wearing a 'slip of oak'. The **Royal Oak** also operated for market traders and farmers, and must have competed for similar trade and custom as the inn opposite.

The Royal Oak is now a licensed restaurant

1855 advertisement for the Royal Oak

The Harp sale in 1923

James Cope was running the inn during the mid-18th century followed by William Bevan. In 1847 James Powell was serving the needs of the market carters and vanners; by 1855 Simon Powell was offering 'Excellent Accommodation' at 'Moderate Charges'. After this the inn seems to have gone gradually downhill under a series of innkeepers. The **Royal Oak** only just survived into the 20th century, for by 1914 the former inn was housing the Ross Conservative Club. To a certain extent it has reverted, now being a licensed restaurant featuring a recently installed glass panel depicting life in Ross.

In Old Gloucester Road, known earlier as Arthur's or Hatter's Lane, a cider and beer retailer opened the **Trumpet** in the mid-19th century. This was part of a row of houses between

The Harp in retirement in 2001

Perrock's Almshouses and the former Walter Scott Charity School. Like the **Peacock**, which was known to have stood on the opposite side of the road, it was short lived. This was unlike the former **Harp Tavern** in Alton Street, which stands at the end of the footpath leading from Old Gloucester Road. Thomas Webb, another cider retailer, had opened this inn by 1840. Only cider was served until it became a beer house when Charles Smith took over in the 1860s. It was yet another one that was eventually acquired by the Forest Brewery. Although the beer house was sold in 1937, the tenant E.L. Lloyd remained there until it was closed around 1941 by the Cheltenham Original Brewery.

A story exists that was repeated in the *Ross Gazette* of December 2000. A highwayman named William Lester frequented a 'little tavern on the Gloucester Road known then as the **God Encompasseth**, but corrupted to the **Goat and Compasses**'. On Christmas Eve in 1729, Lester held up a stagecoach on the Ross to Ledbury road, but 'before the robber's attention was drawn to the occupants of the coach, a well-aimed bullet pierced the highwayman's shoulder. William Lester reeled in the saddle at the shock, and his horse bolted and set off at a mad gallop towards Ross with the stagecoach in pursuit'. On the way he found sanctuary in a chapel but 'the highwayman's time had arrived. His lips formed themselves once, twice in a word, and as the stars, the moon, and the world of 1729 proclaimed Christmastide he muttered "Father forgive —" then shuddered and died'.

James Evans opened the **Oddfellows Arms** in 1851 at an unknown site in Copse Cross Street. This street leads south onto the Walford Road, where the area around Ashfield was transformed into a leafy suburb during the 19th century. By 1876 a corner site between Walford Road and Archenfield Road was occupied by the **Prince of Wales**. In a building typical of this period, the proprietors were offering 'Good Accommodation for Tourists [and] Cyclists' in the 1890s. This was another licensed premises that was taken over by the Forest Brewery and like others was sold in 1937. It remained under the same tenancy with Mr. H.C. Freeman providing his 1930s guests with 'Good Cooking' at his 'Pleasantly situated' hotel. The **Prince of Wales** still provides a useful service to the residents of this part of Ross.

The Walford Road continues through the suburbs of Ross to the junction of Fernbank Road, originally known as Puckeridge or Puttridge Lane. In 1791 it was discontinued as a toll road because its narrow and hilly route to Deep Dean was unsuitable for wheeled traffic. At this junction 'lying back from Puttridge Lane was a heap of stones overgrown with scrub bushes ... the

ROSS, HEREFORDSHIRE.

To LICENSED VICTUALLERS & CAPITALISTS.

ASHFIELD,

Within a quarter of a mile of the Town of Ross.

MESSRS. ROOTES and WINTLE have been favoured with instructions from Mr. T. H. COUNSELL, to offer for SALE by AUCTION, at the PRINCE OF WALES INN, Ashfield, Ross, On FRIDAY, the 16th day of JULY, 1880, At 4 o'clock in the Afternoon.

Lot 1.—All that valuable FREEHOLD FULL-LICENSED INN, DWELLING-HOUSE, and PREMISES, with Gardens and Pleasure Grounds thereto belonging, situate at Ashfield, Ross, and known as the " Prince of Wales."

The House, which is built of brick and roofed with slate, is most beautifully situated at Ashfield, at the junction of the roads leading from Ross to Goodrich Ferry, and Walford, quarter of a mile from the town of Ross, and containing Taproom, Bar, Smoke-room, Bar Parlour, Parlour, Kitchen, Back Kitchen, Larder, 2 Store-rooms, 7 Bedrooms, W.C., good dry Cellarage. There is Stabling for 4 Horses, Brewhouse with every arrangement for Brewing, and large Yard with Workshops, good Kitchen Garden well stocked with choice trees, and large Bowling Green. The whole has a frontage to the road of 142 yards, and covers an area of about half an Acre.

For further particulars, apply to the Auctioneers, Bank Offices, Ross ; or Messrs. Minett and Piddocke, Solicitors, Ross.

The sale of the Prince of Wales in 1880

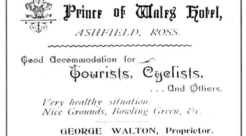

1896 advertisement

The Prince of Wales in 1905

The one time Plough in 2001

remains of a house called **Whip Willers'**. It was believed to have been a public house and had been 'a call for gangs of poachers that came out of Ross to prowl Chase Wood'. The name probably originates from dog whippers who were employed to stop livestock from being harried by dogs. They presumably met at the willow trees.

Further along the Walford Road in the Tudorville suburb, the **Plough** and **Noah's Ark** were both open by 1876. When Winifred Cresswell took over the **Plough** from her parents, it was in its heyday. This was during the 1940s and 50s and she is still remembered in the area as 'a very well known pub landlady'. Although the **Plough**, a former Alton Court Brewery pub, until recently displayed a fading sign, it was closed during the 1980s.

The **Noah's Ark** is easy to miss, as it is tucked away in a building probably erected when Chapel Road and Tudor Street

The well hidden Noah's Ark is still serving its local customers in 2001

were developed in this part of Ross. Mrs. Catherine Evans was retailing beer at the **Noah's Ark** in 1876, Mary Townsend in 1890 and George Morris in 1891. From the beginning of the 20th century Henry Ayers was the innkeeper for several decades. The name is derived from an ark featured in the arms of the Shipwrights Company, which bears a motto 'Within the Ark, safe for ever'. This appealed to innkeepers as a suitable name for a pub and must be relevant, for the pub is still open. The only other pub at Tudorville was Edward Bullock's **True Heart** listed in 1914, but its whereabouts is not known by the locals or the author.

The 2001 Noah's Ark sign

Past Tudorville on the Walford Road at the Ross parish boundary is the **Vine Tree Inn**, a free house which now includes a Caravan Park. This high–gabled three-storied freehouse has been an inn since around 1840 when John Bailey, a gardener and seedsman, aptly called it the **Vine Tree**. The inn marks an ancient site previously known as the **Deadwoman**, a name possibly derived from 'boundary stone'. Its situation below the steep wooded slopes of Chase Hill is on a prehistoric route from a crossing over the Wye at Wilton to the Iron Age hill fort on Chase Hill. Due to its name and situation it is hardly surprising that legends exist about the death of a woman, which have two versions. Either a woman died after being chased by hounds and torn to pieces, or

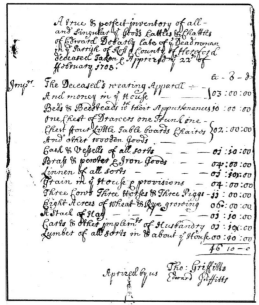

Inventory of the Deadwoman in 1708, later the Vine Inn

The Vine Tree sale in 1923

The Vine Tree, on the Ross boundary, in 2001

a woman was murdered while fetching water from the well in the woods above. However, the factual history of the **Deadwoman** dates from 1551 when the property passed from Kyrle to Parry. Following this, other familiar Ross names were associated with the **Deadwoman** including the Merricks, the Dubberleys and the Freres. The Baileys ran their market garden here together with the inn until 1873 when Mortimer Overton became the victualler, followed by a succession of licensees. Like other pubs in the vicinity the **Vine Tree** was purchased by the Forest Brewery and sold to the Cheltenham Original Brewery in 1937 when it was occupied by Mr. H. Crossley.

The Vine Tree sale in 1937

This completes the history of the known past and present inns, taverns and beer houses in Ross parish, and represents over 90 names that existed at different periods. It is worth noting that in 1822 there were 16 inns and taverns in Ross and this number had increased to 30 by 1835. With the additional opening of beer and public houses in the 1850s, the number of licensed properties rose to 36 and this remained more or less constant until the First World War. Since then the number has gradually declined to 20, a total that does not include the hotels, restaurants and clubs in the town.

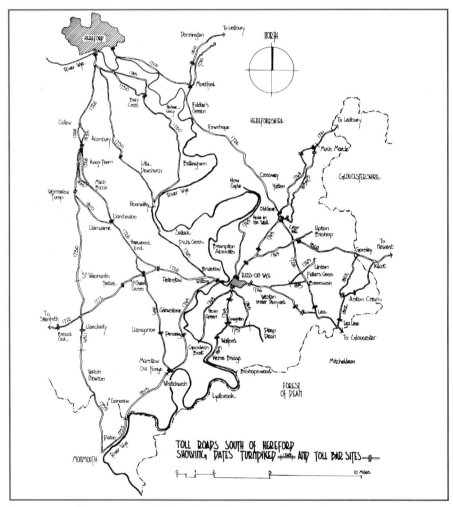

South Herefordshire turnpike roads

CHAPTER SEVEN

From Ross-on-Wye to Hereford
THROUGH HAREWOOD END

Below Ross the river Wye is crossed by Wilton Bridge, a handsome six-arched structure built of red sandstone. It was completed a couple of years after the 1597 Bridge Act, but has been extensively repaired and restored over the centuries. From Wilton in Bridstow parish two traditional routes lead to Hereford, one goes through Harewood End, and the other to Hoarwithy where another choice of two roads has always been possible. Inns and beer houses were established on all these routes, some in villages and others in quite isolated places, with many remaining open today.

Wilton in the early 19th century 'might properly be called the quay or wharf to Ross, by furnishing a convenient accommodation for the shipping and landing of goods sent up and down the river'. With all this activity two riverside inns catered for the bargees, travellers and traders. The main one was the **King's Head**, originally called the **Bear**, which was run by the 'men of the river'. One of these was the adventurous Luke Hughes, who, in the 1730s for a wager, navigated a coracle down the Wye from Ross to Lundy and back, and William Gilpin wrote 'the account of his expedition [which] was received like a voyage around the world'.

The river trade declined in the mid-19th century, initially due to the opening of the Abergavenny to Hereford tramway in 1825, then the completion of the Hereford to Gloucester canal in 1845, and, finally, the opening of the railway between the two cities and through Ross in 1855. Joseph Davies, the victualler, grocer and general shopkeeper at the **King's Head**, managed to survive all these changes and by 1881

KING'S HEAD HOTEL,

WILTON, NEAR ROSS.

Good Fishing.   Fine Views.

PLEASANT APARTMENTS.

DINNERS AND TEAS PROVIDED.

BOAT ON THE RIVER.

Wines, Spirits, Ale, and Cider

OF THE BEST QUALITY.

CHARGES MODERATE.

R. ACOTT, Proprietor.

1894 advertisement

Mary Nicholls was the licensee. Within a few years she was replaced by Uriah De La Hay, who moved from the nearby **Lion Inn**, where his mother, Anne had been licensee. The inn continued through the 1890s offering 'Pleasant Apartments' with 'Fine Views' to fishermen and holiday makers. It was about this time that Wintle's Forest Brewery purchased the inn and like their other licensed properties it was included in their grand sale particulars of 1923 and 1937 complete with a 'good Skittle Alley' and a 'Two-stall Stable'. The inn eventually passed to Whitbreads, but lack of business during the 1980s led to its delicensing and conversion into holiday apartments.

The other inn at Wilton was the **White Lion**, which was first recorded in 1735 and was rebuilt in 1779. The adjoining building, which is called the 'Prison House', was built in 1600 at the same time

Two boys looking at the sundial on Wilton Bridge about 1900, with the King's Head Hotel in the background

110

as the 'Great House' with its court room, which now forms part of Wilton Court and stands opposite the inn. Both buildings replaced the functions of the manor court and goal which had been housed in Wilton Castle until Charles Brydges revamped the building. The Great House was large enough to provide living accommodation, and it is possible that Charles Brydges and his family lived there while the work was undertaken at the castle. The '**White Lyon**', like the castle, had been purchased by the Governors of Guy's Hospital in London to add to their massive estate in Herefordshire. In 1754 William Barron was the publican and keeper of the Vineyards, and Mr. Vigor, a Bristol merchant, was at Wilton Court. Susan Webb was the young innkeeper at the **White Lion** in 1841. Apart from running the inn, she had three young children to look after, but by 1851 she was helped by William Amos, a hostler, and Helen Wall, a house servant. Anne De La Hay was at the **Lion** in 1881. Her husband had apparently died and she was helped by her son, Uriah who was eventually to move to the **King's Head**.

Edward Ellis was a colourful publican at the **White Lion** during the 1920s and 30s. He was a cricketer from Gloucester who had served and been honoured in the First World War. His children were all born in the 'top bedroom' at the inn, and his two daughters recall their father entertaining fishermen, travelling by pony and trap, cooking sides of meat on a spit, allowing gypsies to stay in the barn, and placing drowned victims from the Wye in his cellar. By the 1980s the Whitbread pub was serving 'Excellent Meals' in the former Prison House which was by then called the 'Old Jail Restaurant' before the inn's name was briefly changed to the **Hereford Bull**. Thankfully it reverted back to its original name and remains open as the **White Lion**, a popular riverside pub amongst the array of private hotels at Wilton.

The nearby buildings include the **Castle Lodge Hotel**, formerly called Wilton House, where Charles Dickens stayed in 1867 with his friend

The White Lion at Wilton in 2001

111

George Dolby. Dolby lived at Ashfield Lodge in Ross, and also at Wilton House and at both places he entertained Dickens on more than one occasion. Of the visit in January, 1869, Dolby recorded 'He had heard so much of the beauties of the scenery in and around Ross, and expressed a wish to be taken for a walk along the prettiest road in the neighbourhood. I chose the one which is supposed by old travellers to be the "prettiest in England" from Ross to Monmouth, about eleven miles'.

Leaving Wilton, the main Hereford road was realigned by the Ross Turnpike Trust in 1795 to its present route through Bridstow and then up the hill to Peterstow. In this small village with a population of only 304 in 1887, drinkers were well catered for by four licensed premises. In the middle of Peterstow village the **Vine Tree** was a short lived inn adjoining the village shop. In 1881 the licensee was Michael Hall who was also a plasterer. He lived there with his wife, Jane, who doubtless looked after the inn as well as their three children. The establishment changed hands and was run by Hannah Meek in 1891 then by Joseph Chance in 1902. The **Yew Tree Tavern** was serving beer as early as the 1830s and in the 1880s Michael Hall apparently moved there from the **Vine Tree** and stayed for some 35 years. It was in 1937 that Wintles Forest Brewery sold the **Yew Tree** with its coach-house, stabling, barn, granary and five acres of land occupied by

The Vine at Peterstow around 1900
(Druce collection)

The Yew Tree at Peterstow around 1930 (Druce collection)

W. Byard. It was taken over by Whitbreads and has survived into the 21st century as a local pub offering a beer garden and a site for touring caravans in addition to all normal services.

Beyond the village, but still within the parish, the **Red Lion** stands on an ancient crossroads on the A49 and marked as Winter's Cross on Bryant's map of 1835. Crossing the A49 is a minor road described by Fosbroke in 1822 as:

> From Hentland there runs a British Trackway to the Meend, thence to Wilzon, thence to Whitfield, where it falls into the Turnpike road at Pencreek; but probably went further.

---

70. PETERSTOW.—YEW TREE INN.

ALL THAT messuage or Inn known as the Yew Tree Inn situate at Peterstow near Ross in the County of Hereford and all outbuildings and appurtenances thereunto belonging comprising at side and in rear coachhouse stabling for three pig cots store room urinal closet etc. and separate detached brick and stone building comprising wash-house loft over timber erection of barn and granary cart shed etc. and garden TOGETHER with land containing in all about five acres and all other outbuildings and appurtenances thereunto belonging TOGETHER with the site thereof and the land occupied therewith which said premises are now in the occupation of W. Byard as tenant.

Wintle's Brewery sale of the Yew Tree in 1937

113

1932 advertisment for the Red Lion

*The Red Lion at Peterstow at the
beginning of the 21st century*

The building that is the **Red Lion** dates from the 17th century and in 1839 was recorded as the 'Red Lion and Garden'. During its later years various victuallers also worked as a coal dealer in 1858, a threshing machine proprietor in 1867 and a tiler and plasterer in 1902. It was delicensed in the late 1970s and converted into a dwelling called the Chestnuts, but for once the conversion did not succeed and it was reopened as an inn a few years later.

Still within Peterstow parish, at the junction of a road that leads through Skenfrith to Abergavenny, was the site of the **Rising Sun**. The inn probably emerged after the road to Abergavenny was turnpiked in 1772 with the inn named after a coach called the 'Rising Sun'. In 1833 this junction was known as 'the Old Turnpike, otherwise Cross Hands, on the Turnpike Road from Ross to Hereford'. By 1839 the 'Rising Sun Public House and part of Yard and Cottage adjoining' was occupied by Thomas Smith. From the pub another route called the Green Lane led to Sellack, but was closed by Quarter Sessions in 1871 as it was considered 'inappropriate for public use'.

At the time of the 1881 census, the establishment was called the **Rising Sun Inn** and described as being at **Old Pike**, which was apparently used as an alternative name. The 75-year-old Thomas Smith was the landlord. A few years later in 1889, Sidney Smith, a carpenter of 35 years was sentenced to six months hard labour for stealing '80lbs. clover fodder, pig food and a bucket, the property of Mr. Harold Scudamore'. Thomas Hall, keeper of the **Rising Sun**, gave evidence that 'the morning in question was very dark; he could not have seen anyone 10 yards off'. When cross-examined, he added 'May have recognised him if he had been out of the dark; the prisoner is my landlord'.

Although the inn survived as the **Rising Sun** into the 20th century under Thomas Higginson, it was eventually closed and the site became the Everstone Garage. In recent years this has been replaced by a small, rather smart housing estate.

Before reaching the next road junction, a well-signed entrance leads off to the right to **Pengethley Manor**, a hotel since the end of the Second World War. The original Tudor house with its 'quaint old hall' was damaged by fire in the 1820s and was replaced by the present building erected by the Rev. Thomas Powell Symonds in 1826. The ancient cellar survives as a picturesque feature in the hotel garden and dates back to 1546 when

The ancient cellar in the garden at the Pengethley

John Pychard from Paunton owned the house, which at that time was apparently fortified with a tower. In 1580 Thomas Higgins made a survey of all 'Erable Lands, Pastures, Woods and Meddowes belongynge to the Mannour of Pengethley'. The house then consisted of 'Hall, Parlour, Buttery, Kytchne and Chambers'. In 1583 the estate was purchased by John Powell who later married into the Symonds family who remained at Pengethley until 1947.

1950s advertisement for the Pengethley Hotel

Pengethley Park was renowned for its oak, elm, lime, ash, and spruce trees, but when visited by the Woolhope Club in 1867 it was noted that:

The absence of large trees seems explained when it is remembered that the Colonel Symonds of the last generation was a member of Parliament for 23 years in succession. He represented the city of Hereford from the year 1796 until his death in 1819. He was elected five times, and on the last occasion, the year before his death, in 1818, he fought a long struggle successfully. Let entomologists say what they please as to the great ravages of *Zeuzera Æsculi*, the *Lucunas cervus*, the *Dorcus paralle'opipedus*, or other insects, but beyond all question the *Æstus politicus* is infinitely more fatal than any of them in its effects on timber trees. A contested election often cuts off all the finest and soundest trees on an estate with one fell sweep, and whole centuries are sometimes required to restore the effects produced by its insatiable demands.

Now under the care of the National Trust, Pengethley Park features a few magnificent trees in a beautiful setting.

Travelling towards Hereford on the A49, the next pub is the **Harewood End Inn** which enjoys a well-documented history from the time of King Charles I. In the mid-17th century it was known as **Harewoods Inn** and leased from John Browne of Harewood to David Furber in 1627 for a rent of 'one cowpole [pair] of capons at Christmas'. When the Browns sold the Harewood Estate to Bennett Hoskyns in 1651 the inn was included in the sale. By 1815 **Harewoods Inn** with 40 acres was rented by William Taylor, but when the Hoskyns offered the Harewood Estate for sale in 1876 the inn was let to Samuel Collins along with 77 acres of land. In 1891 the landlord was Joseph Frederick Scudamore, who was also a farmer.

When the Harewood Police Station was opened in the mid-19th century the County Magistrates Petty Sessional Court was

---

HAREWOOD END FARM,

WITH

PUBLIC HOUSE, known as " HAREWOOD END " INN,

WELL SITUATE FOR BUSINESS,

And comprising Two Attics, Three Bed Rooms and Store Room, Club Room, Parlour, Bar Parlour, Bar, Kitchen, Wash-house, Out-door Coal-house,

GARDEN AND ORCHARDING.

AND THE FOLLOWING OUTBUILDINGS,

Old Malt-house with Rooms over, lean-to Shed, separate Yard with Stable for Five Horses and Loft over, Chaff-house, Cow-house, Barn, lean-to Waggon Shed, open Cattle Shed, Stable for Four Horses, Coach-house and Granary over, Poultry-house, lean-to Shed, and separate Yard in back fold.

The sale details for the Harewood End Inn in 1876

transferred from the **Harewood End Inn**, where cases of petty theft and poaching had previously been heard, to the new Magistrates' Room where they met every alternate Monday at 11.00 a.m.. The culprits were either fined a few shillings or served a prison sentence. By 1931 Mrs. Kinch at the **Harewood End Inn** was offering 'Board Residence, Luncheons, Teas' to 'Small

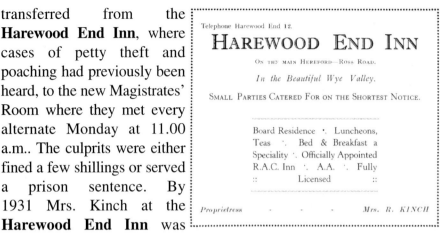

The Harewood End in 1931

Parties'. In the 1980s the pub blossomed into an 'excellent roadside inn', which has continued to the present day under the supervision of its landlord. The Free House now offers accommodation and a restaurant and function room in a nicely converted barn that features the original well, still containing water.

On the opposite side of the Hereford road in the parish of Pencoyd was the **Plough Inn**, run for several generations by the Gretton family. In 1860 they sold the 'dwelling house now and for many years past used as a public house and called or known by the name or sign of the Plough Inn with the gardens, mill house, stables and outbuildings' to Chandos Wren Hoskyns of Harewood, who

The Harewood End Inn at the beginning of the 21st century

promptly delicensed the premises. The building, now split into two houses, still survives on the side of the main road.

The **Axe and Cleaver** is in Much Birch parish about half way between Ross and Hereford. According to local tradition this used to be run by a

The Plough is now two houses

Lot 2

All that old established and fully licensed public house known as the 'Axe & Cleaver' situated in the parish of Much Birch in the County of Hereford upon the main road from Hereford to Ross. The house comprises, Bar, Kitchen, Sitting Room, Three bedrooms, 2 cellars and washhouse and there are attached, Cider Mill with loft, Barn piggeries, capital garden and two parcels of productive orcharding the whole comprising 1. 2. 37 and is now held by Mr. Miller as tenant.

Sale of the Axe and Cleaver in 1888

butcher, and when West Country Breweries designed a sign the poleaxe had to be shortened to match the cleaver. Although part of the building dates from the 17th century, the first known beer and cider retailer was John Jones in 1851. In 1888 the 'old established and fully licensed public house' containing a 'Bar, Kitchen, Sitting Room, Three Bedrooms, two Cellars and a Wash House' together with outbuildings including a cider mill and piggeries was sold by auction.

In 1892, when Alfred Weaver was the landlord, the following incident was recorded in the local paper:

ASSUALTING THE POLICE.— Edward Tomkins, a young man from Much Birch, was charged with having assaulted P.C. William Proctor, near the Axe and Cleaver, Much Birch, on April 25th.—The police officer said he was ordering two drunken men to go home, when the defendant challenged him to fight, and when witness refused he struck him. — Corroborative evidence was given by Thomas Wilding, carpenter of Much Birch. — Supt. Cope said this was the defendant's first appearance.— The defendant was also given

HEREFORDSHIRE.

Much Birch, Little Birch and Kingstone.

Valuable FREE PUBLIC HOUSE and FREEHOLD PROPERTIES.

Messrs. HILES - SMITH & SON

will offer the following Lots for SALE BY AUCTION, at

The Law Society's Hall, East Street, Hereford,

On Wednesday, 26th November, 1919,

at **THREE** o'clock in the Afternoon, subject to Conditions of Sale to include the Common Form Conditions of the Herefordshire Incorporated Law Society.

Lot 1. All that Freehold Fully-licensed Inn, known as

"THE AXE & CLEAVER"

situate in the Parish of Much Birch on the Main Road between Hereford and Ross.

The house contains bar, tap-room, smoke-room, parlour, kitchen, 5 bedrooms, beer-cellar and offices; the outside buildings comprise club-room, stabling, barn, cider-house and cow-house; with garden, grass paddock and orchard, the whole containing about

TWO ACRES

This is one of the Oldest-Established Licensed Houses in the district, and is an ancient picturesque hostelry.

The house is Free and a good business has been carried on for many years, and is now in the occupation of Mr. Walter Brewer as a Yearly Tenant.

Tithe 10/11,

Sale of the Axe and Cleaver in 1919

a good character reference by his master, John Watkins. — The magistrates said it was a serious offence to interfere with the police whilst they were in the execution of their duty. The defendant would be fined 15s. including costs.

By 1902 Henry Jones was offering 'good accommodation for cyclists', but by 1919 the brewers Godsall and Son had acquired the inn and, under the tenancy of Ernest Wheatstone, it was 'delightfully modernised'. From about 1930, the **Axe and Cleaver** belonged to the

Axe & Cleaver Inn
MUCH BIRCH
HEREFORD

Proprietor:
E. H. WHEATSTONE

A FULLY-LICENSED old-world country Inn delightfully modernized. Situated in beautiful country half-way between Hereford and Ross. Ideal for walking or as a centre while touring the WYE VALLEY. On a good 'bus route with an hourly service each way. All bedrooms are very well appointed with h. & c. water, Slumberland beds, and electric fires.

There is a very cosy Lounge and pleasant Dining Room. Excellent cuisine and every comfort—ideal for Winter residents.

A nice garden and grass tennis court are at the disposal of patrons.

Good hunting country with South Hereford Hounds and Ross Harriers. Riding can be arranged locally by appointment in advance.

Garage for 6 cars. Petrol and Service Station 50 yards.

TERMS.

Per week : 5½ guineas each inclusive.

Per day : 17/6 (minimum 4 days).

Hot Baths, 1/-. Garage free.

Bed and Breakfast : 10/6 each.

Dinner 4/6. Luncheon 3/6 to 4/6. Afternoon Teas 1/6 to 2/-. Sandwiches and Snacks can be obtained at the Bar at reasonable charges during opening hours, 10.30 to 2.30 and 6 till 10.

Patrons can have packed meals if they wish to go out for the day.

An advertisement card produced shortly after the Second World War

1960s inn sign

Stroud Brewery, a company that was taken over by West Country Breweries in 1962. The **Axe and Cleaver** still presents an attractive façade to the road and, as it can be seen by drivers from a distance, it is well used by travellers as well as locals.

North of the **Axe and Cleaver,** the original road leading towards Hereford took a circuitous route through Much Birch and Kingsthorne and then across the slopes of Aconbury and Callow hills until the present line was constructed by the Hereford Trust following the 1835 Turnpike Act, and then improved in the latter part of the 20th century. Along this route was the **White Hart**, which did not survive later than the mid-19th century when the Much Birch Friendly Society met there. The closure of the **White Hart** would have doubtless been in part due to loss of passing trade following the building of the new road and the opening of the railways.

From this old road there are a maze of winding lanes that lead towards Little Birch where the **Castle Inn** has long served the local community. In 1851, when George Arnold was the 'victualler' at this inn, a James Matthews was a beer retailer and shopkeeper at the nearby **Little Castle Inn**, but this licensed property closed shortly afterwards. Joseph Mason was landlord at the **Castle** in 1891. Some time before 1924 the **Castle**, by then a Wintle's Forest Brewery inn, had been rebuilt. It was described as being

> stone built with slated roof and contains entrance Hall, Cosy Front Bar, Smoke Room (both lofty and well lighted), Licensed dining room overlooking lawn, all fitted with up-to-date Register Grates; Kitchen with double over cooking apparatus, Pantry, ground floor Cellar and Wine Cellar. On the first floor is a Drawing Room, 4 Bedrooms and Landing. Outside W.C. There is a large lawn and Garden about half-an-acre at the back, planted with shrubs and fruit trees. There are ample buildings and a Large Yard, Wash-House, Saddle Room, Garage or Coach-House, Loose box, Cow Shed, French Barn, Range of Piggeries, 3 Stall Stable with loft and outside latrine.

In 1937 Harry Probert was the landlord, and although a notice inside the pub suggested it had been associated with the Alton Court Brewery it belonged to Wintle's Forest Brewery before being taken over by the Cheltenham Original Brewery Co.

The Castle at Little Birch.
Right : Sale of the Castle in 1924
Above : A well-stained beer mat
of the 1970s

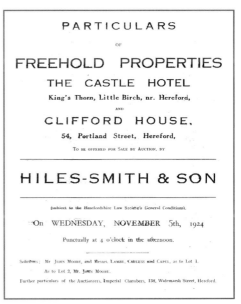

From the **Castle Inn** a sign directs walkers to the 'King's Thorn', which is traditionally associated with the Holy Thorn of Glastonbury which flowers on Twelfth Night. In 1984, the *King's Thorn Community Handbook* recorded:

> The local 'Holy Thorn' is said to have originated from a cutting received by King Charles I when he was staying in the district. The 'Thorn' is situated in the hedge just past the cottages about 120 metres down the lane which starts at the right-hand side of the Castle Inn. Special services used to be held around the tree at midnight on Twelfth Night. These were well attended and wardens were appointed to make sure that no damage was done to crops or hedges. The *Hereford Times* reported that in 1951, 150 people assembled on Twelfth Night braving rain and mud to see the Holy Thorn burst into bloom at midnight. Then, as now, it depends upon the weather to what stage the buds reach on Twelfth Night. In most years the buds are advanced and early stages of flower production can be seen. Usually, however, one needs to spend the evening imbibing at the Castle Inn before setting forth to observe the tree in full bloom at midnight. Botanically the tree is a variety of the common hawthorn, *Craetagus Monogyna praecox* (*praecox* = early flowering). There were also 'Holy Thorns' at Colwall, Tyberton, Orcop, and Bredwardine, but many have since died.

The old turnpike road crosses the present main road as it wends its way towards the small village of Callow. Here, a building opposite the church was formerly a coaching inn called the **Duke of Chandos' Head**. It was presumably named after the Duke who owned vast estates in Herefordshire that were eventually sold to the Governors of Guy's Hospital. In 1754 the 'Publick House at Callow' was let to William Pyefinch at £8 a year, but its name was later changed to **Guy's Head**, presumably reflecting the new ownership. Associated with this former inn is a story about a ghostly figure in the dark carrying something across the road and over the fields to a house. They return empty handed suggesting that a body was taken away and buried, so that the coach left the following morning with one less passenger.

The **Guy's Head** was closed shortly after the opening of the new line of turnpike road and was replaced by the **Angel Inn,** which was conveniently placed to catch passing trade from both roads at Grafton on the north side of the Callow Hill. In 1891 Charles Southall was landlord, and then, and during the early years of the 20th century, when Rose Griffiths was the landlady it was regularly visited by Alfred Watkins the well-known Herefordshire naturalist, archaeologist and inventor. Apart from having a drink, the stop was to top up his Gardner Serpollet steam car with water. In 1902 the **Angel** was an agent for Arnold Perrett & Co., who purchased the pub and resold it to the Cheltenham Original Brewery in 1937. In 1931 the **Angel** offered bed and breakfast and teas,

The one-time Guy's Head in Callow

making it sound more like a guest house than a pub, but by combining with shop and post-office it managed to continue until 1971, when it was converted into a dwelling house.

THE ANGEL INN, CALLOW
Nr. HEREFORD
Bed and Breakfast .· Teas .· Old World Tea Gardens .· All at Moderate Charges .· Small Parties :: Catered For ::

Proprietress - - *MRS. C. M. WALDRON.*

1931 advertisement for the Angel

Directly on the main road, about 2¹/₂ miles from Hereford city centre, is an inn that was originally called the **Brick Kilns**, for it was run by a brickmaker in the mid-19th century. In 1881 Christopher Robinson was the innkeeper, assisted by

The Angel is now a private house

123

Freehold Fully-Licensed Premises and Farm,

KNOWN AS

"THE BRICK KILN INN,"

Situated in the PARISH OF GRAFTON, about 2¼ miles from the CITY OF HEREFORD, on the road to ROSS and MONMOUTH and comprising the

Public House (with good Pull up),

Containing: Bar, Bar Parlour, Kitchen, Back ditto, and Private Parlour on the Ground Floor, with door to Cellarage in the Basement; on the Half-Landing a good Club Room; and above, Three good Bed Rooms and a Lumber Room (could be used as Bed Room).

Near to the House is an excellent,

RANGE OF BUILDINGS,

Including Stabling for Four Horses, Barn with loft over, Cow Houses for Nine, Cider Mill House (with new Press), Piggery, Rick Yard, and outside Shed.

There is a good

ORCHARD AND TWO GRASS FIELDS,

With excellent Frontage to the HEREFORD ROAD, and a capital Pond of Water.

On the further part of the Property from the Public House are

TWO GOOD COTTAGES WITH GARDENS,

The one containing Four, and the other Two Rooms, with Scullery and Out Houses a-piece and a Well of water, together with a small

CLOSE OF MEADOW LAND,

The whole extending to an Area of about

17 a.   0 r.   0 p.,

And forming a most compact and desirable Property.

Sale of the Brick Kiln Inn in 1898

his wife Eliza and their step-daughter Marian. The inn may not have been doing very well, for although John Grinter was officially their servant, he was also working as a general labourer. Towards the end of the century, when Mrs. Sarah Holmes was landlady, nine local men were prosecuted for being on licensed premises during prohibited hours in a case that was recorded in the *Hereford Times* in 1892:

124

CHARGE OF BEING ON LICENSED PREMISES DURING PROHIBITED HOURS. — Robert Cook, John Cook, Thomas Cook, of Ridge Hill, William Cook, of Hereford, Walter Cook, of Gallows Tump, Benjamin Burton, of Hunderton, William Coleman, farm bailiff, of Grafton, Thomas Jones, of Haywood, and Edward Corbett, of Ridge Hill, were charged with having been found on the licensed premises of the Brick Kiln Inn, Grafton, during prohibited hours, on Sunday, April 3rd. Mr. Akerman defended. — P.C. Barnett deposed to visiting the premises at twelve minutes to three o'clock on the day in question, and finding all the defendants there in the yard. He did not see them drinking. He saw that the table in the kitchen was wet as if there had been drinking. — Mr. Akerman called Burton, who said that he went into the yard, and there was a conversation among them about a football match. There was no drink supplied to them after closing time. — William Coleman deposed to leaving the house before closing time. He did not believe that any drink was sold after closing time. — Mr. Akerman having addressed the Bench, the magistrates considered that a technical offence had been committed, fined each defendant 2s. 6d. and costs.

A few years later the **Brick Kiln Public House** with two bars, a club room, parlour and an extensive range of outbuildings including two cottages was leased for £85 a year to George Hill a 'cottage farmer and beer retailer'. In 1920 Police Inspector Wynn charged the landlord at the **Brick Kiln** for overcharging his customers for whisky and beer, and for not displaying a price list. The landlord attempted to defend his case through 'lack of knowledge', but the Inspector replied 'there was no excuse for now knowing the law as the local papers had been full of similar cases'. He added that a bottle of beer selling for $8^{1}/2$d. in the public bar, where the rules governing prices applied, could be sold in another bar for 10d. Shortly after this event the name was changed and

---

GRAFTON.—"GRAFTON INN".

ALL THAT messuage and public house formerly called or known as The Brick Kiln Inn but now known as the Grafton Inn TOGETHER with the outbuildings thereto belonging including cow-houses stables piggeries two sheds enclosed barn and cider mill AND ALSO several pieces of pasture and orchard land occupied therewith and containing in the whole 17·032 acres or thereabouts and which premises are situate in the Parish of Grafton in the County of Hereford adjoining the Turnpike Road leading from Hereford to Ross and are now in the occupation of J. Sweeney

---

The Wintle's Brewery sale in 1937

The Grafton in 2000,
awaiting new owners

The Graftonbury
(Derek Foxton collection)

A page including the Ross to
Hereford section of Paterson's
1828 road book

the establishment became the **Grafton Inn**. By the 1930s, like the inn
at Callow, the **Grafton** was offering lunches, teas, and bed and
breakfast. It closed down in the late 1990s, but the building has now
been restored and reopened.

Grafton Lane leads to a former country house occupied by
Captain R.H. De Winton, J.P., in 1879. By the 1950s it had become a
private hotel run by Mr. and Mrs. R.D. Waddington, and in 2000 the
property was known as the **Graftonbury Garden Hotel.**

CHAPTER EIGHT

From Ross-on-Wye to Hereford
THROUGH HOARWITHY

The 'back' road from Ross to Hereford leaves the A49 at Bridstow, bearing off to the right. Although an unclassified road, it has always been considered as an alternative to the main road. The winding road at Sellack passes Pict's Cross, where a war memorial now stands on the site of an ancient mark stone recorded by Alfred Watkins in 1928. From east to west a road leads from Foy to Pencraig as already described at Winter's Cross in chapter seven. Almost opposite the gates leading to Caradoc Court is the delightfully situated **Lough Pool Inn.** This picturesque building dates from the 17th century when Richard Mynde lived there. It was occupied in 1839 by John Jones as a tenant of Richard Garrold of the Whitehouse estate, which was one of the many properties acquired by the Governors of Guy's Hospital.

It is disappointing not to find any confirmation that there was a beer house at the Lough Pool until 1870 when William Smith was granted a beer house certificate for the **Love Pool**. According to the pub's history he was a butcher and opened the beer house in 1867 with a single room bar that doubled as a butcher's shop. In July 1873 the **Lough Pool** was again recorded as the **Love Pool**, when Richard Davies applied for an extension of hours 'to keep his home open until 11pm on the occasion of a picnic'. However, it was properly called the **Lough Pool** in the 1881 census when the 70-year-old Richard Davies was still recorded as the innkeeper with his wife, Rosetta, also 70. Their daughter helped with the business, but the son, William, then 36 and still unmarried was an under-gardener, probably at Caradoc Court. Charles Yates, an agricultural labourer, was their only lodger. In 1905

The Lough Pool in 1999

Above : general view

Left : The bar

when William son of Richard Davies had taken over, the **Lough Pool** had two tap rooms but no bar. Today the popular hostelry is a typical example of a modest beer house blossoming into a first-class inn during the late 20th century.

Although the **Lough Pool** has been extended and modernised it still retains its old world charm with a warm and welcoming ambience. Recently, a smell of lavender has led the owners to associate this mysterious scent with a former visitor, Margiad Evans, a writer of note who wrote her last book *A Wicked Woman* at the **Lough Pool** before she died in 1958. Her other works include *Country Dance, Creed, The Old and the Young* and *A Candle Ahead.*

From the **Lough Pool** a delightful footpath leads through the valley down to the church at Sellack and from there a short distance across meadows to the bank of the river Wye. Here is a graceful suspension bridge, built by public subscription in 1895 to replace a ferry that joined the parishes of Sellack and King's Caple. An inscribed stone records that the bridge was built 'To the Honour of God and the Lasting Union of these Parishes for the use of All'. Although no documentation has been found, a rumour exists that there was a beer house near the church that was used by those crossing the ford or the ferry to get to King's Caple well before the footbridge was erected. The remote church at Sellack, uniquely (for England) is dedicated to St. Tysilio, a 7th-century Welsh saint and brother of Cynon, King of Powys. During the Civil War the churchyard cross avoided destruction when 'a party of parliamentarian soldiers left Ross for the beautiful and secluded village of Sellack on the Wye with the intention of destroying the cross and chancel window'. The vicar cleverly delayed them by offering them such good food and wine that they almost forgot their mission. However, as they returned one soldier fired a stray shot which made a hole in the chancel window—a hole that was later filled with plain glass.

Sellack, together with the parishes of King's Caple and Hentland, share a curious Palm Sunday tradition that dates back to 1484 when a Sellack vicar left in his will 'Bread and Ale to the value of 6s. 8d. to be distributed to all and singular in the aforesaid churches for the good of my soul'. Over the centuries the founder's name was forgotten so that by the 19th century, the charitable peace gift was recorded as being left by an unknown donor. On Palm Sunday it was distributed in the form of plain bread cakes known as Pax Cakes. These were served with ale and accompanied by the greeting 'Peace and Good Neighbourhood'. The tradition has survived, but the Pax Cakes are now served with cider or tea.

Returning to the **Lough Pool** the drive opposite leads to Caradoc Court, a former Elizabethan mansion tragically and mysteriously burnt down in 1986, but now in the process of being carefully restored. The sale particulars of 1863 describe the Court as being 'formerly a Gentleman's Mansion of some importance, and may be restored at a very moderate outlay to its former character'. The large and lofty dining room featured the Scudamore crest of a 'Bear's Paw and Coronet' on each panel. There was ample room in the 'extensive cellars' for wine, the home-produced cider and beer, both made in the adjoining 'Cider House' and 'Brewhouse'.

From the **Lough Pool** the road to Hereford descends Riggs Hill and follows the Wye to the pretty village of Hoarwithy, recorded in 1851 as 'a neat village in the Parish of Hentland, about six miles from Ross, or nearly midway between the town and Hereford, on the lower road. It is pleasantly situated near the banks of the Wye, and the scenery around is variant and extensive. On an eminence overlooking the surrounding countryside, is erected the Chapel of Ease to Hentland; it is a neat modern brick building, built in 1842, and contains 150 sittings'. As almost everyone now knows, this modest chapel was transformed in the 1880s to its present Italianate style church, cleverly constructed around the existing chapel. This unique church was built for the Rev. William Poole, and designed by J.P. Seddon, to include a campanile tower and cloisters. The elaborate interior features marble columns, pulpit and altar, a mosaic floor and ceiling, and finely-carved choir-stalls and prayer-desk depicting 'S. Dubricius and the miracle of the wine', the cask is inscribed 'Harry Hems, Carver, Exeter, 1884'.

This linear village has gradually developed between the riverside meadows and a steep wooded bank, the northern part known as Wye Hill. In 1851 there were five licensed premises that offered a full range of facilities. Beer came from the **Fisherman's Arms**, kept by Phillip Preece and cider from John Terry at the **Yew Tree**—both on Wye Hill. These were short lived inns, but on the roadside at the foot of the hill was the **Odd Fellows Arms** built in 1834. This became the **Forester's Arms** and, with its skittle alley, was sold in 1887 for £340 to James Preece, but by 1889 the premises were unoccupied, delicensed and sold. Its later name suggests that it became a laundry, but it is now a dwelling house where the name 'Foresters' has recently been revived.

Llanfrother Farm

HOARWITHY

Area : 220·685 acres

TWO COTTAGES

are arranged as follows:—

Yew Tree Cottage overlooks the River Wye, and is built of stone with a slate roof. It contains:—**Sitting Room; Living Room; Two Bedrooms.** Outside **Shed** and bucket closet. **Garden.** Main Electricity.* Farm Water Supply.

The Salmons, Hoarwithy, is built of stone, colour washed, and with a slated roof and contains:—**Sitting Room; Living Room** with Rayburn cooker; **Kitchen; Bathroom** with basin and W.C.; **Three Bedrooms.** Outside **Shed. Garden.** Main Electricity. Farm Water Supply. Hot Water System. Cesspool Drainage.

(The Salmons is subject to the conditions of an Improvement Grant under the Housing Act, 1949.)

(*Claimed by Tenant)

Sale of the Yew Tree and the Salmons in 1961

Further along the road a stone-built cottage called the Salmons was the **Three Salmons** in 1851—a cider house kept by Thomas Evans, but it was closed in 1861 when Chandos Wren Hoskyns purchased part of the Llanfrother estate including the inn. The

The retired Three Salmons in 1961

name was appropriate for outside the inn was a large stone slab where salmon for sale were displayed by the fishermen of Hoarwithy. Several years ago this slab was damaged and it has since been removed, but the cider mill has been preserved in the garden.

The property next door to the **Salmon** housed the most important inn at Hoarwithy. This was called the **Old Harp** in 1851, when Thomas Williams was described as the victualler. In the 18th century it had been known as the **Anchor**, but when Richard Smith, a harpist, took over as innkeeper in 1802 he changed its name to the **Harp Inn**.

Thomas Williams, Innkeeper at the Old Harp in 1851, aged 36

Smith died in 1810 and was buried at Bridstow where his elaborate chest tomb decorated with harps records:

The Harp whilst Mortal aft he strung
To please the gay and jocund throng
With angels now he plays and sings
Glory to God, the King of Kings.

Richard's widow continued to run the inn until 1813 when she advertised the **Harp** (also for some unknown reason known as the **Bolt**) to be let or sold—'All that old established and well accommodated Public House, with the Garden, Stables and Outbuildings thereunto'. By 1819 John Williams was the

Hoarwithy Bridge Act of 1855

Wall painting at the Old Harp

*Pigeon Shoot at the Harp
in January 1880*

innkeeper of what was then called the **Old Harp**, and it was during his tenancy that the inn was extended and altered with picturesque scenes painted on the new interior walls. The wall paintings would have been admired by the committee of the Hoarwithy Bridge Company who regularly held their meetings here following the 1855 Act of Parliament authorising a bridge to replace the ferry. This first bridge was opened in 1859, but by 1875 it was in dangerous condition and was replaced the following year. The present bridge was built in 1990.

For about a hundred years the paintings were covered by layers of wallpaper, but the present owners discovered them and the best parts have since been preserved. The **Old Harp** continued as a 'comfortable house' and in 1861 was purchased by Chandos Wren Hoskyns who lived in Harewood House in the adjoining parish. It was then placed under the tenancy of James Preece, a butcher and timber merchant. Along with the rest of the Harewood Estate the **Harp Inn** was included in the 1870s sale as a 'Dwelling House' with 'Two Attics, Three Bedrooms, Parlour, Tap Room, Bar, Store Room and Cellars' with 'Outbuildings, Brewhouse, Stable for Four Horses and Loft over, open Shed, Piggeries, Yard' and four acres of rich meadow land. After its eventual purchase in 1884 by the Revds. Pigott and Bosanquet, it was converted into the Harp Temperance Hotel under Mrs. Mary Shaw then Miss Fanny Pope, and for one hundred years its extensive cellars were 'dry' until the Hurleys purchased the property in 1973 to run their popular 'Wineweekends' with a well-stocked wine cellar.

In 1816, two Friendly Societies were established at Hoarwithy. One, known as the Hoarwithy Amicable Society, held its meetings at John Terry's **Yew Tree** until 1843, and the Hoarwithy Friendly Society, who transferred their meetings to the **Old Harp** after the **Prussia Inn** was closed in the early 19th century. Before James Preece lost his tenancy of the **Old Harp** he was summoned by Petty Sessions for detaining certain articles of the

THE "HARP" INN and LANDS,

SITUATE AT

HOARWITHY, on the High Road from ROSS to HEREFORD,

With DWELLING HOUSE,

Containing Two Attics, Three Bed Rooms, Parlour, Tap Room, Bar, Store Room, and Cellars in the Basement,

GARDEN.

And the following OUTBUILDINGS,—Brew-house, Stable for Four Horses and Loft over, open Shed, Piggeries, Yard; and the following

VALUABLE ENCLOSURES OF RICH MEADOW LAND,

Abutting on the RIVER WYE.

Sale particulars of the Old Harp in 1876

The former Old Harp

THE POPLARS
HOARWITHY, Nr. Hereford

Proprietors : Miss E. G. MAILES and Mr. A. E MAILES

Large Gardens and Lawns : Own Farm Produce : Bright Pleasant Rooms
——SALMON FISHING PRIVATE WATERS——

THE POPLARS is pleasantly situated in the centre of a very pretty village in the Wye Valley, sunny and sheltered position. Within easy reach of all beauty spots in Wye Valley by rail or road. 1 minute shops, post & church. Hereford 10 miles, Ross 5 miles. Bus passes door to these towns.

Station, G.W.R. BALLINGHAM 2 miles.

Estbd. 1900

The Old Harp under new management by 1931

133

The New Harp about 1900

Hoarwithy Friendly Society in 1875. These included the flags, banners, scarfs, bankbook, and box with key. Preece was dismissed from the society as its secretary—responsible for paying out money to sick members—so the meetings were 'to be held elsewhere'.

The 1881 census shows the 52-year-old James Preece at the **Harp Inn** together with his wife Mary. They had two general servants and two adult boarders, James Roberts and Richard Edwards. They were both labourers born in Hentland and Richard had his 11-year-old son with him. However, Preece managed to overcome the past events and by the late 1880s had established himself as landlord of the by then sole pub in Hoarwithy, This was called the **New Harp** and opened in a dwelling that was formerly called Fishbrook Cottage. Thomas Dance was the landlord in 1902, probably about the time that the **Harp** was acquired by Alton Court Brewery. In 1962 they sold the 'Inn at the Mill Brook Hoarwithy in the Parish of Hentland known as the **New Harp Inn** with the outbuildings yard and land' to West Country Breweries who were eventually taken over by Whitbreads. During the 1970s the **Harp** became 'rather dreary' until 1979 when John and Pauline Keenan took it over. They 'were attracted to Hoarwithy simply for the fishing—John literally eats, drinks, and sleeps angling, but as yet he hasn't caught a single salmon'. In the *Ross-on-Wye Advertiser* of 1980 the new publican explained an unusual use of the bar:

Hoarwithy church tower stands above the old village shop,
once the King of Prussia Inn

Every Wednesday afternoon a doctor from Ross conducts his surgery in our bar. It makes sense really, after all, we are right in the centre of the village and all the locals know he's here — but we are not open while he's seeing patients.

By 1984 the one-bar inn was regularly 'packed with ramblers, rafters, campers, and other visitors from outside the village'. As a result the **New Harp** has been extended and modernised and offers all the usual facilities expected from a typical Herefordshire village pub.

Beyond the **New Harp**, and on the opposite side of the road, is a stone house which in the 18th century housed an 'old and well accustomed inn known by the sign of the **King of Prussia**', named after Frederick the Great. In 1786 he allied himself with England against the French and so became a popular hero. The **Prussia** faced the road leading to the Hoarwithy Horse Boat which crossed the Wye to King's Caple. In the 1820s, long before the ford and ferry were replaced by the Hoarwithy Bridge, the **King of Prussia**, then run by H. Harry was closed. It became a grocers and general stores which likewise closed around 30 years ago.

The Hoarwithy Bridge enabled the inhabitants of Hoarwithy to reach Fawley Station after the opening of the Hereford, Ross, Gloucester Railway in 1855. Following the closure of the railway in

1964, the bridge became more important to the people of King's Caple, providing a reasonably direct access to Hereford and Ross. It has been said that all this travelling in the past was 'thirst provoking', which accounts for a fair share of pubs at King's Caple in addition to those at Hoarwithy. Out of the five known public houses in King's Caple none have survived.

A couple of miles downstream from Hoarwithy at Sellack Boat on the King's Caple side of the Wye was the site of the earliest pub in the parish. Known as the **Old Boar** it was built in 1696 to cater for the river trade, but appears to have been short lived and had closed by the mid-18th century following the death of Margaret Harris who left 'Three hundred gallons of original Cyder' valued at £1. The house still survives and is called Sheildbrook, the home of the late Elizabeth Taylor who ran a nursery garden and wrote *King's Caple in Archenfield.*

The **Yew Tree,** also known as the **Wood Inn,** was run by Henry Terry as a beer house in 1905. It was in a remote situation on an unsurfaced lane leading off the Brockhampton road. The inn sported a skittle alley, and is remembered by older folk as a small thatched property lying high above the Wye. It fell into disrepair and remained derelict for a

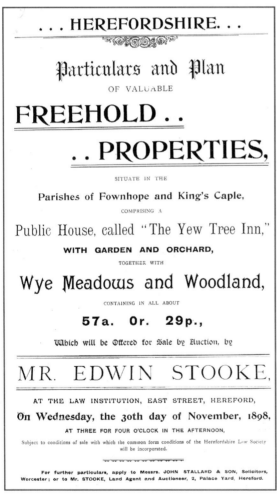

... HEREFORDSHIRE. ...

Particulars and Plan

OF VALUABLE

FREEHOLD ..

.. PROPERTIES,

SITUATE IN THE

Parishes of Fownhope and King's Caple,

COMPRISING A

Public House, called "The Yew Tree Inn,"

WITH GARDEN AND ORCHARD,

TOGETHER WITH

Wye Meadows and Woodland,

CONTAINING IN ALL ABOUT

57a. 0r. 29p.,

Which will be Offered for Sale by Auction, by

MR. EDWIN STOOKE,

AT THE LAW INSTITUTION, EAST STREET, HEREFORD,

On Wednesday, the 30th day of November, 1898,

AT THREE FOR FOUR O'CLOCK IN THE AFTERNOON,

Subject to conditions of sale with which the common form conditions of the Herefordshire Law Society will be incorporated.

For further particulars, apply to Messrs. JOHN STALLARD & SON, Solicitors, Worcester; or to Mr. STOOKE, Land Agent and Auctioneer, 2, Palace Yard, Hereford.

Sale of the Yew Tree at King's Capel in 1898

The Yew Tree or Wood Inn, since replaced by a modern house

number of years, but has recently been replaced with a private house.

Opposite the Barn Stables on the road to Fawley, a cottage was known to have been a beer or cider retailers called the **Cat and Fiddle**. It would seem that the rather odd idea of a fiddling cat was firmly established in the public's imagination by the 16th century, well before the nursery rhyme beginning 'Hey diddle diddle, the cat and the fiddle ...' which has a mid-18th century origin. It could also refer to a once popular game called tipcat, with the fiddle representing the dancing that would attract customers to the inn.

A sole entry in 1851 records the beer retailer William Reece at the **Cross Trees**. If this did not refer to the **Yew Tree**, then it was probably situated at the village crossroads, and only survived until Thomas Gatfield opened the **New Inn**. This faced the former station at Fawley, a mile north-east of King's Caple, and its opening coincided with that of the railway in 1855. Before the end of the century its name had been changed to the **British Lion**, which in later years struggled to keep going. Despite its renovation and modernisation in the late 1990s the **British Lion** was considered to be 'no longer viable' and sadly took on a new life as a

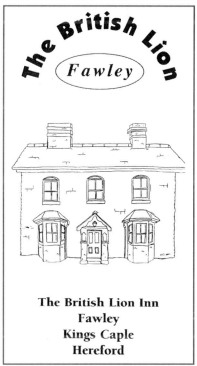

**The British Lion Inn
Fawley
Kings Caple
Hereford**

1998 advertisement for the British Lion, once the New Inn

137

The British Lion at Fawley shortly after closing as an inn

The Plough at Little Dewchurch in 2001

private house in March 2000.

Returning across the bridge to Hoarwithy, there used to be two roads leading to Hereford, but the second has long fallen into disuse. The direct route leads steeply uphill and past the **Plough** at Little Dewchurch. This inn was established before 1839 and was run by Thomas Thomas in 1851. A decade later the landlord had branched out into blacksmithing and shopkeeping as well as innkeeping. Several charges of drunkenness occurred at Little Dewchurch including the time in 1894 when John Tompkins was found by P.C. Jones from Hoarwithy at 10 p.m. after 'he had been down in a ditch, and was very drunk, staggering and making a noise'. Tompkins was fined 10s., or had to suffer 7 days hard labour. The **Plough** has remained open to serve the occasional traveller that takes the minor road to the city and may benefit from the new residents settling in the gradually developing village at Little Dewchurch. The thirsty traveller on this road has no other port of call until he reaches the boundaries of Hereford City

The alternative route from Hoarwithy to Hereford originally followed what is now an almost unknown road of 'Six miles or thereabouts' which was recorded as a turnpike road in the 1730 Hereford Road Act. From Hoarwithy Passage (now the bridge)

the narrow road, which is signposted to Ballingham, passes a corner cottage called Evergreens, which, it is said, served for a short time during the 19th century as another **Yew Tree** in Hoarwithy. It then follows the Wye and leads below a cottage

The Cottage of Content at Carey in 2001

still called the **Forty Steps** for obvious reasons. This was licensed in 1870 as a beer house under the name of Philip Preece, but maybe the steep climb led to its early closure. This route was abandoned as a turnpike road around 1840, but at Carey in Ballingham the **Cottage of Content**, formerly the **Miner's Arms** with its wayside smithy, made a welcome break on the old road. It is now an attractive and popular pub housed in a timber-framed building dating from the 17th century. A totally undocumented story suggests that the inn was built as 'three labourers cottages for the Mynor family, and it was a condition that one of the tenants maintain an ale and cider parlour in one room'. The only doubtful connection with the Mynors occurred in the late 17th century when this family were associated with property at Witherstone on the Carey brook.

Another outrageous explanation, which was given in 1948 by the new landlord Mr. C. Scott, was reported in the *Hereford Times*. Scott considered the **Miner's Arms** to be too reminiscent of the Rhondda Valley, so as he had discovered a tablet in a church depicting a 'mediaeval miner' he planned to change the pub to the **Mediaeval Miner.** He added that there had been an 'iron foundry' at Carey, so he 'felt such a sign was more appropriate' and was to be designed by his son, a Planning Officer in Dorset. It seems unlikely that this latter name was used as it became the **Cottage of Content**. In 1985 it was an 'idyllic country pub, popular with the locals and tourists alike, with heaps of atmosphere in its timber-framed interior'. The **Cottage** then offered an 'interesting, varied and adventurous menu', and was 'a truly magnificent little place, thoroughly recommended and well worth finding. The same still applies at the beginning of the 21st century.

The old road from Carey can now only be followed on foot, but a newer driving route leads through the parishes of Bolstone, Holme Lacy and Dinedor. Apart from a cider retailer listed at Dinedor in 1851 the other two parishes apparently remained 'dry' throughout recent history. They formed part of the Holme Lacy estate, and by tradition the Scudamores, Stanhopes and Lucas-Tooths would not tolerate licensed premises on their land, although they brewed beer and made cider for their own consumption.

In 1639 John Scudamore's cellars at Holme Lacy House were stocked with hogsheads of beer, cider, ale, sherry and claret with gallons of sweet wine and white wine available for the Christmas festivities. After Scudamore's absence during the Civil War, he returned to his estate and introduced a new cider apple which he called

John Philip's brass in Hereford Cathedral shows a brance of an apple tree

the Redstreak. He was advised that the Redstreak 'was to be preferred for your Plantation to any other apple whatsoever, especially remote from your House. First, because it yields the best of British Drinks. Secondly, because the fruit is harsh and unpleasant, not tempting the Palates of lewd Persons'. The poet, John Philips, who died in 1708 aged 32 and is buried in the entrance to the north transept of Hereford Cathedral, wrote of the Redstreak in his poem 'Cyder':

Of no regard till Scudamore's skilful hand
Improv'd her, and by courtly discipline
Taught her the savage nature to forget,—
Hence styl'd the Scudamorean plant; whose wine
Whoever tastes, let him with grateful heart
Respect that ancient loyal house.

From Holme Lacy the 18th-century road went over Dinedor Hill, but as it was 'dangerous and inconvenient to Passengers and Carriages'

Early 1930s advertisement for the Wye Hotel

The Wye Inn in 2001

an alternative route was turnpiked below the heights of Rotherwas Park Wood to Lower Bullingham. Here travellers once found the tiny **Nag's Head** on the banks of the Wye. This was later replaced by the present brick building, which by 1891 was grandly called the **Wye Hotel** with Henry Stephen Buckeridge as landlord. In May 1892 the new licensee, Marianne Thomas, had a tough time with the following incident as reported in the *Hereford Times*:

A DOUBLE CHARGE — John Thomas, Farmer, Bullingham, was charged with assaulting Marianne Thomas, his wife, on March 27th. — Mr. Garrold appeared for the wife and stated that arrangements had been made for a deed of separation and on his application the case was allowed to be withdrawn. — There was a further charge against defendant of being drunk on the licensed premises of the Wye Hotel, the license of which was in the name of his wife. — Defendant admitted the offence, and was fined 2s. 6d. and 10s. 6d. costs.

DRUNK ON LICENSED PREMISES — James Price and James Harris, labourers, were charged with having been drunk on the licensed premises known as the Wye Hotel, at Ballingham on April 20th. — P.C. Preece stated that the men were drunk and trying to fight. — Fined 2s. 6d. and 5s. costs each.

141

17¼	Lea, *Herefordshire*	42¼
	¼ m. farther, Forward to Hereford, by Mordiford, 16½ m.	
	To Gloucester 12 m.	
15½	Weston	44
13¾	*to * ROSS*	46¼
	To Newent 9 m. / *To Ledbury 12 m.*	
	Cross the river Wey	
	¾ m. beyond Ross,	
	to Monmouth 9¾ m.	
	½ m. farther,	
	to Hereford, by Much Birch, 13 m.	
10	Pig's Cross	49½
8	Hoarwithy	51½
6	Little Dewchurch	53½
4½	Aconbury	55
1	Junction of the Road	58½
	to Monmouth 16¾ m.	
	½ m. farther,	
	to Hay 20½ m.	
	Cross the river Wye	
	* HEREFORD	59½

The Lea to Hereford via Hoarwithy page from Paterson's 1828 road book

As Dinedor did not have a licensed house, some of the villagers such as Mansel Preece used the **Wye Hotel**. He was fined 10s. and costs in 1894 for assaulting Albert Lyddiatt with a beer glass by 'striking him in the eye with a glass of beer', which broke and turned out to be empty. It was a 'practical joke' that became out of hand and took place outside the inn. The **Wye Hotel** was a City Brewery pub and the landlord in the latter part of the 19th century acted as agent for Arnold Perrett's ales and stouts. This brewery acquired the hotel and in 1937 it was sold to the Cheltenham Original Brewery with a 'Cider House garden yard and orchard and all other outbuildings'. It is now called the **Wye Inn.**

CHAPTER NINE

From Ross-on-Wye to Hereford
EAST OF THE WYE

There is another choice of routes to follow from Ross to Hereford, which is to the east of the river Wye, passing a host of past and present inns, taverns and beer houses. Investigating the first of these involves following a meandering road beside the river through the quaintly named Hole-in-the-Wall hamlet in Foy parish, whilst the busier route follows the B4224 to the Wyeside village of Fownhope, home of a former brewery.

The riverside route starts with a minor road from Ross that crosses over the A40 and then winds through Brampton Abbotts, a village without any record of a public house, but where the sawyer, John Partridge, was retailing beer in 1867. The river Wye divides the parish of Foy into two parts, with the church on the western side and the former school and licensed houses on the east bank. The two sides were always linked by a ford and ferry crossing, but this was replaced by a foot and bridle bridge in 1876. The first bridge was washed away by a high flood in 1919 to be replaced by the present suspension footbridge in 1921.

In the eastern part of Foy the Tommys kept a small beer house called the **Boatman's Rest** until 1858. This was obviously opened to cater for the river trade and the thirsty bargees who, before the 1809 Horse Towing-path Act, had hauled the boats along the Wye. Nearby was the **Anchor and Can,** also associated with the river and the important ford and ferry crossing. In 1844 the **Anchor and Can** was described as a 'pot-house called the **Hole-in-the-Wall**' near the 'ferry

The 'holy well' at Hole-in-the-Wall

where the horse boat was moored to the shore'. In 1852 the 'dwelling house and inn' was occupied by Sarah Hardwick, the victualler and ferry boat keeper. Before the ferry was replaced by the bridge in 1876 the **Anchor and Can** had been closed and the household furniture and shop fittings sold by auction. Even so, the building still remains as an attractive cottage that is now part of an adventure holiday complex. In the garden is a picturesque well which formed part of a large grotto recorded in 1805. This 'Holy Well' is fed by spring water spilling from a stone arch draped with ivy, ferns and wild flowers. According to Arthur Lamont, writing in the Woolhope Club *Transactions* in 1921:

Long before the Thames Tunnel was thought of, there existed a sub-way under the Wye at Foy. It was constructed for the convenience of two religious houses, which stood opposite to each other near the river banks. The entrance on the right bank was from the cellar of the former Ingestone House [rebuilt as a farm about 1835], the outlet on the Ross side, or left bank, may still be seen in the rick yard of the Court Farm, occupied by Mr. Cole [and almost next door to Hole-in-the-Wall]. When inspected, the appearance was that of a filled-up well to within about three feet of the surface. There are several large stones in the garden, which presumably formed part of the building which housed the Brampton Abbots. A native questioned about 40 years ago said he ventured in, when a young man, to about the middle of the tunnel, accompanied by his dog. Either his courage failed or some obstruction prevented his further research. The old cellar on the Ingestone side has long been filled up.

Could this supposed tunnel be the reason for the place being called the **Hole-in-the-Wall**, or was the name derived from the holy well?

CLERGY, GENTRY, TRADES, FARMERS, ETC.

Jones Rev. John, Vicar, Vicarage
York Colonel Phillip, Perrystone Court
Bennett James, farmer, Ingestone
Burgum Thomas, farmer, New House
Davis Charles, Constable
Hardwick Joseph, victualler and ferry boat keeper, *Anchor and Can*, Eaton Tregoes
Hart Francis Henry, farmer, The Cole's Farm
Hooper Richard, farmer, Court Farm
Jones Wm., farmer and Constable, Hill Eaton

Overton John, victualler and farmer, *Old Gore Inn*
Rock Josiah, farmer, Carthage
Rudge James, farmer, Coppice Farm
Stock Charles, farmer, Underhill Farm
Symonds James, fisherman and coracle maker, Eaton Tregoes
Tommy George, beer retailer, *Boatman's Rest*, Eaton Tregoes
Watkins John, blacksmith, Old Gore
Woodhall John, farmer, Park Farm
Woodhall Thomas, farmer, The Park

The principal residents of Foy and Sellack in 1851—Inns highlighted

Hole-in-the Wall in 2001

Brockhampton Court in the 1970s

The back road from Ross through Hole-in-the-Wall was turnpiked by the Ross Trust in 1749, but after alterations in 1773 it was abandoned as a toll road due to the small amount of tolls being collected. This resulted in a toll-free way from and to Ross, which was much appreciated by the farmers and drovers who were the main users. The road continues from Hole-in-the-wall to How Caple and from there to Brockhampton where the **Plough and Harrow** was run by a blacksmith called William Townsend in 1851. Although William continued at the smithy there is no further record of the **Plough**. A short distance away is **Brockhampton Court**, now a home for the elderly. It was an 18th-century rectory redesigned in the 1890s, and described by Pevsner as 'a big composition in a neo-Tudor style,

145

The Old Gore in 1990

decidely pre-Lethaby. Much sculptural decoration'. It was used as a hotel for many years from around 1950 until recent times. Lethaby's beautiful Arts and Crafts church of All Saints stands opposite one of the entrances to the Court; the old church, now in ruins but with plans for conversion to a house, is in the grounds. From Brockhampton the road rises steeply over the edge of Capler Hill before dropping down into Fownhope village close to the church.

If the more obvious road—the B4224—is taken from Ross towards Fownhope, it passes through the ancient crossroads at Old Gore where the road ahead rises steeply up Perrystone Hill towards Ledbury and the Fownhope road bears off to the left. At the junction a former smithy, toll house and inn stood around a wayside cross that has since been re-used as a war memorial. In 1812 the **Old Gore Inn**, occupied by Ann Bird, was offered for sale as a 'capacious well-built and well established Inn'. It consisted of 'a lofty roomy and convenient kitchen, with extensive arched Cellaring underneath, Brewhouse, Wash-house, Dairy, Large Garden, Coalhouse, Barn, Granary, Hay Lofts and Stables for nearly Thirty Horses'. There were also two parlours, 8 bed-chambers and two flights of stairs.

Before the construction of the purpose-built turnpike road from Ross to Ledbury in the 1830s, the **Old Gore** was conveniently placed at the main crossroads for Hereford and Ledbury. Coach travellers heading for Ledbury were requested to alight at the inn and 'ascend the higher ground by the pleasant footpath' thus lightening the load for the horses struggling up the steep slopes of Perrystone Hill. The **Old Gore** must have suffered a loss of trade when the new road which circled round the hill to the south, was built, but the inn did not close until the late 1870s. Today the building is easily recognised as a former coaching inn, which at one time formed part of the Perrystone estate.

From Old Gore the former toll road, turnpiked in 1726 by the Gloucester and Hereford Trust, almost follows an unaltered route through Crossway to Sollers Hope. 'Hop' indicates a 'remote place' in a valley and the manor was in the hands of the Sollers family in the 13th century. Here Charles Halford and Andrew Mailes, from their farm called the **Pounds**, were retailing cider during the mid-19th century. Just over the boundary in Woolhope parish there was a cider-mill unseen from the road at New Gore.

At **Gurney's Oak**, Edwin Jones was retailing cider from a building which became 'ruinous and partly demolished' and was replaced by the **Gurney's Oak Inn** in the early 20th century. In 1902 Thomas Pugh a farmer and beer retailer was selling Arnold Perrett's Ales and Stouts supplied by the City Brewery in Hereford, but it was not until 1960 that the **Gurney's Oak** acquired a full license. It was recently closed and has been converted into a private house, but the name 'Gurney's Oak' is carved on the building.

At the end of the First World War in November 1918 a 'disorderly gypsy' called Valentine Holland from Sollers Hope was locked up for creating a disturbance outside the Hereford Recruiting Office. She was had up for being drunk and at her hearing it was declared that 'her condition was due to distress and excitement in

Gurney's Oak in 2000

fear her brother should be taken for the army'. A more likely reason at this date was to celebrate the end of this horrific war.

The **Gurney's Oak** was always used as the place for the local hunt to meet. On 4 December 1920 the South Herefordshire Hunt was due to meet at the inn, but owing to the sudden death of the landlord the meeting place was changed. The hunt spent a day in Yatton Woods which was 'full of foxes but there was no scent and the weather was very much against hounds'.

Fownhope is one of Herefordshire's larger villages, pleasantly situated between the Wye and a range of wooded hills. There are still several shops, a post office, a school, church, chapel, but now only two public houses survive of the six licensed houses listed in the mid-19th century *Directories*, to serve a population employed in milling, tanning, brewing, lime burning, boat building, fishing, farming and many other trades. The Fownhope Brewery dates from at least the late 18th century, but was moved to Hereford in the early 19th century and became the Hereford Brewery and later Watkins Imperial Brewery. Apart from the beer production this was cider making country, with five cider mills recorded in 1843.

The oldest Fownhope public house is the **Green Man**, which the landlord claims to date from 1485. It is housed in a building that has been much modernised and extended since its known origins in the 17th century. A bundle of deeds in the Hereford Record Office, which cover the years from 1693 to 1778, describe the inn as 'All that house formerly called **The Naked Boy**'. The inn's long past is surrounded by stories of the Civil War, magistrates' courts, the coaching era, and Tom

Spring a champion bare-fist fighter. Over the fireplace in the restaurant is a mural painted by Trevor Makinson. It depicts Colonel Birch, who by tradition halted overnight at the inn after his seige of Goodrich Castle

Fownhope about 1900, with the Green Man the first building on the left

148

in 1845. Also shown are members of the magistrates' court, a coach and horses on the turnpike road, a Heart of Oak customer with his beflowered stick, and the boxer Tom Spring. He was a native of Fownhope and, after becoming England's Bareknuckle Champion in 1823, he kept the Boothall Inn at Hereford before moving to Holborn where he died in 1851. A century later a monument in the form of a cider mill was erected near his childhood home at Rudge End in Fownhope. The inscription reads:

Invictae Fidelitatis Praemiual
This Memorial Commemorates
Thomas Winter,

Born at Rudge End, Fownhope, Herefordshire,
February 22nd, 1795, and died at the Castle Tavern,
Holborn, August 20th, 1851. Buried at
West Norwood Cemetery, London.

Erected by his countrymen of the land of Cider,
in token of their esteem for the manliness and
science which in many served contests in the
pugilistic ring, under the name of Spring, raised
him to the proud distinction of the
Champion of England, 1823-24.

Tom Spring and his memorial at Rudge End

In 1788 the **Green Man** was occupied by William Fountain who let the premises a year later to Mary Powell and Elizabeth Fountain. During the 19th century several generations of women related to 'King-Connop' ran the inn. Connop acquired this royal name because he owned and worked most of the numerous lime-kilns in the district before the industry was supplanted by the Radnorshire lime works. In

The Green Man about 1960

1881 Eliza Frances Connop was the licensee and lived there with her 77-year-old mother, her unmarried sister, Harriot, and her daughter, also Harriot. She was the last member of this family at the **Green Man** and was still there in 1891. In the 20th century the Samuels were followed by a succession of landlords who gradually increased the size of the inn from eight bedrooms in 1931 to 20 in 1999. In 1948 the **Green Man** underwent extensive renovations under its landlord J.P. Nicholls, who gutted the building and put the building back as a timber-framed inn. He sold the inn to Osmond Edwards who continued the improvements under the name of Welcome Inns. It obtained a full licence, as opposed to a simple beer and cider licence, in 1953.

The **Green Man** is still the meeting place of the Heart of Oak Society, which has its roots in an Amicable Society founded in 1791 and became a Friendly Society around 1839. Members of the society paid a regular subscription which provided a payment to them during sickness, injury and death. Although the funeral side of the society ceased in the 1980s, the members at Fownhope were committed to keep the tradition alive. The annual Club Walk Day is held on the Saturday nearest to Oak Apple Day at the end of May and this parade, which always starts from the **New Inn**, is well supported. The **Green Man** also serves as a popular stop for walkers following the Wye Valley Walk and ramblers exploring an excellent network of footpaths, who should not fail to read the sign over the entrance to the former coaching yard:

You travel far, You travel near,
It's here you find the best of Beer,
You pass the east, you pass the west,
If you pass this you pass the best.

The usual sign for the **Naked Boy** and the **Green Man** both represent a foliate head, which either symbolises sadness and sacrifice, death and ruin, or the preferred life and renewal. The green man of inn signs usually stem from Jack-in-the-Green, a spring ritual dating from the 18th century. It is interesting to note that this Fownhope's inn change of name from the **Naked Boy** to the **Green Man** falls within the century of this tradition and the founding of the Fownhope Amicable Society with its May Day celebrations. Another explanation is that it became known as the **Green Man** when John Greene was innkeeper in 1707.

The New Inn in 2001

Nearby is the **New Inn,** which appears to have been opened in the 1860s by William Evans, a painter and decorator who came originally from Ludlow, together with his wife, Elizabeth and their son, also William, and continued by a

1931 advertisement for the New Inn

151

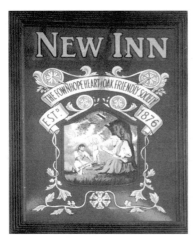

The New Inn still celebrates the Heart of Oak Friendly Society on its sign

carpenter called John Bailey in the 1890s. By 1930 the **New Inn** provided accommodation for 'Tourists and Anglers' under the proprietor Mr. W. White. In the 1950s Geoffrey Longman ran the **New Inn**, succeeding Charlie Edwards, 'in whose days there was a bowling green'.

Between this inn and the church is the site of the **White Horse** which closed its doors long ago and was rebuilt as Whiterdine Place in Victorian times. Possibly opposite was the **Plough,** a cider house only listed once in 1851.

From the crossroads towards the northern end of the village the lane leading down to a former river crossing passes the **Forge and Ferry**, a recent name reflecting past activities. Its original name was the **Highland Home** when 'newly erected' by the wood-dealer, James Mayo, in 1872 as a simple beer house. Indeed, the inn was not even named in the 1881 census, where it is simply described as being in

The Forge and Ferry, closed in 2001

Ferry Road. Throughout the first half of the 20th century the Williams family ran the inn, but around the Swinging Sixties it had an unfortunate name change to the **Flamenco** for a short period. Sense prevailed, and in 1973 it became the **Forge and Ferry**. Hidden from the potential passing trade down a side lane, it has recently closed.

VALUABLE PROPERTY.

TO BE SOLD BY AUCTION,

By order of the Representatives of the late Miss Elizabeth Bird, and under the power of Sale, contained in the Mortgage Deed, by

MR. J. Y. STEPHENS,

At the GREEN MAN INN, Fownhope,

ON TUESDAY, JULY 7, 1863,

At 4 o'Clock in the Afternoon, subject to conditions to be produced, and in the following or such other Lots, shall be agreed upon, the undermentioned

FREEHOLD, COPYHOLD, & LEASEHOLD

PROPERTY.

LOT 1.—A DWELLING-HOUSE, called "The King's Arms Inn, with the Buildings, Garden, Cider-mill, and Two Parcels of very productive LAND adjoining, containing 2r. 29p., pleasantly situated in the village of Fownhope, by the Turnpike Road leading from Hereford.

LOT 2.—A BARN, FOLD-YARD and OUTBUILDINGS, and TWO COTTAGES and Gardens, a Piece of ORCHARDING, containing 1a. 1r. 17p., opposite to Lot One.

LOT 3.---TWO PARCELS of ORCHARDING, adjoining Lot 2, called "The Upper and Lower Crimes," with Two Substantial COTTAGES and large Gardens, containing together 3a. 2r. 38p.

LOT 4.---A small ESTATE, called "New Gore," situate at Buckenhall, in the Parish of Woolhope, on the road leading from Hereford to Ross, consisting of a Stone-built DWELL-ING-HOUSE, with Barn, Stable, Cider-mill, and other Buildings, and Five Pieces of LAND, containing 7a. 0r. 11p., in the occupation of Mr. Philip Williams.

Lot One is Freehold, as is Lot Three, with the exception of the Upper Crimes, which, with Lot Two, is Copyhold of the Manor of Fownhope. Lot Four is Leasehold for a long term of years at a nominal rent, one of the Pieces being held for a term of which 180 years are now unexpired, and the remainder being held for a term of which upwards of 3600 years are unexpired.

For viewing the Premises at Fownhope apply to Mr. GANGE of that place, and at Woolhope to the Tenant; and further particulars may be obtained, and Plans of the Lots seen at the Offices of Mr. Symonds, Solicitor, Hereford.

Dated 18th June 1863

Sale of the King's Arms at Fownhope and other properties in 1863

153

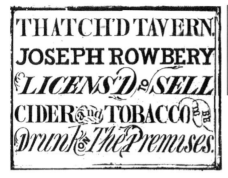

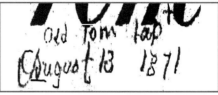

Left : The Thatched Tavern sign
Above : A memo recording the
tapping of 'Old Tom',
a 500 gallon cider pipe

FOWNHOPE.—THE ANCHOR INN.

ALL THOSE two pieces or parcels of land part arable and part pasture and planted with fruit trees situate at a place called Hollyfast in the Parish of Fownhope in the County of Hereford and commonly called "Hollyfast Croft" containing by admeasurement two acres more or less upon portions of which are erected and standing a messuage or Inn called The Anchor Inn situate between Westwood and Hermans House with the millhouse and outbuildings and appurtenances thereunto belonging and occupied therewith.

Sale of the Anchor in 1937

To the north of the crossroads on the main road was the site of the **King's Arms,** an 'Inn with the Buildings, Garden, Cider-mill, and Two Parcels of very productive Land', which, after its sale in 1863, was delicensed and later demolished.

Fownhope's population of over 1,000 in the mid-19th century were well catered for with inns scattered throughout the parish. On Common Hill the **Orange Tree**, now a pleasant cottage, and the **Thatched Tavern**, a tumbling ruin in a nature reserve, both 'supplied ale and cider to the lime-burners in their thirsty work' together with the almost forgotten **Horn** at Rudge End. By 1881, the **Orange Tree** had become the home of William Anthony, a stone mason, and his family, and James Badham, an agricultural labourer, and his wife, Mary, were at the **Horn**.

On the Capler road is a Yew Tree Cottage, possibly the cottage where William and Marshall Apperley lodged in 1861, and the home of the **Yew Tree Inn** of 1881 kept by the 28-year-old Thomas Davies. He was married to Emma from Brockhampton and father to their three-year-old son. Their lodger was one William Godwin, described as a station master from Wiltshire.

To the north of Fownhope, and close to the Wye at Even Pits, the **Anchor** was established near the ferry crossing for Holme Lacy, before it was replaced by a bridge in 1858. It was on ground described in 1728 as 'all that piece or parcal of arable land called Holly Fast Croft'. It was purchased by Nathaniel Purchas, a brandy merchant, in 1800, who possibly used the site for storage. After his death, his daughter sold the land to Richard Wheatstone, a barge owner, who erected a messuage, millhouse and building by 1849, known as the **Anchor.** It is remembered by older folk as a small cottage selling Arnold Perrett's ales and stout and Bulmers' draught cider and was sold by the brewery in 1937. When the bridge was rebuilt in 1973 the **Anchor** was demolished to make way for road improvements. Across the road from the **Anchor** was **Luck's All**, a beer house which in 1855 was described as 'a messuage now used as a public house in the occupation of Charles Wheatstone'. It did not survives as an inn for long into the 20th century, but the cottage is still there.

Within the northern extremity of Fownhope parish, on the left hand side of the road, just before crossing the Pentaloe brook, is a red brick cottage called Bell House. This was recorded as a beer house known as the **Bell** in 1867 and 1876. It seems to have closed before the

Mary Soulsby's painting of the Anchor Inn before it closed

155

Luck's All and the Bell in 2001—both long retired as inns

end of the 19th century, possibly due to competition from the **Moon Inn** which stood almost directly opposite, but in Mordiford parish.

Mordiford is a village sitting between the rivers Wye and the Lugg, where flooding has always been a threat. The great flood of 1811, which claimed lives and destroyed property, is recorded in the church porch. Before this date the west wall of Mordiford church displayed the picture of a fierce 12 feet long dragon which led to a host of lurid tales. It is said that the dragon was eventually destroyed by a criminal called Garson, who was promised his freedom if he slayed the monster. He cleverly hid in a cider barrel and through the bunghole managed to kill the hideous creature, but unfortunately he died from the dragon's noxious breath. The following verse dates from 1670:

The Mordiford Dragon

Left : Shown on the church as drawn by R. Clarke c.1808

Above : The much more ferocious dragon illustrated by Dingley in the mid-17th century

156

This is the true effigies of the strange
Prodigious monster, which our woods did range,
In Eastwood it by Garson's hand was slain,
A truth which old mythologists maintayne.

The **Moon** at Mordiford is an attractive property that was built in 1602, with later additions. It may date as an inn from this period, and was certainly open in 1813 when auctions were held there. The **Moon** has experienced a long list of landlords including John Goodman in 1881 together with his wife, Louisa, and her two children from a previous marriage. It was Goodman who changed the name to the **Full Moon**. In

---

THE MOON INN

situated in the village of Mordiford, in the occupation of MR. DANIEL HUGHES, and held by him on an annual tenancy subject to 6 calendar months' notice to quit, expiring at 2nd February. The accommodation is as follows :

In the Basement.—Suitable beer cellars.

Ground Floor.—Bar, Club Room, Kitchen, Back Kitchen, and Sitting Room.

First Floor.—Five bedrooms.

There are also the following buildings :—Mill house with stone cider Mill and press, Trap house, cowhouse for four with loft over and a lean-to shed, two-stall stable with loft over with lean-to pigscote at rear, Fowl and coal houses. (N.B.—The corrugated iron shed is the property of the tenant).

There is also a large enclosed yard adjoining the buildings and a good kitchen garden, the whole containing an area of **0**A. **1**R. **38**P. more or less.

There is no Land Tax, it is part of No. 177 on the plan.

The commuted tithe shall be taken as apportioned at 2/6.

Sale of the Moon Inn in 1910

The Moon Inn at Mordiford in 2001

157

the early 20th century. During the occupation of Daniel Hughes the **Moon** was offering 'Good accommodation for cyclists, tourists and fishermen' before it was put up for sale in 1910. In 1918 Thomas Eldridge, licensee of the **Moon Inn,** was fined £15 for having 'misappropriated two casks'. They had not been returned to the Anglo Brewing Company because one was being used as a 'pig-wash tub' and the other was 'fixed as a rain water butt'. In 1949 James and Mary Hereford sold the **Moon** to the Alton Court Brewery, who sold it on in 1962 to the West Country Breweries and like many other pubs in the area it was taken under the wing of Whitbreads.

Another one-time beer house in Mordiford parish is at Priors

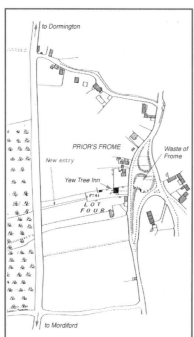

Frome on the old main road leading from Mordiford towards Ledbury. The **Yew Tree Inn** was run for half a century by the Huffs as a 'comfortable little Wayside Inn licensed for Beer, Cider and Tobacco'. By 1910 it was leased to the Alton Court Brewery, who purchased the pub in 1949. It is now a free house and has been greatly extended with an improved access to the main road leading from Mordiford to Dormington. Also in Mordiford parish was a beer retailer at Checkley run by Emma Weaver in 1891.

From Mordiford a 14th century stone bridge leads over the river Lugg

A comfortable little Wayside Inn (Licensed for Beer, Cider, and Tobacco) known as

"THE YEW TREE"

situated at Frome in the parish of Mordiford, and recently put into good repair at a considerable expense to the owner. It is let on lease to the Alton Court Brewery Company for 14 years from the 2nd February, 1910.

The accommodation is as follows :—Capital and extensive cellarage. Tap room, parlour, kitchen, bar, and 4 bedrooms. There is also a good piggery, a small orchard and garden in all 0A. 1R. 9P. or thereabouts.

The commuted tithe shall be taken as apportioned at 2/6. It is part of number 41 on the plan.

There is no Land Tax.

Proposed sale of the Yew Tree at Prior's Frome in 1910

The Prior's Frome side of the Yew Tree at the beginning of the 21st century

and into Hampton Bishop parish and the **Bunch of Carrots**. It was known as just the **Carrots** in 1842 and apparently acquired its name from a carrot-shaped piece of sandstone seen in the river Wye below the inn. In the past it was mainly frequented by fishermen, and a boat called the *Stank Ferry* conveyed passengers across the Wye. A story relates that many years ago an upturned boat was kept in the orchard and occupied by a tenant who called it Noah's Ark. From the latter part

The Bunch of Carrots in 2001

159

of the 19th century the Wheatstone family were associated with the **Bunch of Carrots** before Dick Marshall took over a dilapidated property in the late 1940s. During the Second World War, Dick worked at the Royal Ordnance Factory at Rotherwas. He 'fell in love with Herefordshire' and when the **Carrots** came up for sale he purchased the property. While Dick Marshall 'pulled pints at one of Herefordshire's best-loved pubs, the conversation with customers often led to his collection of remarkable cars! Apparently, he was quite simply car crazy, and had turned the pub's outbuildings into what he called his stable for a collection of valuable veteran vehicles', which included an 1897 Dion car presented to him by the ciderman Len Weston from Much Marcle, a Leyland Thomas racer of 1922, and a 1936 Wolseley.

The **Bunch of Carrots** is now a popular roadside inn which has doubled in size with bars, servery and a function room. In the 1990s it was 'altered with many rooms and cosy snugs with walls covered with a most eclectic selection of pictures, everything from military scenes and bird prints to amusing fishing sketches'. Within three miles of Hereford, the **Bunch of Carrots** attracts a good trade from the city.

CHAPTER TEN

Marcle & the Woolhope Dome

The countryside lying to the north-east of Ross still retains an atmosphere of old England. It is a delightful landscape of sheltered valleys, wooded ridges, apple orchards and sheep pastures with attractive stone, brick and timber-framed farms, houses and cottages. A stiff climb up Marcle and Ridge Hills are rewarded by offering stunning views of this scenic area lying between Ross and Ledbury.

Before the establishment of the turnpike system, Ledbury appears to have been almost totally isolated from south Herefordshire, which may have prompted the inhabitants in 1721 to form the first turnpike trust in the county. One route led from Ledbury to Much Marcle and was continued to Ross in 1749 by the Ross Trust with their toll road leading from the 'Town Brook, to a place called the Smith's Shop, in the parish of Much Marcle'. This was the only main route between Ross and Ledbury and wayside inns would have been a necessity.

The Ross to Marcle turnpike road originally followed a hilly

The former Higford Arms in the 21st century

cross-country route from Old Gore, up Perrystone Hill, through Yatton, and past Bodenham Bank to Much Marcle. However, it was found to be too steep for horse-drawn vehicles so the turnpike was re–routed along a purpose-built road in

The Higford Arms had already closed when the farm was offered for sale in 1890

the late 1830s and a new roadside inn called the **Higford Arms** was opened at Yatton in Much Marcle parish. The Price family of farmers ran this inn for several generations, but eventually they reverted back to just farming. During the 1970s and 1980s the extensive buildings were used for the sale of antique and second-hand furniture; it is now a cattery.

The new turnpike road did not alter the prominent position of the well-established **Walwyn** (or **Wallwyn**) **Arms**, dating from the 17th century and known as the **Ship and Castle** in 1797. Earlier it was referred to as **Baker's**, but it is not clear whether it was an inn name or a reference to a baker's shop. When William Robinson sold the premises to Edward Walwyn from Hellens in Much Marcle in the early 19th century the inn took the name of his well-known family. Throughout most of the 19th century the inn had a secondary function as a butcher's shop and slaughter house run by the Mailes family. An inquiry was held at the **Walwyn Arms** in 1873 concerning a 'Fatal Accident' when a seven-year-old boy fell from an iron roller. It was reported as an accidental death. In 1881, Richard Mailes was the landlord and also the village butcher. Business must have been reasonably good, for he had two 'live in' servants, one as barmaid and the other a 15-year-old 'domestic'. Much Marcle was unusual in having two Friendly Societies for females. From 1884 the Ross and Archenfield Branch of the Girls Friendly Society appear to have held their meetings at the **Walwyn Arms** as well as the later Much Marcle Female Friendly Society formed in 1924.

In 1902 the inn was for sale as 'one of the best known country houses in Hereford, being much frequented by Coaching and Shooting Parties, Cyclists, and others from which a large trade is derived'. In 1927 the **Walwyn Arms** was purchased by the Ross-based Alton Court

MUCH MARCLE

HEREFORDSHIRE,

Five Miles from Ledbury, and Three from Dymock Railway Stations.

To Capitalists, Brewers, Wine Merchants, and Others.

MESSRS.

W. MANTON & Co.

Have received instructions to SELL BY AUCTION, at the

NEW INN HOTEL, LEDBURY,

At 3 for 4 o'clock precisely in the Afternoon,

ON TUESDAY, JULY 29TH, 1902,

Subject to Conditions of Sale to be then produced, the Old-Established and

FULLY-LICENSED

FREEHOLD HOTEL,

KNOWN AS THE

"WALLWYN ARMS,"

With Large and Productive Kitchen Garden, Butcher's Shop and Slaughter House,
Extensive Stabling and Coach House, Cow Houses, and Sheds, Poultry House,
Coal House, Piggeries, &c., adjoining, together with 10 Acres or thereabouts
of very Rich PASTURE LAND, the whole comprising an Area of

11a. 0r. 0p.,

Or thereabouts.

For further Particulars apply to

C. E. LILLEY, Esq., Solicitor, Ledbury;

· Or to the AUCTIONEERS.

Offices, New Street, Ledbury.

Sale of the Walwyn Arms in 1902.
Capitalists, brewers & wine merchants welcome!

The Walwyn Arms in 2001

Brewery from Thomas James Porter, and in 1936 the brewery was questioned by the Licensing Sessions about a sign displaying the inn as a free house. In no uncertain terms they were told to take it down and also to improve the sanitary arrangements at the inn. The **Walwyn Arms** is now an attractive feature of the crossroads in Much Marcle, and when the annual Steam Rally is held there, steam and traction engines line up in the car park where refreshments are served to the drivers and spectators.

The Much Marcle Amicable Friendly Society was formed in 1794 and held their meetings at the **Swan**. By the mid-19th century this inn

The Royal Oak at Much Marcle in 2001

had closed which is hardly surprising due to its secluded position north of Much Marcle church; it is now called Swan Cottage. The Much Marcle Friendly Society met at John Taylor's house from 1815 until 1854 after which the meetings were held at the **Walwyn Arms**. In 1948 F.C. Morgan wrote:

> Annually upon the feast day, the 29th May, through for a time this was changed to 29th September, a date found to interfere with the hop-picking, the men preceded the women in procession to church, and after service with a sermon the former dined at the Walwyn Arms and the latter had a meat tea in the schoolroom.

The **Royal Oak** is on the Ledbury road at the northern end of Much Marcle parish. It started life as a fairly small beer house in the mid-19th century and was eventually acquired by Wintle's Forest Brewery. In 1923 the brewery offered for sale the **Royal Oak** as an 'Attractive Stone-built Premises' with a bar, smoke room, tap room and beer store on the ground floor. Outside were a cider house, stabling and pigcots, now all completely transformed'.

By Messrs. COOPER & PREECE.

MUCH MARCLE.
(7 Miles from Ross and 5 from Ledbury.)
FREEHOLD INN AND LAND.

MESSRS. COOPER & PREECE will SELL by AUCTION, at the KING'S HEAD HOTEL, ROSS,
On THURSDAY, 16th MARCH, 1916, at 4 p.m.
The ROYAL OAK INN, fronting the main Ross and Ledbury Road, with the Outbuildings, Garden, and Pasture Orchard, containing 2a. 2r. 27p., in the occupation of Mrs. Elizabeth Williams.
For further particulars, apply to the Auctioneers, Ross, or to Messrs. Collins, Solicitors, Ross. 1066

THE ROYAL OAK, Freehold Beer House

MUCH MARCLE, HEREFORDSHIRE.

Attractive Stone-built Premises, with Rough Cast, well placed on Ross-Ledbury Road, comprising :—

FIRST FLOOR :—Three Bed Rooms, Sitting Room, Store Room.

GROUND FLOOR :—Bar, Smoke Room, Tap Room, Kitchen, Scullery, Pantry, Beer Store.

OUTSIDE :—Good Yard, Brick-built Stabling for two with Loft over, Cider House, Closet, Urinal, Timber erection of Sheds, Pig Cots, etc., and Garden.

Two Orchards are included in this Holding, making in all an Area of nearly Three Acres.

The Property is of Freehold Tenure, and let to Mr. John Lowe on Quarterly Tenancy, at

Per   £34   Ann.

Tithe Rent Charge, 13s. 7d. per Annum.   Compensation Charge, £1.

MUCH MARCLE.—ROYAL OAK.

ALL THAT messuage or Inn known as the Royal Oak situate at Much Marcle in the County of Hereford and all outbuildings and appurtenances thereunto belonging comprising yard brick built stabling for two with loft over cider house closet urinal timber erection of sheds pig cots etc. and garden AND ALSO two orchards containing in all an area of nearly three acres and all other outbuildings and appurtenances thereunto belonging TOGETHER with the site thereof and the land occupied therewith which said premises are now in the occupation of John Lowe as tenant.

The Royal Oak was for sale several times:
Upper : 1916 , Middle : 1923 , Lower : 1937

165

However, it was not sold until 1937, when it was purchased by the Cheltenham Original Brewery. From the garden and terrace are extensive views, and the pub with its window boxes makes a pretty picture.

Much Marcle is famed for its cider, which has been produced by Westons since 1880 when Henry Weston developed his traditional cider and perry making into a commercial operation. For over a century this family-run firm has made cider and perry using traditional methods, and now welcomes visitors for tasting and tours around the cider mill. Previously there had been a 'Cyder House' recorded in 1797 on the Kempley road and a 'cider merchant' trading from Stocking Farm in 1867 and 1891. At Lyne Down, a smaller establishment sells farmhouse cider and perry made from unsprayed cider apples and perry pears milled in a hundred-year-old scratter mill.

A worker at Westons recalls in *Within Living Memory*, 'I started work at Westons in 1921 straight from school at 14 years old, starting at 7.30 a.m. until 6 p.m., working in the Bottling Department, where all jobs were done by hand, moving bottles and cases. Only the cider mill and presses were driven by a huge oil engine, also the pumps, but all other work was manual and very different today when all the work is done by machinery'. Before a lorry was purchased the cider was conveyed by horse and dray to Dymock station, on the Ledbury to Gloucester line, and the apples were transported by horse and waggon. Although the 'work was hard and the hours were long' he enjoyed working at Westons and stayed there for many years.

Much Marcle has a wealth of historic sites to investigate—the beautiful Norman chapel at Yatton; Hellens, a Jacobean manor house; the church dating from the 13th century with its massive yew tree in the graveyard; the motte and bailey of Mortimer's Castle near the church; and Oldbury Camp an Iron Age hillfort on Ridge Hill. On the west side of Marcle Hill near Rushall, there is what is now an insignificant site called the Wonder. It is where in 1575 'the earth opened up revealing a hill with a rock underneath which rose to a great height making a bellowing noise. As it travelled along it bought down trees, sheep folds, cattle, flocks of sheep and Kynaston Chapel with its steeple and bells. This remarkable landslip made the tilled ground pasture, and turned pastures into tillage'.

This frightening event has not been forgotten as a nearby inn in Much Marcle has been renamed the **Slip Tavern**. It is reached from the village along a minor road to the west and turning north on the Rushall road. In 1839 this was simply a

THE SLIP TAVERN

Free House
Watery Lane, Much Marcle, Ledbury, Herefordshire
Telephone 01531 660246

cottage and garden, which, towards the end of the 19th century, became a beer house known as the **New Inn**. Before the census day of 1881 it was conveyed from Richard Cox and others to Henry Cox, a wheelwright. He lived with his wife Elizabeth and their six children aged 11 and under. The 15-year-old Catherine Carver was their only help with domestic duties and child care, whilst Henry ran the inn and continued to work as a wheelwright. It remained with that family until 1926 when Mrs. A.E. Randall took over. In 1935 she sold the inn to the Stroud Brewery which was taken over by West Country Breweries in 1962 and later passed to Whitbreads. The **New Inn** gained a full licence in 1960 and its name was eventually changed to the **Slip Tavern** to relate to the 1575 landslip. The colourful garden won an award in 1983 and the inn is still surrounded by cider orchards and

provides a splendid place to visit on a summer evening.

From the **Slip Inn** at Much Marcle a winding lane rises through Rushall and Kynaston to the site of the Wonder. Extensive views overlooking hop-growing country to the north-east, where the

The Slip Tavern at the beginning of the 21st century

cottagers and farmers of Aylton and Putley must all have brewed their own beer, for there are no records of licensed houses in these villages. Woolhope Cockshoot is further along the road, within a mile of the Wonder, at the northern end of Marcle Hill. Here, the **Oak**, a 'Public House, Smithy, garden and Fold', was occupied by a beer retailer and timber merchant in 1851, but appears to have gone out of business around 1870. A refurbished cottage called Woolhope Cockshoot stands on its site from which there are spectacular views.

Woolhope village is set in a scenic landscape of ridges and valleys, the result of a geological upheaval millions of years ago. Layers of sandstone, limestone and shale were pushed into a dome which was gradually worn down by rain and weather. In 1851 the *Woolhope Naturalists' Field Club* was founded and named after this quiet secluded backwater with its rich variety of rocks, fossils, flora and fauna. Woolhope is surrounded by a maze of lanes with no major roads, and the ancient ridgeway from Woolhope Cockshoot to Yatton is preserved as a right of way.

Between the ridge and the Malvern Hills is a scenic plain described in 1892 by Thornhill Timmins as:

> a district that has long been famous for the fine quality of hops raised within the grounds, the bines being protected from the rough gales by lofty hawthorn hedges, twelve or fourteen feet in height, which attract attention by their unusual appearance.

This hop-growing industry is still very much in evidence, and makes a distinctive feature in the landscape.

Woolhope manor was presented to Hereford Cathedral by the two sisters Wulviva and Godiva, the famous naked equestrienne. In Coventry there is a pub called Lady Godiva, named after the wife of Leofric, Lord of Coventry in the 11th century. He was very severe on his tenants so Godiva made an agreement that if she rode naked through the streets of the city he would remove his impositions. The church at Woolhope, founded in Norman times, retains many interesting features including a modern window depicting Godiva on a white horse.

From Woolhope Cockshoot a lane descends past Winslow Mill to the **Butcher's Arms**, a popular pub at the eastern end of Woolhope village. The pretty timber-framed building dates from the 17th century,

The Butcher's Arms in 2001

and during much of the 19th century it was two separate cottages housing a butcher's shop and a beer house. In its deeds, dating from 1819 to 1910, there is a fire policy of 1820 insuring the dwelling house for £70, and the barn, cow-house and cider mill for £30. It was Henry Hodges who combined the two to form the **Butcher's Arms** and in 1881 his wife, Louisa, was described as a beer retailer, whilst he was a gardener in addition to being the innkeeper. They had six children ranging in age from 14 down to two and the eldest daughter was working as a 'mother's help'. Since obtaining a full license in 1960 the **Butcher's Arms** has attracted a regular clientele, tourists and an increasing number of walkers.

In the centre of the village and opposite the church is the former vicarage which dates from around 1640. It was altered in 1841 and vastly extended to its present size in 1882 when it was surrounded by a high stone wall. The old vicarage, together with the **Crown Inn**, which stands next to the church, share in the origins of an Easter charity dating from 1648. It was a surgeon, John Jones, who left in his will 'for ever a house called the **Crown**, with garden, building, and an acre and a half of land called Martin's Cross. He also gave his house and yard called the Wall-house, adjoining to the vicarage, to use of the poor of the parish of Woolhope'. At the time of the Charity Commissioner's Inquiry in 1837 it was reported that 'The first of the above-mentioned properties is still used as a public-house', but the 'Wall-house was taken down, and the ground on which it stood thrown into the vicarage garden'.

Property auction sales were held at the **Crown** in 1808 and 1813. It was described as a house and malthouse kept by Peter Mailes in

169

The Crown at Woolhope in 2001

1851, and by 1867 the innkeeper was brewing his own beer. The Mailes were of long-standing at the **Crown** and in 1881, Richard, in addition to being the inn keeper, was a farmer of 40 acres employing one man. He and his wife Frances had six children and employed a 16-year-old domestic servant. When Arthur Sherratt was the innkeeper in 1902 he also ran an adjacent shop. In 1920, William E Porter of the **Crown Inn** was summoned for working a horse in an unfit condition, but the case was dismissed because the horse's raw wound was caused by someone's careless harnessing. Since then it has been greatly refurbished and has become a thriving and popular inn. Outside a mounting block is inscribed with 'I. H. 1829', maybe the initials of a former innkeeper.

From Woolhope a road leads westwards across Broadmoor Common and through Haugh Woods to descend to the B4224 at Mordiford. In the past the inhabitants of these wild woods and commons did not 'enjoy a high reputation for honesty' hence the saying 'Beggars at Weston, Thieves at Woolhope'. Broadmoor Common covers 35 acres of rough pasture with grazing rights for sheep, cattle and horses. Since 1987 it has been managed by the council as a Local Nature Reserve. Cottages are scattered around the edge of the common and in the 19th century three of these were occupied by a shopkeeper, a beer retailer and a maltster.

CHAPTER ELEVEN

Ross to Newent

If the M50 is ignored there are three cross-country routes that lead from Ross towards the Gloucestershire market town of Newent. Through Upton Bishop, Linton or Aston Ingham these three roads follow stretches of former toll roads that were turnpiked by the trusts of Ross and Newent. By 1822 there was a weekly carrier and a daily coach service between the two towns, and Newent was described as a:

> small irregularly built borough and market town, in the hundred of Botloe, and county of Gloucester, and immediately on the verge of the counties of Worcester and Hereford; distant 112 miles from London, and eight from Gloucester, Ledbury, and Ross. Its communications with the metropolis are regular, owing to coaches running from the place, lately established on this road, which communication is likely to be the means of bringing the place into notice, and ultimately tend greatly to its advantage. Indeed, from the spirit of improvements which has begun to pervade, it is probable ere long that it will rank very respectably in the scale of towns. The principal ornaments of the town are the spas and gardens. It appears that the component parts of these springs (which have been fully explained by Dr. Reece, in a treatise on the nature and properties of medicinal waters) are similar to those at Cheltenham, and equally beneficial in similar cases. The Well Cottage, surrounded by enlivening and interesting scenery, is within an easy walk of the town; to which the approach is through Mr. de Visme's delightful pleasure grounds, accompanied part of the way by the Herefordshire and Gloucester canal, and two large sheets of water from in the spring and summer a most enchanting promenade. The church is a handsome and venerable pile; is very clean and neat, and contains many singular monuments, particularly one of great antiquity to the

memory of Baron Grandison. The families employed in agriculture are 310; in trade and manufacture 148. Families not comprised in the above are 98; amounting in the whole, according to the census in 1821, males 1,330, females 1,330 total 2,660, which is an increase since 1811 of 122. 'Tis astonishingly singular and worthy of remark, that the sexes are equal in number. Fairs are Wednesday before Easter, Wednesday before Whitsuntide, August 12th, and the Friday after the 19th of September. Market day is on Friday. A court leet is held here in the month of November annually.

The northernmost route leads from the **Travellers Rest**, at the junction with the M50, along the B4221. This closely follows the course of the 18th-century toll road to the ancient crossroads at Crow Hill in the parish of Upton Bishop. Crow Hill was a busy place in 1851 with a collection of varied trades including a carpenter and agricultural implement maker, a grocer and provisions dealer, a butcher, a blacksmith, five boot and shoemakers, a beer retailer at the **Farmer's Boy** and a victualler at the **Wellington Inn** where the Crowhill Friendly Society met.

LORD WELLINGTON INN,

CROW HILL, UPTON BISHOP.

THE ANNUAL

PIGEON SHOOTING

Will be held at the above Inn on

TUESDAY, 31st DECEMBER

(NEW YEAR'S EVE).

SPORTSMEN PLEASE NOTE.

The New Year's Eve Pigeon Shoot at the Lord Wellington in 1895

William Price was retailing beer at the **Farmer's Boy** and was followed by George Lane in 1858, but this establishment had ceased trading by 1867. However, the **Wellington Inn** continued as a pub under publicans named Morgan, Probert and Clarke. Before the turn of the century it became the **Lord Wellington,** probably renamed by Wintle's Forest Brewery who offered the public house for sale in 1923 when Charles Hitchings was the tenant. At that time it consisted of a public bar, smoke room, two kitchens and five bedrooms with outbuildings including a barn, stabling, cow sheds, pig cots, cart sheds, two closets and a urinal.

Like many other Wintle pubs, the **Lord Wellington** remained with the brewery until it was taken over by the Cheltenham Original Brewery in 1937, later to pass to Whitbreads. The 'friendly and

172

unspoilt village pub' of 1985 was sold by the brewery and was suddenly and quickly transformed into the **Moody Cow**, which retains a country warmth with its pine furniture, farmyard pictures, exposed beams and stone fireplaces in the public bar and the restaurant in the former barn.

The **Farmer's Boy** was a popular pub sign in the west country and in south Wales. The **Lord Wellington Inn** was named after the first Duke of Wellington who defeated Napoleon at Waterloo in 1815. He became a national hero and served

Sale of the Lord Wellington in 1923

The Moody Cow, once the Lord Wellington, in 2001

as Prime Minister between 1828 and 1830. The **Moody Cow** was a name chosen by the landlord for personal reasons, which gave the refurbished pub a distinctive title.

Upton Bishop is a scattered village offering extensive views over the surrounding countryside. It is a farming community lying about three miles north-east of Ross. The former hop-yards and cider orchards have been replaced by root and arable crops. The farmhouses of historical note are Felhampton, Tedgewood, Woodhouse and Upton Court, all of which date from at least the 16th century. In 1872 Charles

Robinson recorded that Gayton Hall was the property of Lord Ashburton, and although pleasantly situated had 'no special architectural features' and added that Grendon Court dated back to the Furney family in the 17th century.

At Phocle Farm a tradition was observed probably for the last time on the eve of Twelfth Night in 1879. It involved lighting 12 bonfires arranged in the shape of a horseshoe around a high pole covered with straw. When all was ablaze, cider was circulated and drunk 'in honour of the farmers, with wishes for good crops'. Then 'as soon as the fires had burnt out, an adjournment was made to the farm-house, where an excellent supper of roast-beef and plum pudding had been provided. The men were all waited on by the master, mistress, and friends; and this formed the most silent part of the evening's entertainment. After supper, the cider bowl passed round, pipes were lighted, songs were sung, and the festivities were kept up to an early hour in the morning'.

Beyond Crow Hill a lane on the left leads to Kempley through Upton Crews, where a beer retailer was listed in 1858. Further on, and set back from the road is the 14th-century Upton Court, which, according to the inspector for the Royal Commission who visited in the early 1930s, includes a 17th-century brew-house. It was described as being of 'two storeys, timber-framed on a stone base. The fireplace has moulded jambs'. This was the farm of Thomas Powell, a fruit grower and landowner who retailed cider from a licensed cider house in 1905. He continued making cider at a time when

> prize-winning apples could make money for a few; but cider was an essential part of the economy. Farm-workers assumed, as they had for many centuries, that it was part of their small rewards. Every farm, and many substantial cottages, had a cider-press and a cider-mill. Trees of more or less any kind and age would produce the fruit that went into the circular stone trough to be crushed by the horse-drawn stone wheel. Cider-making was one of the great occasions of the year. In some homes it involved leading a horse through the house to get to the mill in the back-garden. But gradually in the 1930s the supply of cider to the workers became less of an obligation. Fruit was sold to Westons or Bulmers, whose product was so much less powerful that it aroused unprovable suspicions.

On the Gloucestershire border at Fishpool there is still a forge, presumably the one where George Smallman lived and worked in the late 19th century. On his visit to Ross in 1894 he enjoyed a drinking spree, and was found lying on the pavement outside the **Crown and Sceptre** and charged with being drunk and disorderly. At the same court Abiah Harris from Weston-under-Penyard was also summoned for being drunk in Ross. She gave a rambling tale in her defence, but was nevertheless fined for her misbehaviour.

UPTON BISHOP.—THE PHEASANT INN.

ALL THAT messuage or Inn known as The Pheasant Inn situate in the Parish of Upton Bishop in the County of Hereford with the cellar and outbuildings and appurtenances thereunto belonging and the garden and piece or parcel of meadow or pasture land and orchard thereto adjoining and belonging containing together by admeasurement two acres or thereabouts.

Sale of the Pheasant in 1937

Partly hidden by a hedge, this cottage was once the Pheasant Inn

From Crow Hill the B4221 continues towards Newent along a route turnpiked by the Newent Trust after the 1802 Act. On the roadside before crossing the M50 motorway the Ross-on-Wye Golf Club offers the facilities of a licensed bar, but only to club members and visiting golfers. A minor road leads between the golf course and Queen's Wood to a small unkempt cottage. This was formerly the **Pheasant**, described as being 'alone on the hill above Upton Bishop'. In 1851 it was a beer house kept by Edwin Burgess, but it then appears to have been closed for some time until it was re-opened as an Arnold Perrett pub in the 1890s. The licence was transferred to Edwin Mason in 1902, and the brewery sold 'The Pheasant Inn with the cellar and outbuildings' in 1937 to the Cheltenham

Original Brewery. Edwin Mason is listed as the publican in 1941, but it closed around 1970 when Molly Mason served as the last landlady.

Shortly after the Ross Golf Club the B4221 crosses the M50 and heads through Gorsley and Kilcot to Newent along a stretch of road that was entirely new in 1810. It was built and maintained by the Newent Turnpike Trust to replace a meandering way across the legendary wilds of Gorsley Common, a haunt of rogues and vagabonds in the 18th and early 19th centuries. Workers were required for road building, stone quarrying and lime burning. Lying mainly in Herefordshire and partly in Gloucestershire, Gorsley grew into a more civilized area with a chapel, shop, inn and school, and in 1872 it was formed into an ecclesiastical district with Clifford's Mesne.

It is traditionally known that the end cottage at Blindman's Gate was a beer house before the **New Inn**, also at Blindman's Gate opened in 1847 to serve the community. Joseph Fishpool was the beer retailer and postmaster in 1851 followed by John Drew a few years later. After this there was a succession of beer retailers who also doubled as shopkeepers throughout the 19th century and into the early 20th century. Eventually it was purchased by Arnold Perrett and Co. who were taken over by the Cheltenham Original Brewery and eventually the **New Inn** became a Whitbread pub.

Arnold Perrett & Co. was a Gloucestershire-based brewery that was established in 1887 after Arnold & Co. from Wickwar had acquired H & A Perrett in Wotton-under-Edge. In 1937 Arnold Perrett & Co. ceased to brew following the take-over by the Cheltenham Original Brewery. At this time the company owned over 90 pubs, hotels and other properties in Monmouthshire, Gloucestershire, Herefordshire and Devon.

In 1976 Whitbreads ran a competition to find a different name for the **New Inn**, and 'one enterprising local made the connection between

GORSLEY.—THE NEW INN.

ALL THAT messuage or Inn known as The New Inn situate at Gorsley near Blindmans Gate in the Parish of Linton in the County of Hereford with the Ciderhouse pig-shed and all other outbuildings and appurtenances thereunto belonging TOGETHER with the site thereof and the land occupied therewith including a piece of arable land and orcharding thereto adjoining containing one acre or thereabouts.

Sale of the New Inn, now the Roadmaker, in 1937

the pub's first customers and their occupation, and the pub became the **Roadmaker**'. It was described as being 'homely and welcoming right down to the vases of fresh flowers' in 1985 when the 'tiny tavern in the Herefordshire countryside' was stocked with Whitbread's beer and Weston's cider. The **Roadmaker** has since been extended to form a spacious restaurant and bar and continues to serve food and a selection of beer, wine and spirits.

The earlier road from Crow Hill to Newent takes a more southerly course through Linton and meanders across Gorsley Common to Kilcot. Linton enjoys an historic past which is well appreciated by the Linton History Society who have produced a brief account of Linton

The Roadmaker at Gorsley in 2001,
once the New Inn

and its land from 1600 to 1900. In the village centre is the church, a pub and the village hall housed in the former school. Opposite the church is the old vicarage built in 1867 for the Rev. Edward Palin who was featured in *American Friends*, a film made in 1991. The actor Michael Palin played the part of his great grandfather.

In Linton village there was only the blacksmith, William Pitt, retailing cider at Shutton before two pubs opened around 1867. They were the **Alma** and the **Plough**, but the latter did not survive long after John Penny's occupancy. On the other hand, the **Alma**, originally kept by James Cole is still open. In 1876 Henry Hodges was the publican competing with John Marfell at the post office and stores who was selling Wintle's Ales and porter. By 1905 Wintle's had acquired the inn, which, like the other pubs owned by the Forest Brewery eventually became a Whitbread house. The **Alma** is named after a river in the Crimea, where in 1854 the first battle was won against the

Sale of the Alma in 1923

Russians. After this event the name became widely used, not just for pubs, but also for the daughters of those who had fought in that war.

Three Friendly Societies were founded at Linton between 1817 and 1851, but none of their meetings were held at licensed premises. The Linton Provident Friendly Society established in 1817 was not allowed to hold their meetings at a public house contrary to the majority of Friendly Societies. The Gorsley Friendly Society met at Gorsley Schoolroom, and the Linton Mutual Benefit Society met at Linton Hill.

During the 1890s the Rev. Palin was still serving as vicar of Linton and was the 'third eldest Magistrate in the Ross Petty Sessional division, having been appointed in 1878'. This was a decade of considerable drunkenness in the area. It was when Joseph Taylor, a labourer, was charged with an assault that took place in Linton; and when Charles Gilbert, another Linton labourer, was charged with being drunk on the highway at Aston Ingham he pleaded guilty to 'drinking

The Alma at Linton in 2001

too much whisky with a friend when returning from the stock sale'. In addition, the *Ross Gazette* of 1892 reported that William Price was charged for being drunk on the highway at Aston Ingham, when 'he was found lying down with his head in a ditch and his body lying over the road, and he was fast asleep'. The following year Sarah Davies, the wife of a hawker, was found drunk on the highway at Linton in charge of a donkey and cart. Her son was covered in blood caused by her falling over a pile of stones. She admitted to drinking home-made wine that she had obtained from a cottager, and said she had not visited a public house.

About two miles south-west from Linton church and the **Alma** is the site of Eccleswall Castle, which by 1869 was 'occupied by a substantial farm-house'. At that time 'the traces of the original building which have survived are too slight to form a basis upon which to erect a surmise of its size and extent'. Previously, in 1823, when the old farmhouse was rebuilt and the buildings modernised, the owner decided that 'the tower and the mill house adjoining were to be left unaltered as the tower was useful for keeping cider'. A document of 1704 to 1717 names the **Golden Heart** and the **Royal Oak** suggesting long-lost inns in Eccleswall and Aston Ingham, both in the manor of Lea.

The third and longest cross-country route from Ross to Newent leads north from the A40 at Lea Line along roads turnpiked by the Newent Trust after 1802. At Aston Crews one turnpike road closely followed the existing B4222 to Kilcot, whilst the other led further north past Withymoor Farm and Beavan's Hill to reach the B4221 at Gorsley. At the junction of the two turnpike roads at Aston Crews the **White Hart** served travellers and locals from at least the early 19th century, and the **Crown** had opened by 1858, but both have since been renamed.

The original names for these two pubs are both very traditional— the **White Hart** was a common sign that was associated with Richard II in earlier times. The continual use of this distinctive and visual sign in later centuries was favoured by innkeepers because by that time it had become a generic term for taverns. The **Crown** was also a very popular inn sign that had been in use for many centuries showing loyalty to the monarchy. Charles Hindley in his *Tavern Anecdotes* records a poem probably composed in a public bar:

> Come my lads and Crown your wishes
> With glee come Crown your greatest joys
> Come to the Crown and drink like fishes
> Spend each a Crown my jovial boys.

Aston Crews in the mid-19th century was a busy road junction where two forges, a shop, a carpenter and wheelwright's shop, a builder's yard, and two pubs were serving the community. It was William Lewis the carpenter and wheelwright who opened the **Crown** and stayed there until after 1867. He was followed by George Pearce, and in 1902 William Cook, one of the blacksmiths, was running the **Crown** before Wintle's Forest Brewery acquired it. In 1923 it was described as a 'Stone-built Premises on Ross-Newent Road, about three miles from the Brewery'. The property comprised of four bedrooms, a store room and club above a bar, tap room, smoke room, kitchen, sitting room and cellarage in the basement. Outside was a yard, garden, two stables, a smithy and two pig cots.

In 1937 the **Crown** was taken over by the Cheltenham Original Brewery later acquired by Whitbread. By 1985 Whitbreads no longer had connections with the pub, for Hook Norton, Bass, and Sam Smith's beers were served at the newly named **Penny Farthing**. This is a pub name that became very popular in the 1980s and makes an interesting sign. The

THE CROWN INN, Freehold and Fully Licensed

ASTON CREWS, HEREFORDSHIRE

Stone-built Premises on Ross-Newent Road, about three miles from the Brewery, and comprising :—

FIRST FLOOR :—Four Bed Rooms, Store Room, Club Room.

GROUND FLOOR :—Bar, Tap Room, Smoke Room, Kitchen, Sitting Room and Cellarage in Basement.

OUTSIDE :—Yard, Small Garden, Stabling for Two, Smithy, Pig Cots, Two Closets, Urinal, etc.

The Property is of Freehold Tenure and let to Mr. G. MacDonald, on Quarterly Tenancy at the low Rent of

Per   £14   Ann.

Land Tax, 18s. 4d. per Annum.   Compensation Charge, £1.

The Crown sale in 1923

The Penny Farthing, once the Crown, at Aston Crews

The White Hart in 1985 before becoming the Countryman

Penny Farthing remains open unlike its neighbouring pub, the **White Hart**.

James Cole a road surveyor kept the **White Hart** in 1851, and was followed by Enoch Little a farmer and butcher. By the beginning of the 20th century Inde Coop and Co. from Burton-on-Trent had taken over the pub. This was about the time that Thomas Lewis was offering 'Accommodation for travellers, Good Stabling, Charges Moderate', but he was soon replaced by a brewery tenant called Walter Woodhouse. He was succeeded by other tenants and the **White Hart** became known as a 'quiet and select place with business type diners', with Wadworths beer drawn 'straight from the barrel'.

Since 1985 the **White Hart** has changed its name and its image. However, after tales of drunkeness and misbehaviour its reputation has suffered and it has been closed. In 2001 the sign for the **Countryman** is still in place and the pub appears to be a Marston pub but the empty building now stands forlornly by the roadside waiting for a new lease of life.

From Aston Crews the B4222 meanders through Aston Ingham, a parish described by Margaret Watson in 1991 in her *History of Aston Ingham*:

Aston Ingham boasts a Church, a Village Hall and a Scout Hut. Apart from the neat new development of Aston Bank there are no two cottages immediately adjacent to each other. All are scattered along the narrow lanes or unmade tracks, separated by fields and orchards or neatly tended gardens. Make your way through the lanes to the northern side of the parish and you will come to Beavans Hill. Here the cottages cluster more closely under the eye of Beavans Hill House. Then away through the lanes again and back past Knightshill Farm to Aston Crews where the houses gather closely round the two Pubs of the parish and down the hill back to Aston Ingham again.

In Aston Ingham the field names include 'Barrell Ditch', 'Hopyard', 'Tankard Field' and many 'Orchard' names, so it is not surprising to find an early reference in 1616 to a 'dewelling house thatcht of many smale rowmes, a cider house, a stable, a must myll house, a swynescott, a shepcott, a beasts house, a wayne-house, a host house and three small barnes'.

The White Hart at Aston Crews,
renamed the Countryman,
awaiting a new lease of life in 2001

Beyond Aston Ingam a winding lane climbs in a south-easterly direction through spectacular countryside to Clifford's Mesne and May Hill, which in 1858 was considered to be 'an object of curiousity; on the top is a clump of fir trees, which has a very singular appearance when seen from a distance, from the otherwise barren appearance of the hill'. May Hill rises to 1,000 feet and forms a distinctive landmark with its circle of pine trees replanted in 1887 to celebrate Queen Victoria's Golden Jubilee. Sheep, ponies and pigs graze the rough hillside now under the care of the National Trust. Various legends and traditions surround this beautiful hill, including the story of a local drunk, who, having heard that treasure was buried in an underground chamber, discovered the opening and 'went in drunk and died there'.

A mile below the summit of May Hill is the **Yew Tree** at Clifford's Mesne, which before 20th-century boundary changes was in Herefordshire. The **Yew Tree**, despite its modern front, is an old building with interior features dating from the second half of the 17th

The Yew Tree at Clifford's Mense in 2001

century. It was a dwelling that seems to have emerged as a beer and cider house kept by Mrs. Louisa Parsons around 1900. It became an Alton Court Brewery house, and in 1905 the pub had one tap room and five living rooms. In 1914 Henry Wheeler was serving beer and cider at the **Yew Tree**, and in 1941 William Blakemore was behind the bar.

Alton Court Brewery sold the **Yew Tree** before 1960, but fortunately it remained open. During the 1980s and 1990s it became popular for refreshments after an energetic ramble over May Hill. In 2000 Paul and Anna took over and refurbished the pub, revealing some of its original features. If found in the maze of lanes of Clifford's Mesne this old building is worth viewing while savouring Paul's fine food and wine.

The old road from Aston Crews to Kilcot passes an attractive property called Beavan Hill House which dates from the early 18th century and is said to have been an inn. It is more likely that the cottage opposite was the inn, as it was a smithy and James Preece, the blacksmith in 1867, was at the **New Inn** in Aston Ingham. After this date it was not listed again, but in 1876 Philip Palmer was retailing beer from a carpenter and wheelwright's shop, which could have been at the same site.

Beavan Hill House was called Glenmore in the 1930s and 1940s when Rutland Boughton, the famous composer, lived there. He was born in 1878 and after a long creative life he retired from public life to live at Aston Ingham and spent time farming, writing and composing, although he remained an active member of the Communist Party.

Before his death in 1960 he moved to London, but his work is commemorated on a blue wall plaque on the outside wall.

In 1902 at Babylon, near Beavan's Hill, a horse dealer called Thomas Overton had, by 1914, become a cider merchant. Aston Ingham was a parish where 'great cider orchards produced the best cider in all South Herefordshire', and traditional cider makers at the beginning of the 21st century are still convinced that 'the finest cider is made within sight of May Hill'.

CHAPTER TWELVE

Ross to the Gloucester Border

From the outskirts of Ross the A40 leads through Weston-under-Penyard, Ryeford and Lea to the Gloucestershire border. This route through Ross was important for it included traffic from Hereford and South Wales heading to Gloucester and from there on to London. The road between Ross and Gloucester was first turnpiked by the Gloucester and Hereford Trust in 1726. The Hereford Trust took over the section from Ross to Lea in 1730; the section finally being taken over by the Ross Trustees from 1749. Since then the road has undergone extensive improvements including realignments at Lower Weston, Ryeford, Lea and Lea Line.

In 1863 Dr. George Strong, from the Chase in Ross, observed that after the opening of the Hereford, Ross and Gloucester Railway, the road became quiet, which previously had 'teemed with life and noise and motion: 23 coaches bowled along it daily, besides van and obstructive coal waggons; for the use of other travellers, more than 50 pair of horses were kept at the two principal posting houses [in Ross]'. With all this traffic, it is surprising that only two coaching inns have been identified on the Gloucester road between Ross and the county boundary; they are the **Weston Cross** at Weston-under-Penyard and the **Crown** at Lea.

Weston-under-Penyard, the 'Garden Parish of Herefordshire' has a long and fascinating history dating from Roman times when an iron-making centre was established at *Ariconium*. In the late 18th century this site was discovered by Mr. Merrick from Bollitree 'who owned the soil, resolved to level it, and in doing so an immense amount of Roman coins, and some British were found, together with many antiquities, among which were fibulæ, lachrymatories, lamps, rings, and fragments of tessellated pavements. Some pillars were also discovered, with stones having holes for jambs of doors, and a vault or two in which was wheat of a black colour, and in a cinereous state'.

The parish derives its name from its position, west of *Ariconium* and below Penyard Hill, the site of a Norman castle 'commanding an extensive prospect, and yet surrounded by a dense and tangled wood, would give it favour in the eyes of a feudal lord who divided his time between the chase and the sterner field of war'. From the Talbots, the great Earls of Shrewsbury, it devolved to the Countess of Kent, and was purchased by Mr. Partridge the iron master at Bishopswood in 1740. The castle had fallen into ruins during the 17th century, but on this remote hill, a cottage that adjoined the old castle was inhabited by a woodman until about 1928. 'He used to strip the oak trees for bark and charcoal burning. He also made cleft-oak gates and hurdles and wheel-spokes and ladder rounds'.

There are many interesting properties in Weston including Street House, Weston Hall, the Rectory and Bollitree Castle—a late 17th-century house transformed by Thomas Hopkins Merrick into a mock gothic castle by adding picturesque walls and towers in the 1780s. The property was inherited by William Palmer who entertained the radical journalist, William Cobbett in the 1820s. Cobbett in his *Rural Rides* described the surrounding landscape as 'very rich, the pasture the finest I ever saw, the trees of all kinds surpassing upon an average any that I have before seen in England'. He also made the comment that as 'a country of cider and perry; what a shame it is, that here, at any rate, the owners and cultivators of the soil, not content with these, should, for mere fashion's sake, waste their substance on wine and spirits! They really deserve the contempt of mankind and the curse of their children'.

William Palmer also owned the **Weston Cross Inn** which was occupied by John and Frances Rix in 1832. In the 1850s Richard and Grace Dayer took over and lived there with their children, a servant and an agricultural labourer, and eventually were able to buy the inn from the Bollitree estate. After Richard died in 1858 at the age of 54 his widow continued to run the pub until about 1870 when Richard Reid took over. It was in the late 19th century that the Forest Brewery from Mitcheldean purchased the Weston Cross, and, like their other

Sale of the Weston Cross in 1923

establishments, it was offered for sale in 1923. The 1923 sale particulars describe the inn as 'Freehold and Fully Licensed' with four bedrooms, club room, spirit room on the first floor, and a bar, tap room, smoke room, sitting room and kitchen on the ground floor. Outside there was a coach house, stables and four cottages sub-let by the tenant William Andrews. It was at this date that the Ariconium Lodge of Buffaloes was founded by A. Davey, A. Bird and L. Ayers. Twenty-two men were initiated and the lodge held their meetings at the **Weston Cross** until 1939.

Morris Dancers at the Weston Cross Inn in the mid-20th century

In 1937, when Horace Pettit was the landlord, the Cheltenham Original Brewery Co. took over the premises which later passed to Whitbread. The **Weston Cross** is a traditional stone-built pub still offering food and drink in pleasant surroundings. The adjacent building features arched gothic windows—a touch of the picturesque copied from Bollitree.

Jessie Stonham, in her *Daughter of Wyedean* published in 1978, recalled that:

> At the bottom of Church Lane there were three cottages, attached to which there is an interesting tale. It was said that a man who was a heavy drinker decided to 'give it up' and save the money he would have spent in drink; and for the sum of one hundred and fifty pounds he built these cottages. How delighted one would be now to be able to build three cottages for anything like the same amount; but at that time, of course, it represented a considerable sum. These were called 'Temperance Cottages' and bore a sign with these doggeral lines:
>
>
>
> Who'd a thought it
> Temperance bought it.
> If a like freehold
> You would buy
> Then this plan
> You should try.
>
>

In 1980 there were two country house hotels in Weston-under-Penyard—the **Wye Hotel**, formerly Penyard House, which now houses the Leadership Trust, and the **Hunsdon Manor** which is still open. It was originally called the **Sandiway Hotel**. Further along the A40 at

The Wye Hotel about 1950

Ryeford a converted and restored 19th-century Baptist Chapel stands in front of its earlier counterpart, which is soon to be transformed from its derelict state. On this corner in 1838 was a malthouse, which has since been demolished, and the site

1950 advertisement for the Sandiway Hotel

incorporated into the grounds of the former chapels.

From Ryeford a lane leads south-west through Pontshill to the Castle Brook valley, passing Parkfields a residential centre and art gallery. For many centuries this estate had been the home of the

Hunsdon Manor in 2001,
earlier the Sandiway Hotel

Bonnors, Trusted and Southall families. The lane then makes an exaggerated bend around the derelict buildings of Bill Mills standing on a site which has been in continuous industrial use since mediaeval times. The swift clear waters of the Castle brook has powered a mill for ironworking, papermaking, cornmilling, malting and finally the bottling of beer, and the manufacturing of mineral water before the adjacent factory was built to package soft drinks.

It was during the 1890s that Alfred Wintle expanded his malting and milling business at Bill Mills into bottling beer and producing mineral water. Cask beer was delivered by rail to Mitcheldean Road or Ross Station from Bristol and Burton-on-Trent. From the station it was conveyed by horse-drawn wagons to Bill Mills. The old mill rattled and shook with the machinery that bottled, labelled and corked bottles of Guinness, Bass, and Allsopp, which were placed in wooden cases and delivered to local pubs and private houses.

189

Wintle's advertisement in 1891

In September 1892 Herbert Hyett, employed by A.J. Wintle and Sons at Bill Mills, was summoned at Ross Petty Sessions for 'furiously driving two horses and a van at Weston-under-Penyard, along the road as fast as they could gallop'. For dangerous driving he was fined £1 or 14 days imprisonment and for beating the horses 'unmercilessly' he was charged with 'cruelly ill-treating horses' and given 14 days hard labour. Tom Wintle was the beer retailer at **Bill Mills** in 1905, as recorded in the Return of Licensed Houses to the Herefordshire Constabulary.

By the 1930s Bill Mills was only being used for manufacturing mineral water and bottling Bass, Worthington, Guinness and Marston ales and Whiteways cider. The old water wheel became more rickety, eventually broke and was replaced by a six-horse-power diesel engine. Under new management from 1958, the company specialised in bottling soft drinks under the Wintle brand and in 1979 the company changed its name to Dayla Soft Drinks Western Ltd., moved into a new factory in 1983, and in 2001 plan to relocate the packaging of soft drinks into Ross.

Although a mere hamlet, Pontshill was important enough to have an entry in the Domesday Book. Now it is developing into a village suburb with few facilities, but in 1851 there was a tiler; a carpenter and wheelwright; a miller; a cottage farmer; a coal dealer and shopkeeper; two farmers; Thomas Robbins, who was a cider retailer; and John Cole, a victualler, shopkeeper and coal dealer at the **Castle Inn**, also known as the **New Inn**. William Howells, the miller, took over the inn some time before 1867 when it was advertised for sale as 'All that Inn or Public-House called or known by the name of the New Inn with the Gardens and Premises thereto belonging. And also all that Steam Flour Mill with the Machinery and Fixtures'. At this date the mill was unoccupied and Mrs. Morgan was running the inn.

In 1870 the sale particulars of the Hownall and Ryeford Estates included: 'Lot 9 — All that Freehold Dwelling House used and called the New Inn with the Gardens, Yard, Stables, Outbuildings and Appurtenances thereto adjoining and belonging situate at Pontshill, late in the occupation of Mr. Walters as tenant thereof'.

In 1881 Joseph Roberts was the innkeeper at the **New Inn**, living with his wife Maryann and their seven children. The eldest daughter helped in the house and the eldest boys assisted with the horses. He was followed in 1902 by Thomas Stephens then Frank Chapel until the 1930s when Charles Powles took over. Before 1905 it had become an Alton Court Brewery pub and was taken over by West Country Breweries in 1962. Powles was kept on as the publican, and in 1965 he renamed the pub the **Travelling Hen** due to the following report in the *Hereford Times*:

> Clara was her name and with her antics 'on a wing and a tyre' she found fame not only in her home village of Pontshill, near Ross-on-Wye, but also far and wide. It was in 1963 that Clara the curious, one of the half-dozen hens belonging to village licensee Charles Powles, decided to hop on board his son's lorry and take a trip to Bristol. On the return journey the son spotted the bird, placed her in the cab and continued to Ebbw Vale where she presented him with an egg.
>
> A year later, Clara was on the move again, stowing away on a lorry chassis and heading for Cardiff where, presumably, she intended to seek her fortune. Once again, the driver espied the feathered passenger which he transferred to the cab where she duly delivered another egg as the vehicle motored along the M5.

West Country Breweries were so impressed when they heard about Clara's escapades that they decided to re-name Mr Powles's New Inn pub 'The Travelling Hen'. The brewery claimed there were so many hostelries with the New Inn tag and they had asked landlords to come up with alternative suggestions. Mr Powles—mine host at the Pontshill watering hole for 35 years—mentioned his heroine hen and changes were soon under way.

The replacement sign depicted the rear of a lorry with a hen sitting on the spare wheel. The vehicle's registration number was HEN 007. The new sign was officially unveiled by the chairman of Ross and Whitchurch Rural District Council, Bernard Hackett, on October 27, 1965, and guest of honour at the ceremony was, of course, Clara.

Inn sign for the Travelling Hen

Despite the publicity and the unusual name, the **Travelling Hen** did not survive into the 1980s, but the building can still be identified by its name.

It is confusing to learn that a second **New Inn** was established at Pontshill, at Knightensfield, only a few hundred yards from the Gloucestershire border. In an isolated building that was originally owned by Jonathan Marfell, it appears that a Thomas Robbins, already trading as a cider and beer retailer, opened the **Villa Inn** around 1876. By 1881 it had become the **New Inn** with Thomas Hatton as publican. He later moved to the **Crown Inn**, Lea, with his wife and children, but left his eldest son, George, to run the **New Inn**.

The Travelling Hen in retirement

In 1885 George married Jane Cooper, of Treberron, St. Weonards, a lady some 15 to 20 years his senior. They had two children by 1893, when Mrs. Hatton was shot dead, under confusing circumstances, by her husband. The *Ross Gazette*, on 27 July 1893, reporting on the inquest, described how Mrs. Hatton had been shot in the head, in graphic and bloody detail, and such was the local interest that 'During the time that the police were in charge of the house hundreds of people visited the scene of the murder'. The newspaper offerred conflicting evidence that Mr. and Mrs. Hatton had each been, variously, drunk or sober, and arguing, or not, prior to the shooting, which Mr. Hatton claimed to be an accident. Various witnesses stated that the couple had 'always been regarded as exceedingly respectable people', yet they were reputed to live 'on very bad terms'. The *Gazette* appears to have given fuel to the scandal, with a headline of 'Murder of a wife near Ross', calling the event a murder throughout the article, until the end when it offered 'The jury, after a short deliberation, returned a verdict of "Manslaughter" against George Hatton, the prisoner'.

After this unpleasant incident the licence was transferred to John Roberts at the other **New Inn**, and then J.J. Lewis took over as the beer retailer. During the 20th century Joseph Hales was running this **New Inn** until the Kearney family purchased the property in 1928, and in the 1930s and 40s the Chandlers became the tenants of the tiny pub. In 2000, after 70 years of family ownership, the Kearneys sold the pub, and the new owner renamed it the **Wonky Donkey** after his herd of donkeys that grazed in the adjoining paddock.

Continuing towards Gloucester from Ryeford, 'Two more miles brings us to Lea, where the pretty chapel and parsonage are worth notice. The chapel is small and of some antiquity: it consists of a Belfry Tower

The Wonky Donkey still keeps its New Inn sign in 2001

and Spire, a Nave, a Chancel, and a North aisle terminated by a chapel, probably erected by the family of Grey of Wilton, whose arms are placed there' wrote George Strong in 1863. At this date Lea was a 'small parish and village situated on the Ross and Gloucester Turnpike-road, and on the Hereford, Ross and Gloucester section of the Great Western Railway. The Mitcheldean Road Station on that line is in the parish. Part of Lea was in Gloucestershire until 1844, and the township was divided into Lea, Hereford, and Lea, Gloucester, but by the Act of 7 and 8 Vict. the Gloucestershire part was added to Herefordshire. The population in 1861 was 226 inhabiting 49 houses'.

The present A40 zig-zags somewhat dangerously through the village along a route that was designed for horse-drawn traffic. It was altered from its original straightforward course in 1842 by the Ross Turnpike Trust. At various dates there was at least three turnpikes along this stretch of road, each conveniently placed to collect the maximum amount of toll. This was never a popular payment and often led to hostility. In the 1730s riots occurred at Gloucester, Over, Ledbury, Hereford, and at Lea. One riot is recorded in the Quarter Sessions:

> Wednesday July the 28th 1731, between 11 and 12 at Night, Came to the Lea Turnpike in the County of Gloucester, to the Number of 20 persons or more, with Horses and arms, which They fired off Severall times Charging all that were in Bed to Keep there and forbid any of them to Look out at their windows upon pain of Death and there Cutt down and Destroy'd the Gate Erected upon the Road ... And Swore if any more was Erected they would then Come again and Cutt that down also, and Cutt down Burn or Destroy the House or Houses thereto Ajoyning, By Which meanes The Keepers are Soe Terrified, that they will not ask, nor Demand any Toll, But the Travellers pass free.

Lea, being '12 miles from Gloucester, 20 from Hereford, 19 from Monmouth by the old ferry at a Goodrich', was a convenient stopping place for travellers which led to the establishment of a mediaeval hospice at the crossroads:

> From thence by the way which is called
> La Lewey by the vills of
> Netherlie and Overle as far as the cross
> Next the old hospital

Brian Cave, in his booklet *Weston and Lea*, suggests it stood opposite the existing **Crown**, which is known to have been an ancient inn standing on the junction of the old and new roads from Ross to Gloucester. The **Crown** is a listed building which has developed into its present form from its origins in the 14th century. In 1995 it was described as a 'hall in the middle retaining its timber framing at the rear and was originally open from the ground to the roof'. The existing dining room was heightened in the late 16th or early 17th century, and this wing features 'a good staircase of oak with bell finials and stout vase-shaped balusters'. There are later additions at the rear and the bar includes exposed beams and stone fireplaces.

Documents at the Gloucestershire Record Office dating from the early 17th century refer to 'The Crowne in the Streete'. In 1614 Morgan Young paid rent, and this was transferred to David Probert for the 'Messuage called the Crowne'. In 1712

The Crown at Lea in 2001

there were '20 Houses in this Part of the Parish, and about 80 Inhabitants, whereof 3 are Freeholders' when Maynard Colchester was Lord of the Manor. Between 1810 and 1842 there were four cottages and a blacksmith's shop near the **Crown**, and a malthouse, which is a house called the Old Granary.

Charles Heath, visiting in the 1820s found the **Crown** 'a respectable Inn, should the traveller be disposed to take advantage of its hospitality'. In 1851 John Lodge, a farmer, was the victualler at the **Crown.** He continued until the 1870s when William, presumably his son, took over. In 1890 the Colchester-Wemyss estate sold the **Crown** to the Alton Court Brewery, and from thereon a succession of Hattons—Thomas, Abiah, Alfred and Alice—continued as tenants into the 1930s. Thomas was the father of the infamous George, who murdered his wife at the **New Inn** at Weston-under-Penyard in 1893.

In 1962 West Country Breweries acquired the 'Crown Inn, the shop, dwelling house, outbuildings and farm buildings erected thereon'. The shop may have been where a butcher named William Dowding also kept a beer house called the **Butcher's Arms** in the mid-19th century when the neighbouring blacksmith was 'licensed to let horses for hire'. Mrs. Dowding continued at the **Butcher's** in 1858, but shortly afterwards it was closed. The memory continues, even into the 21st century, for one of the side bars at the **Crown** is called the Butcher's Bar.

When a new landlord took over the **Crown** in September 1999 he reported to the *Ross Gazette* that 'There's lots of rumour and local gossip about this place. On cold winter mornings, when its misty, you can hear carriages as they come up Cut Throat Lane', and he added 'There's supposed to be the ghost of a lady haunting upstairs, and a man in the pub one night'.

Following the opening of the Hereford, Ross and Gloucester Railway in 1855 there was a dramatic decline in traffic on the Ross to Gloucester road. The railway company built a station in Lea parish called Mitcheldean Road,

---

THE RAILWAY HOTEL, Freehold and Fully Licensed

LEA, HEREFORDSHIRE

The Property occupies a Good Position for Business outside Mitcheldean Road Station, on the main Mitcheldean-Ross Road. The Premises are Brick-built and comprise:—

FIRST FLOOR :—Four Bed Rooms, Box Room.

GROUND FLOOR :—Bar, Smoke Room, Two Sitting Rooms, Kitchen, etc.

IN REAR :—Outhouse, partly brick and stone, consisting of Beer Store, Wine Cellar, Barn, Wash-house, Store Rooms, etc., Two Closets, Urinal, Pig Cots, &c., Stabling for four with Loft over, Good Garden and Approach. The whole extending to an Area of over 3 acres.

The Premises are of Freehold Tenure, and let to Mr. James Hawker, a tenant of about fifteen years' standing, on Quarterly Tenancy at

Per   £50   Ann.

Tithe Rent Charge, 24s. 6d. per Annum. Land Tax, 27s. 6d. per Annum. Compensation Charge, £3.

ALL THAT messuage or Inn known as the Railway Hotel situate at Lea in the County of Hereford and all outbuildings and appurtenances thereunto belonging comprising outhouse partly brick and stone consisting of beer-store wine cellar barn wash-house store room etc. two closets urinal pig cots etc. stabling for four with loft over garden and approach containing in all over three acres and all other outbuildings and appurtenances thereunto belonging TOGETHER with the site thereof and the land occupied therewith which said premises are now in the occupation of Robert Scott Taylor as tenant.

Sale of the Railway in 1923 (top) and 1937 (bottom)

The former Railway Inn at Lea in 2001

and a local cider retailer called John Skinner was quick to open the **Railway Inn**, which he and his wife ran for a number of years. Some time before 1905 the nearby Forest Brewery at Mitcheldean purchased the **Railway Inn** and James Hawker was their tenant from 1914 to 1923 at a rent of £50 a year. The brick-built property consisted of a bar, smoke room, two sitting rooms and a kitchen on the ground floor, with four bedrooms and a box room above. In the grounds was a beer store, a wine cellar, a wash house, pig cots and stabling for four horses. Then in 1937 the **Railway** like other Wintle pubs was taken over by Cheltenham Original Brewery. It appears to have closed soon after 1960.

Just over the county border at Mitcheldean in Gloucestershire was the site chosen by Thomas Wintle in 1868 to establish the Forest Brewery, which expanded into a huge enterprise. Alfred at Bill Mills was the brother of Thomas Wintle and, after Thomas died in 1888, he was succeeded by his son Francis. In 1904 the Forest Brewery was featured in *Industrial Gloucestershire*:

> Practically all of the barley used in the brewing is obtained from Herefordshire, which is one of the best barley growing districts in the Kingdom. Before malting, the barley is put through a cleaning apparatus, and all the small, broken and imperfect grains are rejected. The hops are obtained from Worcestershire. It need scarcely be said that absolutely no adulterant is used in any process, though frequent laboratory tests are made to insure uniformity of product. Mr. Wintle has made himself thoroughly familiar with the art of brewing, in which he takes great interest apart from any questions of profit, devoting almost his whole time to the brewery.
>
> He brews mild and bitter ales and stout, all of which are sent out in casks. He has throughout the district between sixty and seventy

public-houses, at which his ales are sold exclusively, and also agents in all the neighbouring towns. Many private families also obtain their supply direct from this brewery, and to such we can say, after careful inspection of the plant, that they are served with a beverage which for purity and wholesomeness is not excelled anywhere.

Francis Wintle retired from business in 1923 due to ill-health, and the Forest Steam Brewery which he had 'most successfully carried on, and his father before him, for nearly Sixty Years' was offered for sale together with 72 licensed properties. However, it appears that the Forest Brewery continued to operate until 1937 when 'it was resolved that the Company be wound up voluntarily and that the Liquidators be appointed ... and he was thereby appointed Liquidator for the purpose of such winding up'. The Cheltenham Original Brewery Company then took over Wintle's Brewery and 93 licensed premises situated in the counties of Gloucester, Hereford, Monmouth and Brecon.

Francis Wintle retired to live at Lea and the brewery at Mitcheldean closed, but the buildings were later re-used by Rank Xerox, and are now occupied by various small companies including Performance Related, who have organised the Ross International Festival every August since 1996.

CHAPTER THIRTEEN

From Ross to the Forest of Dean

Amongst the 11 routes turnpiked by the Ross Trust in 1749, two led towards the Forest of Dean. Both roads initially shared the same route through the tollgate at Copse Cross, but they then divided at Tudorville on the outskirts of Ross. One followed Puckeridge Lane, which led from the top of Fernbank Road, and followed a rugged course between the hills of Chase and Penyard to Deep Dean. After the 1791 Road Act came into force it was discontinued as a turnpike road and replaced by a more convenient route along the Walford road and through Coughton. Although closed as a road, the line of Puckeridge Lane has been preserved as a footpath and survives as a good example of an 18th-century toll road.

Before the road closed it was used by carters and waggoners hauling coal, lime, timber and stone from the Forest of Dean, so a wayside inn would have been essential. This was provided at **Castle Brook**, traditionally the site of an ancient inn. After the road was diverted the **Castle Brook** closed as an inn and became a smallholding occupied by a Mr. Mills. At the end of the 19th century it was purchased by the Cobrey Estate and the building was extended and converted into a 'comfortable Farm House' to accommodate the farm bailiff.

CASTLE BROOK

Comprises a comfortable Farm House, two Sitting Rooms, five Bedrooms and convenient Offices, small Stable, Pigstye and Lean-to Shed, in the occupation of the Farm Bailiff. There are two excellent Labourers' Cottages in No. 328, and Cottage and Garden in No. 350.

The Mansion and Premises are amply supplied with excellent Water, and Hot and Cold Water is carried over the House.

The above is let on a lease to J. L. Piddocke, Esq. (expiring on the 2nd of February, 1892), at a rental of £568 per annum, tenant paying Tithe Rent-charges.

The sale of the Cobrey estate including Castle Brook in 1887

Deep Dean lies sheltered below the wooded slopes of Howle Hill, which is crowned with an Iron Age hillfort. In 1871, William Onions, a haulier, was serving beer from the **Traveller's Rest** at Deep Dean, but it only remained open for 10 to 15 years. From Deep Dean, steeply ascending paths lead past scanty remains of lime kilns, pits and quarries which serve as a reminder of the past brick and lime industries. Cider for the thirsty workers was produced at a cider mill on Howle Hill, which was replaced in the mid-19th century by the **Crown Inn**. For 45 years this pub remained in the hands of the Morgans, until in 1894 it was advertised for sale as a 'Desirable Free Full-Licensed Inn'. The property was described as a stone-built house with convenient outbuildings all in good repair and situated in a 'populous district adjacent to large Quarries and Limekilns and within easy distance of Ruardean and the Forest of Dean'.

CROWN INN, HOWLE HILL, WALFORD,

3 Miles from Ross. and about 2 Miles from the River Wye.

DESIRABLE

FREE FULL-LICENSED INN.

FREEHOLD INVESTMENT.

MESSRS. COOPER and PREECE (late Cooper and Morris) are favoured with instructions from Major J. S. Collins to SELL by AUCTION, at Albion Chambers, Gloucester-road, Ross,

On FRIDAY, the 22nd day of JUNE, 1894,

At 3.30 o'clock in the afternoon, subject to conditions of sale to be then read, all that Old-Established and Full-Licensed Inn known as "THE CROWN," situate at Howle Hill, in the parish of Walford, together with 7a. 2r. 8p. of LAND, of which 5a. 1r. 28p. are Pasture and Orcharding.

The House is Stone-built, with convenient Outbuildings, consisting of Stable, Barn, Pigstyes, and Sheds, all in good repair, and situate in a populous district, adjacent to large Quarries and Limekilns, and within easy distance of Ruardean and the Forest of Dean: and the same has been in the same hands during the past 4 years. There is no other public-house nearer than two miles ot the above. and the premises are well adapted for a dealer, or other person requiring some occupation in addition to the business.

Possession may be had on the 2nd July, 1895.

The tenant, Mr. Geo. Morgan, will point out the Land, and all other particulars, and a plan of the property may be had of the Auctioneers, at Ross.

1894 sale of the Crown at Howle Hill

The **Crown** was purchased by Wintle's Forest Brewery, and was largely rebuilt in the 20th century to provide a 'Bar, Tap Room, Club Room, Beer Store, Kitchen, Scullery, Wash-house, Bakehouse etc'. Under the tenancy of Frederick Stacey the **Crown** survived further sales of 1923 and 1937 when it was taken over by the Cheltenham Original Brewery. Fortunately for Stacey, he remained as the publican well into the 1940s. Forty years later the future of the **Crown** was in jeopardy until a former hotelier carefully restored the old pub. It became a favourite place to meet for a delicious meal washed down with a pint of beer or a glass of wine. Then the hotelier left and his replacement, the owner of 2000, eventually closed the pub.

Not far from the **Crown** at Kiln Green was another licensed premises called the **New Buildings**. It was run for a long period of time by John Gwatkin and his successors who held a multiplicity of trades in the buildings at various times including ones as beer

The Crown at Howle Hill in 1987

retailers, shopkeepers, carpenters, builders and quarry proprietors. It was in the1880s that the Bench granted a licence for the sale of beer and cider for consumption off the premises to John G. Gwatkin, and in 1898 the *Ross Gazette* reported the following:

AN ON LICENCE GRANTED.

Mr John Gwatkins, of New Buildings, Walford, applied for an on licence to sell beer and cider at his premises, he at present only holding an off licence. A similar application had been made four years ago and had been acceded to by the Bench, but it was refused at the Quarter Session on account of there not being sufficient accommodation. Since then the house has been enlarged in order to meet the requirement of the Quarter Session, and as Supt. Cope had no objection to the on licence being granted, as the police would then have a better supervision over the house, the Licensing Justices conceded the request.

The New Buildings in 2001

In 1946 the **New Buildings** was purchased by the Alton Court Brewery, who sold the premises for £2,000 in 1957 to A.E. Bundy who was granted a full licence in 1960. It continued as a free house for about 30 years before being closed, sold and converted into a dwelling. Prior to the opening of the **New Buildings** as a beer house, there were two other beer or cider houses remotely sited on the northern slopes of Bull's Hill. One was at a place that is no longer identifiable called Pusy or Pusty, where the **New Inn** was kept by Benjamin Jenkins in 1841, and the other was at **Mark's Well**. Both were 'approached only by footpaths from the Bull's Hill and Howle Hill roads', and are long since closed.

From Deep Dean, winding lanes lead towards the Forest of Dean through Hope Mansell, a small parish attractively situated amongst wooded hills. In 1851 the population of Hope Mansell was 189 with seating in the church for 200. Forty children attended the church school before the building of the National School in 1868, which has since been closed. At the southernmost tip of the parish, adjoining the Gloucestershire boundary, was the **Crown**, now closed, but memories survive for the building is called the Old Inn, standing near the crossroads at Hawthorns, just north of Drybrook. Being adjacent to the Forest of Dean it is not surprising to learn that the

The Crown at Hope Mansell in 2001

202

Miners' Friendly Society, established in 1844, held their meetings at the **Crown**. In the 1850s Thomas Brain kept the pub and William

Sale of the Crown at Hope Mansell in 1937

Brain retailed beer—one had an 'on licence' and the other had an 'off licence'. Then Charles Hodge took over for a while before John Richard Sharp became publican from around 1891 to 1914. He was followed by Frederick Evans, who was licensee when the **Crown** was purchased by Arnold Perrett & Co., who were taken over by the Cheltenham Original Brewery in 1937. Despite all these changes the pub remained open until well after the Second World War, but was eventually closed around 1970.

In the delightful and secluded parish of Hope Mansell, a former ale and cider house was situated in the thick woods at Bailey Brook lying east of Hope Mansell church. No known date for its existence is known by the author, but it was a ruined building until rebuilt and named Jacob's Orchard. Nearby and in a more prominent position is a large ugly mansion called Euroclydon, built in the late 19th century by a colliery proprietor. The tall tower enabled him to keep watch on the workers in his colliery in the Forest of Dean. The

Euroclydon—A Country House Hotel for sale in 1949

property was sold in 1909 and by the 1930s Euroclydon had become a **Country House Hotel**. After the Second World War the house became neglected, but was eventually refurbished and converted into a residential nursing home, still known as Euroclydon.

Returning to the turnpike road leading from Ross to the Forest of Dean, the diverted and easier route replacing Puckeridge Lane followed the present B4234 road to Coughton corner where it turned east 'through Coughton Street to Dib Dean'. With an increase in passing trade, the **Travellers Rest** opened as an inn at the Barn House in Coughton. In 1851 and 1858 Esther Attwood was listed as the victualler, but after this date the establishment appears to have closed as an inn. The attractive old building survives with a quaint cobbled yard, a well house, and a barn.

Long closed as inns: the Travellers Rest in 2001 (left)
and the Pig & Whistle in Coughton in 1965 (right)

Coughton is a pretty hamlet in the parish of Walford lying beside the Castle Brook and below the heights of Chase Hill. It has obviously enjoyed an industrial past with a blacksmith's forge, a tan house, a wheelwright's shop and a corn mill that was operated by Thomas Bright before he moved to Bill Mills in 1832. The mill continued in use under different millers until around 1914. At Coughton the property now called the Cider House has been transformed from its 1965 description:

One extremely old cottage, the Old Pike House at Coughton, still stands and is affectionately known locally as the **Pig & Whistle**. It has served as a local to a number of older parishioners, who gather there to drink their home-brewed rough cider.

The other turnpike road from Ross to the Forest of Dean also followed the present B4234 to Coughton and then continued through Walford to a 'Place called the Quern' now known as Kerne. After the 1815 Road Act, the turnpike road was extended to William Partridge's Iron Furnace and the terminus of a Forest of Dean tramroad at Bishopswood at the county boundary.

The 1879 Directory records Walford as 'a large parish and village ... situated on the river Wye and Ross and Forest of Dean road; the situation of this village and the scenery around are very beautiful. The name is a corruption of Welsh Ford. The Ross and Monmouth railway has a station at Kerne bridge in this parish'.

During the final quarter of the 19th century several large properties in Walford were offered for sale. The sale particulars show that ample provision was made for the storage of beer, cider and wine, and the making of cider. At Hill Court there was 'extensive dry Cellarage, composed of brick arches' and at the newly erected Walford House there was a 'Brew House' and 'Good Cellarage for Beer, Cider and Wine'. Hom Lodge was described in 1890 as 'A Pretty Villa with Gardens and Grounds' that also had a 'Cider House', and so did Warryfield Farm, Hom Farm and Cobrey in 1887. When Edmund Bond of Cowbrey died in 1710 a 'true and perfect inventory' was made of his belongings which included:

> In the Brewing House—one Brass Furnace and one iron pott with hooks, Tubbs and other utensils.
> In the Mill House—one malt mill and hogshead and two other old vessells.
> In the Mault Chamber—dryed mault, Hopps, Corn Baggs, One Horse Skin.
> In the Outward Cellar—Five hogsheads one full of Beere, a powdring cribb and graines and a chopping block.
> In the Inner Cellar—four hogsheads of Cyder and Casks, eleven empty Casks one Tapp Tubb.
> In the Upper Vault next the Garden Stairs—Three vessels of Harvest Beere.
> In the Lower Vault—Two hogsheads of Cyder and Casks and one hogshead of Beere and Cask.
> Behind the hall doors—one still and Limback.
> [Alembic indicates a pot still, probably used by Bond to distill brandy.]

In the early 1990s Walford was 'an expanding village with a school, inn, shop, garage and church dedicated to St. Michael and All Angels. From the lych gate an avenue of limes leads into the graveyard where the tip of the spire stands as a reminder of damage caused by lightning; monuments include the Rev. Thomas Dudley Fosbroke, vicar of Walford and Ruardean for 32 years, who died on New Year's Day 1842. In the literary world he attained a degree of eminence as a scholar, antiquarian and local historian. His books include a guide to the Wye Tour and a useful account of Goodrich Court written in the first half of the 19th century'. Since the 1990s the shop and garage have closed but the inn at Walford has remained open.

This building was formerly the New Inn at Walford

Beyond the village church and opposite the **Mill Race** is an attractive house dating from the 17th century which was the original village hostelry called the **New Inn** in 1840. This was replaced by the existing **Mill Race** formerly known as the **Spread Eagle,** built in the 1860s with pitched roofs and decorated barge boards in the Picturesque style. The inn was then run by the Taylor family who had previously retailed beer and cider at Brook Farm, now Brook House which is adjacent to a converted Cider House and is approached by a footpath from the preserved stone pound opposite Walford Court.

In 1881, the Spread Eagle was the home for the local Oddfellows

In the 1870s several cases of drunkenness were reported at Walford, including four labourers who were summonsed for being drunk and riotous on a Saturday night. Two of them were sentenced to seven days imprisonment without being offered the option of a fine, as they had previously been summonsed and sentenced on many occasions. A few years later in 1881 John Miles and Henry Higgins, both labourers of Bull's Hill, were charged with 'being drunk'. They were each fined 5s. 6d. plus 9s. 6d. expenses. Then in 1894 Edward Toomer, Leonard Reding, John Weaver, John Hughes, Henry Hughes and William Hughes were all 'charged with being found, unlawfully, on the licensed premises of George Morgan, landlord of the Crown Inn'.

In the mid-19th century the Mill House was the **George Inn** run by Charles Smith, who secured a mortgage on the property in 1865. He died in 1870 and was succeeded by Robert Smith, the millwright and miller, who closed the **George** and took over the **Spread Eagle**. In 1881 Robert, described as a 'Wood Turner and Master Millwright', was at the **Spread Eagle** with his wife Elizabeth, their seven children, his brother-in-law and a lodger.

Robert Smith was a colourful character who kept the **Spread Eagle** for 44 years. On the second Monday of each July he organised 'Bob's Rumpus; a great day for Walford and District, for this was the festival of the Loyal St. Michael's Lodge of the Independent Order of Oddfellows (founded 1880). From 11 a.m. the band from Lydbrook led the procession with members in full regalia from the Spread Eagle Hotel to Bishopswood'. A traditional lunch was served, toasts were made, and plenty of drink was consumed, before tackling the tug-of-war, skittles and other competitions, eventually followed by dancing.

Unfortunately for Bob, he experienced a tragic accident in February 1894. The *Ross Gazette* reported that an inquiry was held at the **Spread Eagle** respecting the death of Sydney Smith, 28, a wood turner, who lived with his father at the inn. Sydney had met his death while fishing on a brook at Walford.

Later that year, on 18 July, the Oddfellows Fete and Gala was held at the **Spread Eagle.** The *Ross Gazette* reported that after Divine Service at the parish church, the members returned to the **Spread**

The one-time Spread Eagle is now called the Mill Race

Eagle where 'there being plenty of roast and boiled joints, with all other necessaries, the utmost satisfaction was given to all who sat down to it'.

During the First World War the **Spread Eagle** changed hands and Bob's Rumpus was not revived, but the Oddfellows Club held a Hospital Sunday on the first Sunday of August in each year until the National Health Service was established.

In 1951 Tom and Mabel Jones from the **Gamecock** in Ross took over the tenancy of the **Spread Eagle**, which by then had been taken over by the Alton Court Brewery. In 1962 the brewery sold the 'Spread Eagle with the cottage known as Kerne Cottage outbuildings gardens and lands adjoining' to West Country Breweries. The pub continued as a rather dingy local before changing hands in the mid-1990s. It was then transformed into a comfortable inn with a mock gothic interior and renamed the **Mill Race** after the nearby brook associated with Walford corn mill, now a saw mill.

From Walford the B4234 follows the Wye to Kerne Bridge, a graceful five arched stone structure built as a toll bridge in 1828. It formed a much needed link between Herefordshire and the Forest of Dean instead of using the

ROSS AND MONMOUTH.	1,2,r	1,2,3	1,2,3	1,2,3	1,2,3	1,2,3
	a.m	a.m	a.m	p.m	p.m	p.m
Hereford dep.	6 20	6 20	9 45	12 50	1 15	6 30
Ross arr.	6 49	6 49	10 15	1 18	4 45	7 2
Gloucester dep.	...	7 30	10 53	1 50	3 55	6 15
Ross arr.	..	8 21	11 37	2 39	4 42	7 0
Ross dep.	6 55	8 25	11 45	2 50	4 55	7 10
Kerne Bridge..	7 7	8 38	11 57	3 2	5 7	7 22
Lydbrook	7 12	8 43	12 2	3 7	5 12	7 28
Symonds' Yat	7 17	8 49	12 9	3 14	5 19	7 37
Monmo'th (May h	7 30	9 3	12 23	3 29	5 33	7 53
Monmo'th (May h	9 34	12 34	3 59	7 6	6 19	8 15
Symonds' Yat	9 46	12 46	4 11	7 15	6 31	8 28
Lydbrook	9 53	12 53	4 18	"	8 6 38	8 35
Kerne Bridge ..	9 58	12 58	4 23	7 33	6 43	8 40
Ross arr.	10 8	1 8	4 33	7 45	6 53	8 50
Ross dep.	10 16	1 18	4 45	——	7 2	9 3
Gloucester arr.	11 3	2 10	5 27	..	7 47	9 55
Ross dep.	11 37	2 39	4 42	7 0	7 0	9 41
Hereford arr.	12 6	3 10	5 10	7 30	7 30	10 2

NO SUNDAY TRAINS.

The Ross and Monmouth Railway, with trains stopping at Kerne Bridge, had connections from and to Hereford and Gloucester in 1884

unreliable ford and ferry crossing at Goodrich. In 1873 the Ross to Monmouth Railway opened with a station at Kerne Bridge used by many tourists visiting Goodrich castle, a short distance across the bridge. All these improvements led to the development of Kerne Bridge with a number of inns, beer and cider houses being established, together with a hotel. Unfortunately the railway closed in 1964, leaving the traders in the area largely dependent on tourists in cars and on foot.

In the past Kerne Bridge was very much associated with fishing on the river Wye. Local fishermen made and used coracles—small boats made of wicker and canvas and water-proofed with pitch. The seat was formed by a plank across the middle and the craft was light enough to be carried on a fisherman's back. William Dew at Kerne Bridge between 1889 and 1910 was the last known coracle user on the Wye, and his coracle is now in Hereford Museum. Later, fishing became more of a sport, when Robert Pashley from Kerne Bridge became known as the 'Wizard of the Wye' due to his record catches of salmon and grilse between 1908 and 1947.

1962 advertisement for the Castle View Hotel, now the Inn on the Wye

Overlooking the Kerne Bridge is the **Inn on the Wye**, a much extended and modernised version of the former **Castle View Hotel**. It was originally a modest barn or coach house converted into a 'boarding house' by John Clayton in the early 20th century. It soon became known as the **Castle View Hotel** famed for its view of Goodrich Castle. In 1977 a tragic fire caused the death of a child and damaged the property, but business continued under new ownership until the recession of the late 1980s. The hotel was left derelict with its windows and doors boarded up, which gave a poor impression of the Wye Valley to visitors.

The Inn on the Wye in 2001

However, in the early 1990s the deserted hotel was purchased and transformed into the **Inn on the Wye** with theme bars, restaurant, function rooms and accommodation available in ten bedrooms. The inn opened in 1995 and offered 'Peaceful country walks, idyllic scenery, close to local attractions—the ideal place for touring, walking, fishing, canoeing, golfing etc'.

In the 1980s the dismantled remains of the railway track and viaduct at Kerne Bridge were developed into a much needed picnic spot and canoe launching site. It is a riverside site conveniently placed on the route of the Wye Valley Walk, a long distance trail of 150 miles following the Wye from its source on Plynlimon to its mouth at Chepstow. From the Kerne Bridge Picnic Site a riverside path leads south behind Stafford House, which stands on the site of the **Plough Inn**, a pub which was open in 1840 but did not survive into the mid-19th century. The **Plough's** riverside site suggests an association with the river trade and fishing, and another ferry which crossed the river to Goodrich. The **Plough** is one of the commonest pub names in the country and the name has certainly been in regular use since the 16th century.

On the opposite side of the road to the Kerne Bridge Picnic Site is a compact stone house called Lumleys, the former **Kerne Bridge Inn** which was opened by William Sillett, a coal merchant, when the

---

WALFORD.—THE KERNE BRIDGE INN.

ALL THAT messuage or Inn known as The Kerne Bridge Inn situate at the Leys in the Parish of Walford in the County of Hereford with the gardens orchard and premises and all outbuildings and appurtenances thereunto belonging and containing by estimation one acre and thirty-three perches or thereabouts TOGETHER with the site thereof and the land occupied therewith.

Sale of the Kerne Bridge Inn in 1937

railway arrived. In 1891 Mrs. Elizabeth Little was the landlady, whilst Arthur Webb was there in 1902 selling Arnold Perrett's Gold Medal Ales and Stouts. In 1937 'The Kerne Bridge Inn situate at the Leys ... with the gardens orchard and premises and all outbuildings' were taken over, like many other pubs, by the Cheltenham Original Brewery, and eventually

The Kerne Bridge Inn closed in 1993 and now only provides accommodation

became part of the extensive Whitbread holdings.

During the 1980s the **Kerne Bridge Inn** was renovated into 'an attractive two-bar pub with a good line in snacks and beer'. In the comfortable and traditional pub one bar was decorated with pictures of fish and Guinness prints and the small public bar featured original furniture, a wall clock, a piano and a darts board. Despite an attempt to keep the pub open, it closed around 1993 and was converted into the bed and breakfast establishment now called Lumleys.

The route of the Wye Valley Walk from Kerne Bridge towards Ross ascends Leys Hill. Just before the steep climb a property on the left was the **Albion**, a beer house kept by George Davies in 1881. In 1892 George Wolfe transferred the licence to

The Albion closed about half a century ago, but the name can still be seen

211

Emanuel Husbands who continued to keep the house for several decades as tenant of the Alton Court Brewery. In 1941 Mrs. G. Horsley was running the pub, but it appears to have closed shortly afterwards. The name 'ALBION' painted on the outside wall is clearly visible.

The road from Kerne Bridge towards Lydbrook in the Forest of Dean passes another former pub before it leaves Herefordshire for Gloucestershire. This was the **Dry Brook Inn**, where George Taylor was the victualler during the mid-19th century when the Walford Union Benefit Society held their meetings there. Also at Drybrook in the 1850s was Thomas Baker, a cider retailer who also worked as a stonemason. From the county boundary at Bishopswood a winding lane leads up the wooded hills where the **Labour in Vain** existed as an inn for a very short period from the 1860s under Charles Bullock.

CHAPTER FOURTEEN

From Ross to Monmouth

According to Charles Heath in 1828, the distance from Ross to Monmouth was 20 miles by water or 10 miles by land. At that time boats and coaches were hired at Ross for the scenic journey down the Wye Valley, where a plentiful number of inns offered suitable refreshments. Today, the Wye's lengthy meanders through the picturesque gorge at Symonds Yat presents a problem to the visitor who may well find some difficulty in following the minor roads and easier to use the footpaths, stretches of the Wye Valley Walk and the two traditional passenger ferries at Symonds Yat.

Nowadays the main route from Ross to Monmouth follows the A40 which was reconstructed as a dual carriageway in 1960. This is the only road leading from Ross that has undergone such a dramatic change since its days as a toll road when the Ross, Hereford and Monmouth Trusts were responsible for various sections from 1749 onwards. Another route once led south from Ross to Monmouth through Hom Green, past Hill Court and across the river Wye at Walford either by the ford or the ferry known as the Goodrich Boat. In 1749 the Ross Trust turnpiked this two mile length of road which formed the shortest of its 11 routes. The ancient river crossing with 'its bustling life and incessant passing to and fro' began to decline after the building of Kerne Bridge in 1828. After centuries of use stretches of this road north and south of the Wye have been closed to the public, although never officially shut down.

In 1873 the completion of the Ross and Monmouth railway offered an alternative and attractive journey down the Wye valley through the scenery which had been so much admired by those seeking the Picturesque a century earlier.

Accounts were written by Shaw, Ireland, Farrington, Gilpin, Heath, Bloomfield, and Fosbroke amongst others, and as a result the Wye Tour became commercialised by boat proprietors and innkeepers. Craft were hired from Ross for a leisurely journey, with time to write, sketch, picnic and explore on foot the delightful scenery of the Wye Valley. A permanent visible reminder of this period is the watercolour views sketched by James Wathen between 1788 and 1802. By 1827 a single boat was insufficient to cope with the demand 'since the pleasure of the excursion has been known, they have increased to eight, and more are sometimes wanted to accommodate the company. The price of the boat from Ross to Monmouth is £1 11s. 6d. From Ross to Chepstow, £3 3s. besides provisions for the boatman'.

From Ross to Monmouth the present A40 passes the **Orles Barn Hotel** at Wilton, one of several private residences converted into hotels since the Second World War. At Glewstone, below the steep embankment of the busy thoroughfare lies the former **Boat Inn** on a section of the old road leading from Ross to Monmouth, which had hardly altered its course since its days as a turnpike route. In the mid-19th century the '**Glewstone Boat Beer House and Garden**' was kept by James Price the 'victualler and pleasure boat proprietor', followed by Sarah Price in 1867. Shortly after this the **Boat Inn** was acquired by the Glewstone Court Estate and they closed the inn and used the premises as a boat house. Indeed, the **Glewstone Boat** is shown as uninhabited in the 1881 census although a 'ferry with boat' was still available as late as 1922. By the 1940s Bessie Collins had established a C.T.C. road house offering accommodation and refreshments

to weary cyclists at the Boat House. Since the construction of the dual carriageway the property, now a private dwelling, can only be seen from a right-of-way down a series of steps leading from the A40 or from the riverside path.

The traffic today speeds past Pencraig—

The Glewstone Boat is now a private house

from the Welsh meaning 'head of the rock'—where the Court now serves as an hotel called **Pencraig Court**. From around 1841 the Apperley family appear to have been publicans and beer retailers at the **Pencraig Beer House**, but in 1881 William Williams, an out-door beerhouse-keeper was refused an indoor licence to sell beer and cider. During the 20th century **Mount Craig** opened its doors as a hotel offering 'extensive views over the Wye Valley'.

CROSS KEYS INN
GOODRICH, ROSS-ON-WYE,
HEREFORDSHIRE
Symonds Yat (0600) 890203

BED & BREAKFAST	**FUNCTIONS**
CHILDREN WELCOME	Private Parties
Children under 2 sharing Parents Room	Wedding Receptions
FREE	Sit Down Meals Catered For up to 50 people
Cot Available	Outside Bars
Morning Tea	Large Car Parks
Packed Lunch	Coach Parties by Arrangement
Home Cooked Food	LAWNS: Childrens Swings
Full Bar Menu	GAMES: Skittle Alley, Pool, Darts,
Evening Meal (including Vegetarian)	Table Games
Dogs Welcome	MUSIC: Background for Bars & Meals
	Piano Saturday Evening
	Discotheque by Arrangement for Parties & Functions

PROPRIETORS: TOM & MARILYN COOK

A 1987 advertisement for the Cross Keys

Just beyond the A40 road bridge at Goodrich Cross the **Cross Keys** stands on the turnpike road leading from Ross to Monmouth. It was probably at this inn that the victualler, Samuel Smith, was 'unlawfully' entertaining 'people with poppet shows' in 1759. This was before the long serving Gretton family kept the **Cross Keys** from around 1790 offering 'a neat room and stabling'. From 1794 the Goodrich Friendly Society met at the **Cross Keys** and were still there in 1851 when John Collins was the innkeeper. By the time of the 1881 census, David Williams, his wife, two children, a servant and two lodgers were resident at the inn. In 1905 it was purchased by the Alton Court Brewery and taken over

The Cross Keys in 2000

by West Country Breweries Ltd. in 1962. The pub's name reflects its situation on a former crossroads and its nearness to Goodrich church. The crossed keys is a common sign in Christian heraldry, referring to St. Peter to whom Jesus said 'I will give unto thee the keys to the Kingdom of heaven'—the papal arms include crossed keys as do those of many bishops. Despite its displacement from the main road since 1960 the **Cross Keys** remains open in a building of some antiquity.

Carter's Terrace, Marstow, in 2001

From Goodrich Cross a minor road leads west over the dual carriageway and winds its was to Brelston Green and Marstow church, which was rebuilt on this site in 1855. Facing the church is **Carter's Terrace**, recorded as a beer house in 1838 and kept by Ann Carter in 1841. Some time after 1851, when Cornelius Carter took over the establishment, it closed as a beer house.

From the junction of the A4137 at Old Forge, the original road from Ross to Monmouth can still be followed through Whitchurch, described in 1891 as:

> The village is pretty and contains some good houses, it is surrounded by Welsh mountain scenery of the most picturesque description, the rivers Wye and Garron afford good fishing. The church of St. Dubricius is an ancient building of stone in the Decorated style. Symonds Yat (or Gate) was formerly a pass on the road to Wales, the scenery here is of the most delightful description and splendid views are to be had of the surrounding country.

Above the first section of old road the Plough Farm of 1835 had briefly become the **Plough Inn** during the late 19th century. At Whitchurch the old road passes the **Crown** standing on a prominent corner and still advertising its beers and menus. In 1828 Mr. and Mrs. Williams kept the **Crown Inn**, and in September 'the most respectable families in the surrounding district appoint one evening in the week, to celebrate it [The Village Feast] with a BALL and SUPPER, at the CROWN INN, the house affording very superior accommodations for such meetings, increased by the neatness which pervades the interior'.

In 1870 the publican, John Waters, was fined for assault after an incident involving a labourer from Llangrove who went into the **Crown** for a quiet drink. He was kept waiting and Waters assaulted the labourer and blamed him for disturbing the pub, but he was found to be sober. In 1875, under the same landlord, Thomas and Alexander Richards were charged with stealing a halter and dandy brush from the **Crown's** stables, where they had 'put up their horses'. They admitted to this petty crime and

> **CROWN INN, WHITCHURCH.**
>
> ——∞——
>
> **RICHARD MESSENGER,**
>
> Respectfully informs Visitors and Tourists, that they will find every accommodation at the above Inn, which is most pleasantly situate between Ross and Monmouth, on the high road to South Wales, and within an easy walk of Goodrich Court and Castle, and the finest Wye Scenery ; and is particularly convenient for Anglers, the fishing in the neighbourhood being excellent.
>
> **Charges Moderate.**
>
> ————
>
> COACHES PASS AND REPASS DAILY.

1855 advertisement for the Crown

were tried at Quarter Sessions. A month later George Symonds was charged for being drunk 'in charge of a horse and cart at Whitchurch'. but the case was dismissed.

In 1891 Mrs. Jane Knight was running the 'Crown commercial and family hotel and posting house' providing 'tourists and families ... every comfort ... at reasonable charges in the delightful village of Whitchurch on the banks of the Wye and in view of Symonds Yat'. More recently the **Crown**

The Crown at Whitchurch.
Top : about 1908; bottom : 1990
(Druce collection)

217

has suffered from flooding due to heavy rain. The worst flood happened in September 1999 when the Tudor Bar, the cellar, the hallway entrance and toilets were all under several inches of rainwater.

At Whitchurch a number of Friendly Societies were established in the 18th and 19th centuries. The earliest one—the Whitchurch Friendly Society—existed from 1794 to 1814 at the **Bell Inn**, an otherwise unknown hostelry. The meetings were then held at the **Crown**, where the Friendly Society of Tradesmen had previously met.

It is at Whitchurch that the old A40 runs parallel to the dual carriageway towards Monmouth. The former highway passes Sandyway Lane, where an unnamed public house served the locality. Since 1844 when William Tombs was the owner, no licensees have been recorded. Further along the old A40 a pretty winding lane known as Well Vale Lane leads past buildings at Well Vale the site of 'a substantial Malthouse, Cider Mill-house, and Cider Mill; a Stable and Slaughter-house; with about Eight Acres of rich Meadow Land'. This became the **Malt Shovel** until the mid-19th century. At Crocker's Ash, the Doward House has undergone refurbishment since it closed as a hotel about 25 years ago. The grade II listed building dates from around 1800, but with some 20th-century alterations, and has now been converted into apartments.

DOWARD HOTEL
WHITCHURCH (Nr. Symonds Yat), HEREFORDSHIRE

The Hotel with a Reputation for Good Food, Comfort, Amenities and Service.
FULLY LICENSED
The view from the Hotel extends for many miles over the beautiful Woods, Hills and Pasture Lands of Herefordshire.
PHONE WHITCHURCH (Hfds.) 67

The Doward Hotel in 1950

Before reaching the Monmouthshire border the old and new roads meet at Ganarew which had a population of only 156 in 1931. Next to the church, rebuilt in 1849, the Old Manor House contains beams that date to the mid-16th century. Further down the Wye, Wyastone Leys is now the home of Nimbus Records. It was originally called the Leys, a late 18th-century house that was rebuilt in 1820 by Richard

218

Blakemore, an iron master and Member of Parliament from South Wales. Ganarew does not appear to have had any licensed premises.

Returning to Whitchurch, the B4164 leads south from the A40 to Symonds Yat West, an attractive riverside hamlet largely spoilt by the success of tourism and unsympathetic planning. By 1891 it was emerging as a tourist trap with four licensed premises, two temperance hotels and a coffee tavern already established.

The **Old Court,** now an hotel, stands by the roadside. It is a fine, stone-built manor house of 16th- and 17th-century date although two trusses in the upper part of the west wing may indicate that an earlier building was incorporated. It was the home of the Gwillim family until 1800 when Elizabeth Gwillim died. In 1828 Charles Heath described the **Old Court** as:

> A spacious residence, similar to the generality of these edifices; and having been let, for many years, to private families, who successively took great pains to keep it in repair, preserves both within and without all its former respectability and comfort. Part of the ancient tapestry continues to ornament the walls of the bedchambers, while the oak floors vie with the looking-glass for lustre,—a fate very rare for such premises. In a parlour, on the north side of the house, are these arms in the windows, most beautifully executed in stained glass, and in the finest preservation.

Old Court, Whitchurch about 1930

Heath also made a general observation about the area:

> The soil of Whitchurch, like that of Goodrich, the adjoining parish, is of a fine loamy nature, producing excellent crops of all sorts of grain, with the addition of rich fruit trees, which furnish the farmers' cellars with large quantities of cider and perry; so abundant indeed, as to make those liquors the general beverage of the country.

The narrowing road passes the **Wye Knot**, originally a cottage belonging to Thomas Ballinger, which became a beer house called the **Grove Inn**. In 1878 'All that freehold messuage or dwelling house commonly known as the Grove Cottage and used as a beer house with the outhouses and garden' was purchased by John Jones whose family ran the inn for several generations. During the First World War, when glass was in short supply, the pub's beer and cider was served in jam pots, so it was nicknamed the **Jam Pots**. Some time before 1960 the **Grove Inn** was taken over by the Alton Court Brewery and was closed around 1970, However, a few years later it started up again under new management as the **Wye Knot**, and is still open.

From the **Wye Knot** a maze of twisty lanes and footpaths lead up the steep slopes of the Great Doward, where disused quarries and lime kilns remain as a reminder of its past industrial history. At the **Yew Tree** the Ballingers opened another cider house in the mid-19th century. The **Yew Tree** continued to serve its customers by a succession of Ballingers until its closure around 1960. The property has since been

A 1987 advertisement for the Wye Knot Inn

220

transformed and is now called Yew Tree House.

On the roadside overlooking the Wye Valley is the **Symonds Yat Inn**, the meeting place of the Symonds Yat Friendly Society in 1884 and the female version from 1842 to 1850. In the 1850s the victualler was Walter Pritchard, who was also a lime burner and shopkeeper. It was then taken over by John Ballinger from approximately 1867 to 1914. In the 1950s the proprietress, Dora Bell Scott, was serving her 'excellent cuisine', and in 1971 the refurbished and extended premises was

SYMONDS' YAT HOTEL AND BOARDING HOUSE,
Within Ten Minutes' walk of Symonds' Yat Railway Station,
NEAR WHITCHURCH, HEREFORDSHIRE.

JOHN BALLINGER,
RETAILER OF
FOREIGN AND BRITISH SPIRITS, WINES, &c.,
Home-Brewed Beer, Burton Ale, Dublin Porter, and Prime Herefordshire Cider
(Bottled and Draught).

The above Hotel affords one of the most pleasant retreats for Families and Tourists — the house is situated on an eminence commanding Beautiful and Picturesque views — the rich and fertile valley, with the meandering of the lovely River Wye, and the majestic tower of Rocks called Symonds' Yat. Goodrich Castle and Court are within an easy distance.

PLEASURE BOATS TO ALL PARTS OF THE RIVER WYE.
Well-Aired Beds, Good Stabling, Lock-Up Coach House.

The Symond's Yat Hotel in 1876

The interior of the Symond's Yat Hotel from a 1950s advertisement

1 Soup Roast Spring Chicken Seasoning Seasonable Vegetables Fruit Trifle **60p** ½ BIRD PER PERSON	**2** Soup Roast Leg of Lamb Mint Sauce Seasonable Vegetables Cheese and Biscuits **60p**	**MAR.–OCT.** 1972	**9** Bread and Butter Jam 2 Cakes Pot of Tea **24p** Clotted Cream extra 8p	**10** Plaice and Chips Bread and Butter Pot of Tea Fruit and Cream **55p**
3 Soup Roast Spring Chicken Seasoning Seasonable Vegetables Cheese and Biscuits **60p** ½ BIRD PER PERSON	**4** Soup Half of a Roast Spring Chicken Seasoning Seasonable Vegetables Ice Cream or Cheese and Biscuits **72p**		**11** Boiled Gammon Ham Salad Bread and Butter Ice Cream Pot of Tea **50p**	**12** Plaice and Chips Bread and Butter Pot of Tea **42p**
5 Soup Roast Spring Chicken Seasoning Seasonable Vegetables Fruit Salad and Cream **65p** ½ BIRD PER PERSON	**6** Soup Roast Leg of Lamb Mint Sauce Seasonable Vegetables Fruit Salad and Cream **63p**		**13** Fresh Salmon Salad Bread and Butter Pot of Tea **53p**	**14** Spring Chicken Salad Bread and Butter Pot of Tea **43p**
			15 Boiled Gammon Ham Salad Bread and Butter 2 Cakes Pot of Tea **53p**	**16** Fresh Salmon Salad Bread and Butter 2 Cakes Pot of Tea **58p**
7 Soup Fresh Salmon Salad Bread and Butter Fruit Trifle **62p**	**8** Soup Whole River Trout and Tartare Sauce Salad Bread and Butter Fruit Trifle **62p**		**17** Whole River Trout and Tartare Sauce Chipped Potatoes Bread and Butter Ice Cream Pot of Tea **62p**	**18** Fresh Salmon Salad Bread and Butter Fruit and Cream Pot of Tea **62p**
21 Soup Roast Duck Apple Sauce Seasonable Vegetables Fruit and Cream **87p**			**19** Cold Meat and Ham Salad Bread and Butter Fruit and Cream Pot of Tea **63p**	**20** Boiled Gammon Ham Salad Bread and Butter Fruit and Cream Pot of Tea **56p**

How prices change! The 1972 menu at the Symond's Yat Hotel

catering for coach parties in 'two restaurants on the ground floor seating 120 and 130'. It was not very successful and shortly afterwards the **Symonds Yat Hotel** was converted into a nursing home, but in 1999 it re-opened as an inn once more.

The Symond's Yat Hotel in 1972

One cannot miss the arched and well-signed entrance to the **Paddocks** leading to the large white-washed hotel standing in its own grounds besides the Wye. The original dwelling house of 1844 has dramatically evolved

The elegant Paddocks Hotel of the 1930s
Left : the dining room, right : the lounge

The Paddocks in the 1930s

from being the **King's Head** of 1862 to an elegant hotel in the 1930s, when:

> The Hotel has recently been extended and modernised. Electric Light. Hot and cold running water in bedrooms. Central heating. The Paddocks Hotel is situated in its own well laid out grounds, with Tennis Court and Putting Green, convenient to main road, and has a very extensive view of river and Gorge, with direct south aspect, sheltered from the more prevalent winds, it obtains a maximum amount of sunshine.
>
> The cuisine is made the subject of special consideration, the food supplied being of the very best: meat, poultry, vegetables, butter, cream, etc., all being supplied from the hotel farm.

The Paddocks
SYMONDS YAT (WEST)

FULLY LICENSED

Situated in its own grounds with a very
extensive view of the River Wye

POULTRY, MILK, FRUIT AND VEGETABLES
FROM OWN FARM

20 Bedrooms – All H. & C.   Central Heating
Proprietors: J. G. & E. B. LEWIS   A.A. and R.A.C.

Telephone – Symonds Yat 246

A 1967 advertisement for the Paddocks

Since then the hotel has been almost completely rebuilt and modernised to its present form.

Also beside the Wye at Symonds Yat West is **Ye Olde Ferrie Inne** housed in a building claimed to date from the 15th century. The inn emerged as a beer house serving the bargees using the towpath before the river declined as a navigable waterway in the mid-19th century. William Ballinger was here in 1844 followed by Edwin Ballinger, beer retailer and ferryman. It changed hands at the turn of the

The Olde Ferrie Inne in the 1930s

Ye Olde Ferrie Inne

Symonds Yat West, Herefordshire HR9 6BL
15th Century Free House and Riverside Inne

Accommodation. Restaurant with riverside views.

Open Seven Days a Week

Superb views of Yat Rock, and surrounding
countryside

Afternoon and Cream Teas, Lunches and
Evening Meals

Canoe Launching, Boat Hire, Bike Hire,

Picnic Areas, Boat Trips, Ferry crossing to Yat Rock

Large Car Park facilities

Phone Symonds Yat 890232

A typical advertisement of the 1980s

20th century and only then became officially known as **Ye Olde Ferrie Inne** instead of the simple **Ferry Inn**. In 1920 the 'boat ferry' daily conveyed the postman and his mail across the Wye, and today the pub still operates this upper ferry at certain times. From the 1920s the Sterretts ran the **Ferry Inn** serving 'Hot and Cold Luncheons and Teas' in their 'Fully Licensed Free House' with a capacity to seat 200 in their restaurant.

The Symonds Yat area is a walkers' paradise, for signed footpaths and byways lead in all directions, beside the Wye, up the Doward to old iron workings known locally as the Pancake

Mines, across the river by ferry or Biblins Bridge to ascend Symonds Yat Rock, along the Wye Valley Walk, or to King Arthur's Cave. Sited 100 metres above the river Wye, the cave consists of two chambers, the largest of which is 12 metres long. Excavations in 1925-27 found a hearth and a collection of Palaeolithic flints. Remains of mammoth, woolly rhinoceros, hyena and various other animals were also found.

One quaint feature of **Ye Olde Ferrie Inne**, appreciated by walkers, is the unusual public right of way which leads down a flight of stone steps through the pub buildings. This joins the riverside path, the landing stage for the ferry and the pub's terrace offering 'Superb views of Yat Rock and surrounding countryside'.

From the **Olde Ferrie Inne** a small boat conveys passengers across the Wye to Symonds Yat East, a picturesque hamlet consisting mainly of hotels, guest houses and tea rooms strung along the riverside in the shadow of Symonds Yat Rock. 'This famous panoramic viewpoint has attracted tourists since the dawn of Picturesque appreciation in the 18th century'. Those early Wye Tourists were guided up the steep rock to admire the landscape that William Gilpin had viewed in 1770 including 'the course of the stream round the promontory. Its lower skirts adorned with a hamlet: in the midst of which, volumes of thick smoke, thrown up at intervals, from an iron-forge, as its fires receive fresh fuel, add double grandeur to the scene'.

After the opening of the Ross to Monmouth Railway in 1873 tourists could alight at Symonds Yat Station and, although in 1896 'it was considered that nothing should tempt the tourist to give up the water', the 'speedy transit of a railway journey' attracted more visitors. Sid Wright in *Holidays in Hereford* described Symonds Yat in 1937 as 'one of the beauty spots of the Wye Valley, but alas! it is fast being spoiled for the true nature lover. To see the Yat at its best [the visitor] should go early or late in the year or in the morning, and be sure to avoid Sunday afternoons and Bank Holidays'. The situation has not changed over the 60 or so years since this was written; the loss of the railway has been more than balanced by the increase in private car usage and the many coach tours.

The only pub in the Herefordshire part of Symonds Yat East is the **Saracen's Head,** a riverside inn where one of the two ferries there convey foot passengers across the Wye to Symonds Yat West. In the

*A late 1960s advertisement for
the Saracen's Head*

early 19th century this pub was called the **New Inn**, when it was kept by the Davis family as a beer and cider house and in 1821 the Friendly Society of Gentlemen, Tradesmen and others met there. When the Lloyd Ywarth Brewery from Newport acquired the premises in the 1880s its name was changed to the **Saracen's Head** and after old Mr. Goode and his daughter were there in the early 1880s, John Jones became the landlord. He was followed by Annie Jones as the licensee into the mid-20th century. It now bears no resemblance to its origins in the 19th century as a beer house with a carpenter's and wheelwright's shop, but it still retains the tradition of the barman acting as a boatman conveying visitors across the Wye in a ferry operated by an ancient system of ropes and cables.

A few yards further along the Wye Valley Walk is the **Royal Hotel**, which was established in 1874. In the early 20th century it was run by the Baumgartes who offered guests 'exceptional facilities for Boating and Fishing' with 'Drawing, Smoking and Billiard Rooms' available in the attractive building that overlooked the

Sale of the Royal Hotel in 1957

226

Symonds Yat railway station until the line closed in 1964.

In the early 20th century Goodrich could have been approached 'by way of the ferry situated on the old road between Ross and Monmouth, and reached from Ross by way of Archenfield,

The Royal Hotel from the railway station at the beginning of the 20th century

Hom Green and Hill Court. By this route the Castle is only about 3 miles from Ross, but the ferryman may have to be called from the opposite bank, and it is not always easy to make him hear the summons. Another way to the Castle is by boat from the landing-stage at Ross. A third route is by rail to Kerne Bridge, from which the Castle is only some half-mile distant'. Sadly, none of these routes are now possible, and from Ross, Goodrich is best approached by car from the A40 or through Walford and over Kerne Bridge.

Goodrich attracts many visitors, some to explore the ruins of its Norman castle and others to stay in a holiday apartment at the neighbouring Flanesford Priory, originally founded by Augustinian monks in the 14th century. Visitors also go to the 13th-century church of St. Giles, to seek both the burial place of Thomas Swift, the Royalist vicar of Goodrich during the Civil War and famed for being the grandfather of Jonathan Swift, and the grave of Joshua Cristall, a talented watercolour artist, who lived in the parish during the first half of the 19th century. On the adjoining promontory, and separated from the castle by a deep dingle, was Goodrich Court, built between 1828 and 1832 for Sir Samuel Rush Meyrick, to house his vast collection of armour. Edward Blore designed the fairy-tale castle to produce a dramatic effect above hanging woods which reach down to the river. After the antiquarian died in 1848 the Court and its contents were sold. Between 1940 and 1945 it was taken over by Felstead, an Essex public school. It was demolished in the early 1950s leaving a mock-Gothic gatehouse on the Monmouth road, a lodge house, and gasworks, all now used as dwellings.

Approaching Goodrich from the A40 at Goodrich Cross, the road into the village passes the Court House, where Heath noted:

> the whole building formed half a square, one part being used as a barn, the other the Sessions House, occupied by a farmer', and in earlier times 'there remained against the inside wall the figure of a RED DOG, but this was not the Crest of the Talbot family, though it might allude to the title. At the present day, there exists below the chimney, fronting the road, the figure of a DOG, carved on a large stone, but whether it was placed there when the building was erected, —or carved on it as a Sign for the Public House, which was kept below,—is at this day unknown.

The only other known inn in Goodrich during the 18th century was the **Crown and Anchor** kept by Jonathan Crumpton in 1728 when a writ was served 'to capture and keep in safe custody Jonathan Crumpton, innholder, late of the parish of Goodrich, in order that he may appear before the Justices of Westminster to answer charges of disturbing the peace', but it is not known how serious the disturbance was. By 1819 it had closed, for it was described as a 'Messuage or Dwelling House with the Garden and Appurtenances thereto belonging formerly used as a Public House called the Anchor'. Philip Carter, who occupied the premises, was ordered by the vicar to repair the roof and windows before it was to be used as a parish workhouse.

By 1832 the workhouse had been moved to an adjoining blacksmith's shop, and the former public house reverted to a 'Shop and Beer House distinguished by the sign of the Crown and Anchor' run by Richard Elsmore. In 1845 it was purchased by Sir Samuel Meyrick of Goodrich Court for £400. He completely redesigned the building into a 'romantic inn with a tall Gothic chapel window and a diversity of pinnacles' representing the spirit of Goodrich Court. The inn was renamed the **Meyrick Arms** and became the **Hostelrie** in 1851 with John Evans serving behind the bar, whilst the former publican, Richard Elsmore, was recorded at the **Old Castle Inn**, an unknown site.

The **Hostelrie Inn** of 1869 contained 'Six Bed Rooms, Ball Room, Landing and Water Closet, Two Parlours, Kitchen, Back Kitchen, Bar, with outdoor Larder and Loft over, Malt Room, Coach-

This Agreement, made the tenth
day of October one thousand eight hundred
and forty five Between Samuel Wall of Ross
in the County of Hereford Gentleman of the
one part, and Samuel Rush Meyrick of Goodrich
Court in the said County of Hereford KH of the
other part as follows. that is to say the said Samuel
Wall agrees to sell to the said Sir Samuel Rush
Meyrick and the said Sir Samuel Rush Meyrick
agrees to purchase of the said Samuel Wall for the
sum of Four hundred pounds the Inheritance in fee
simple of all that Messuage or Tenement Shop
and Beer House distinguished by the sign of the
Crown and Anchor situate in the said village of
Kerne in the parish of Goodrich aforesaid together
with the out buildings and Garden thereunto
belonging containing in the whole Thirty three
perches or thereabouts now in the occupation of
Richard Skynner and numbered 304 in the
Tithe Commutation Map of the said
parish of Goodrich And the said Samuel Wall doth
hereby agree that he will cause to be delivered to
the said Sir Samuel Rush Meyrick at his own
Expence an Abstract of the Conveyance to him the
said Samuel Wall of the said premises within ten
days from the date thereof And also will on or before
the first day of November next upon receiving
from the said Sir Samuel Rush Meyrick the sum
of Four hundred pounds at the Expence of the said
Sir Samuel Rush Meyrick's Execute proper
Conveyances and assurances thereof unto the said

1845 sale of the Crown and Anchor, now Ye Hostelrie,
to Sir Samuel Rush Meyrick for £400

229

1896 advertisement card for Ye Hostelrie

House, Stable for Six Horses, Yard, Garden and Land' and was occupied by the landlord William Sillett. The Russell family were there in 1881, but from 1884 David Williams took **Ye Hostelrie** into the 20th century offering the 'best of accommodation for Tourists, with every convenience for entertaining parties on short notice'. During the 1920s the pub was managed by F.E. Smith for Country Hotels Ltd, and before 1941 it became a Trust House. It has since been extended and refurbished, and is now in private ownership as a 'charming, fully licensed Hotel'.

Goodrich Castle was built by the Normans to defend an important crossing over the Wye, part of an ancient road from Ross to Monmouth. Both as a ford and a ferry, it is documented from at least the 14th century when 'Henry IV, then earl of Derby, when crossing this ferry, learned from the ferryman of the birth of his son at Monmouth, and granted the lucky boatman the monopoly of the Ferry for his life and for his family after him'. During the Civil War on 'a dark night in March 1645, Colonel Birch attacked the castle, and on the same night the out-guard at the Boat House protecting the Ferry was attacked, and after two hours stubborn defence it was captured, the defenders receiving quarter'.

In 1787, the Hon. John Byng wrote in his *Torrington Diaries* that he was unable to hire a suitable boat in Ross for the river trip to Monmouth, so he followed a 'bye course, thro' lanes, by the advice of our host, to the ferry near Goodrich, which our horses cross'd without terror'. After investigating the castle 'A narrow lane of a mile led us into the turnpike road, whereon,

Ye Hostelrie at the beginning of the 20th century

for 5 miles, we never exceeded a foots pace, so transcendently gratified were out eyes with the lofty woods, and the river gliding by us ... The road went, often, so near the river, that with the advantage of the hills and views, we fancied our ride to be fully equal to the river journey'.

When Heath visited the area a decade later he followed the same route and noted:

> For the convenience of Walford, and other villages, on the opposite side of the Wye, a horse-ferry keeps open the communication with their neighbours on this side of it. While enjoying the pleasures of a retired hour at this spot, the mind has been diverted by the courage—for I will not say economy—of some passengers. The river is often fordable in the summer months, but it is wide, and rapid on the landing side; and in these dry times up to the saddle-cloth. Regardless of danger, in they ride, and when they reach the middle of its course, are obliged to secure their legs and the skirts of the coat from immersion. Should the horse, by the accident of the loose stones, make a false step, the riders life would, in all probability, fall a sacrifice; for the strength of the stream is too violent to oppose—and if he had the advantage of swimming well, he would be carried to a considerable distance before he could gain a landing. For this risk he saves the sum of a penny.

In 1798 Thomas Bonner also observed the approach to the ferry from the Ross direction:

> the majesty of the castle upon its rocky eminence nearly perpendicular, strikes the observer with an idea of awful grandeur! and a pleasant busyness incessantly attending this spot, much improves it. The company going down to the boat, the man at his station holding to, a long rope, the tackle and pole by which it is suspended, with the usual splashing of the horses getting into it, the neat little white public house on the opposite side, its adjacent shed for basketwork which is the profession of the industrious and obliging landlord. Here, wholesome refreshment is laid out before you with decent civility; and people of respect are frequently seen enjoying the delights of the river, seated at the door.

The Boat Inn with Goodrich Castle in the background

The public house was the **Boat Inn** which stood on the river bank beside a 'Wharf, Tow Path and Bowling Green'. In the late 18th century Mr. Davis, also the ferryman, offered 'a clean room and frugal fare' to the numerous travellers who used this ford and ferry crossing. Despite the building of Kerne Bridge soon after 1828 the 'ford with its ever amusing incidents and not infrequent, alas! loss of life, and a ferry' continued in use with John Evans at the **Goodrich Boat Inn**, which presumably became the **Goodrich Rope Inn** of the 1850s before it closed.

CHAPTER FIFTEEN

Towards the Welsh Border

South of the Ross to Abergavenny road through Broad Oak (Chapter 17), a choice of routes lead through a rural landscape typical of the Welsh borders. The Herefordshire place names reflect a Welsh influence such as Llancloudy, Llanrothal, Llangrove and Llangarron, with Welsh Newton showing an anglicised form. In contrast all the inns and beer houses were given English names, but out of over a dozen licensed premises only the one at Llangrove remains open.

In this fertile corner of south-west Herefordshire, the waters of the Garron, Luke and Mally brooks played an important role in powering the numerous mills and water pumps. Most of the mills ground corn but one or two were paper and tuck mills. Apart from milling the past population of these parishes were mainly employed in farming, building, blacksmithing and beer retailing.

Before reaching Broad Oak on the B4521, a southern turn along the A466 Hereford to Monmouth road leads through Llancloudy to Welsh Newton. In 1730 this ancient highway was described as 'The Great Road to the Town of Monmouth' and by 1769 it had been turnpiked to Llancloudy Hill by the Hereford Trust, with the remainder of the route being maintained by the Monmouth Trustees. At Llancloudy the former **King's Head** still stands on the right of the minor crossroads. It was known locally as the **Bush**, and the present owners have renamed their home 'Hollybush'.

The deeds of the **King's Head** are understood to date from 1701 under the name of Maffia, but unfortunately are not available, so at present no information can be obtained until 1839 when William Watkins was running the pub as tenant of Anne Shuter. A year later an interesting story survives about a man who walked from the

The one-time King's Head at Llancloudy is now a private house called Hollybush

neighbouring parish of St. Weonards to the town of Monmouth. On his way he drunk two pints of ale at the **King's Head**, one pint at the **Elephant and Castle** in Welsh Newton and a further six pints at Monmouth before finishing his drinking spree with several quarts of rum. For his return he purchased a half bottle of rum in Monmouth, then collapsed near the County Gaol. He was taken to Monmouth Police Station where he unfortunately died. It was considered at the time that 'there was nothing remarkable about the amount of drink he had taken', but the event provided useful propaganda for the Temperance Movement.

When George Jones was the publican in 1850, the Hereford to Monmouth coach stopped at the **King's Head** one late spring morning. An American named Fredrick Law Olmsted and his two friends alighted from the vehicle to continue their walking tour. Olmsted was a well-known landscape gardener who, after gaining degrees in both engineering and science, trekked across the United States and Europe studying landscape gardening. In 1857 he became the superintendent of Central Park in New York, and transformed a wasteland into America's first planned city park. Before setting out for England, Law Olmsted was familiar with the writings of William Gilpin and Uvedale Price, and was 'overwhelmed' with his first experience of the English countryside and its rural scenery, which led him to utilise natural landscapes in his urban parks. His tour of England in 1850 is described in *Walks and Talks of an American Farmer*. After leaving Hereford he wrote:

> We pursued our way, guided by the gentleman who had so kindly entertained us for several miles through narrow by-ways. It was a rarely clear, bright, sunshiny afternoon, and while on the broad

highway we had found, for the first time in England, the temperature of the air more than comfortably warm. The more agreeable were the lanes; - narrow, deep, and shady, often not wider than the cart-track, and so deep, that the grassy banks on each side were higher than our heads; our friend could not explain how or why they were made so, but probably it was by the rain washing through them for centuries. On the banks were thickly scattered the flowers of heart's-ease, forget-me-not, and wild strawberries; above, and out of them, grew hawthorn hedges in thick, but wild and wilsome verdure, and pushing out of this, and stretching over us, often the branches mingling over our heads and shutting out the sky clear beyond the next turn, so we seemed walking in a bower, thick old apple and pear trees with pliant twigs of hazel-wood, and occasionally the strong arms of great brooding oaks.

Like Cobbett, Law observed all aspects of country life, the farms, cottages, gardens, stables, paddocks, agriculture, production and consumption of cider, and the condition of agricultural labourers. He quotes:

A correspondent of the Agricultural Gazette mentions that, in Herefordshire and Worcestershire, the allowance of cider given to laborers, in addition to wages, is 'one to ten gallons a-day'. He observes that. of course, men can not work without some drink, but that they often drink more than is probably of any advantage to them, and suggests than an allowance of money be given instead of cider, and the laborers be made to buy their drink. In this was, he thinks, they would not be likely to drink more than they needed, and it would be an economical operation for both parties. In Normandy, the cider district of France, three gallons a-day is the usual allowance of laborers.

As coaches were largely replaced by an increasing number of trains from the middle of the 19th century, the **King's Head** would have seen less custom. Even so, the inn continued under various publicans including David Powell, George Keddle and John Barrell until the end of that century. In 1922 Henry Hill was followed by Oliver Evans into the 1930s, when the inn was refurbished and modernised before passing to R. Jackson in the 1940s. It had become an Alton Court Brewery pub before being closed around 1962. The publican was well known for serving sandwiches and beer to coach

The Elephant and Castle in retirement in 2001

loads of Welsh day-trippers who were avoiding the Sunday closure in Wales.

Continuing towards Monmouth on the A466, the farm named **Elephant and Castle** stands on the corner of a road junction about a mile and a half north of Welsh Newton church. The farm was indeed an inn called the **Elephant and Castle,** where, in 1832 the parish meetings were held. From the mid-19th century Edward Powell was the victualler, and other publicans followed, including John Dangerfield, Richard Francis and Edward Powell, before it closed its doors as a pub well before the end of the 19th century. As the **Elephant and Castle** was the only licensed property open in 1870, it must have been there that John Haines and George Davis were charged with drunkenness and pleading guilty were ordered to pay a fine and expenses amounting to 11s. each. By 1881, Amos Hodges, the head of the household, was registered as a carpenter and lived there with his three children. The **Elephant and Castle** derives its name from the crest of the Cutler's Company, which depicts an elephant with a howdah on its back, looking like a miniature castle.

Welsh Newton is known for its beautiful 13th-century church and the dramatic Pembridge Castle, which dates from the same period. A fascinating story connecting the two sites was written by Revd. Seaton in 1903:

There is an old cross in the churchyard in fairly good order, near the base of which is a flat stone with a cross chiselled on it, and the following simple inscription- 'J. K. August 22, 1679', which covers the remains of the Venerable Father John Kemble; he was born at Rhydycar Farm, in the adjoining Parish of St. Weonards, in 1599, and studied at Douay, where he was ordained Priest on February 23, 1625; after this he was sent on the English Mission in the same year, and ministered to the spiritual wants of his co-religionists in

Herefordshire and Monmouthshire. On December 7th, 1678, the Bishop of Hereford was ordered to examine matters concerning 'The Combe' (a college of the Jesuits in this parish); upon the receipt of which notice he placed it in the hands of Captain Scudamore, of Kentchurch, who sacked The Combe, carried off the Books, Missals and MSS, most of which are now in the Cathedral Library at Hereford, and proceeded to take Father Kemble to Pembridge Castle, and conducted him to Hereford Goal, to be tried at the Lent Assizes, of which no account can be found. In April, 1679, he was ordered to be brought to London by the House of Lords, and was tried there, and sent back to Hereford Goal, and executed at Widemarsh, August 22, 1679, aged 80. He met his death with calm resignation, and when the hour for his execution arrived he requested to be given time to finish his prayers and be allowed a pipe of tobacco, a cup of sack, in which the Under Sheriff joined him. This gave rise to the old Herefordshire saying of calling the parting pipe a Kemble pipe, the parting glass a Kemble cup.

After his execution, his remains were buried at Welsh Newton church, and because of his martyrdom his grave became a place of annual pilgrimage. His left hand is enshrined as a holy relic at the catholic church of St. Francis Xavier in Hereford, and the Blessed John Kemble was canonised as a saint in 1970.

There was another inn at Welsh Newton called the **Lion** or **Red Lion**, which stood next to the church. The **Lion** was mentioned in the parish records of 1819 when it was resolved 'that part of the present old road turning to the left of the **Lion Public House** into the Turnpike road shall be turned to the right of it'. This was followed in 1820 with the 'stopping up' of the old road by Quarter Sessions. After the road alterations the **Lion** remained open during the 1850s under the victualler and mason, John Palmer.

The **Lion Public House** closed in 1866 when it was purchased by Sir Joseph Bailey M.P., the Lord of the Manor, to provide 'educational facilities for the few children of his tenants'. The former **Lion** was split into two tenements to accommodate Miss Gurney, the schoolmistress, in one half, and Christopher Synonds, the parish clerk, in the other. The schoolroom measuring 32 x 13 ft. was situated over the back kitchen, and was reached by a flight of outside steps. The school was replaced in 1875 by a new building and the old inn then became known as Church House.

Church House was the Lion Inn during the first half of the 19th century

From Welsh Newton church a minor road joins a narrow lane leading to Welsh Newton Common. Although this is now a 'No Through Road' it originally formed part of a route from Llangrove, through Welsh Newton Common, and across the Welsh border to Dixton and Monmouth. This typical common settlement is criss-crossed by a delightful network of paths and tracks. About 50 years ago on the southern outskirts of Yew Tree Wood there was a scanty ruin consisting of '3 walls probably at most a metre high which persons were claiming as an old pub' traditionally known as the **Half-way Public House**. It served as a refreshment stop for those carrying their produce from Welsh Newton to Monmouth market, a distance of at least 8 miles.

Llangrove is a common settlement which was formed into a separate ecclesiastical parish in 1856 with its own church built at a cost of £1,500 in 1858. It was formerly a hamlet within Llangarren, and was still treated civilly as late as the 1881 census. On the outskirts of Llangrove is the **Royal Arms**, a wayside pub in a building that dates back to the 17th century. It was a blacksmith's shop and beer house in the early 19th century owned by the Watkins family of blacksmiths and

LLANGROVE—THE ROYAL ARMS INN.

FIRST ALL THAT messuage or Inn at Llangrove in the Parish of Llangarren known as The Royal Arms with the garden and land thereto adjoining and belonging containing three quarters of an acre or thereabouts and ALSO ALL THAT messuage or shop adjoining the above described premises AND SECONDLY ALL THOSE two pieces of land at Llangrove aforesaid containing 4 acres 3 roods and 28 perches or thereabouts

Alton Court Brewery sale of the Royal Arms in 1962

The Royal Arms at Llangrove when William Lewis was landlord

by 1851 became known as the **Smith's Arms** run by James Weale. From around 1858 until 1870 the landlady was Mrs. Elizabeth Burford, and although Charles Mapp had purchased the **Smiths Arms** in 1862 for £300, he did not take over the running of the pub until 1870. During his occupancy of nearly 30 years he changed the pub's name to the **Royal Arms** in 1881 to commemorate Queen Victoria's long reign. In 1890, the **Royal Arms** was sold to Alton Court Brewery, and since then, despite various changes, it has managed to remain open.

At an unknown site in Llangrove was another beer house called the **Plough and Harrow**, which only traded for a short period during the 1850s.

North from Llangrove, is the main village and parish of Llangarron where, in the mid-19th century, a population of 1,217 supported two public houses—the **Malt Shovel** and the **Three Horse Shoes**. Before reaching Llangarron church the **Malt Shovel Beer House**, malthouse and premises occupied a site on the right of the road now known as Lower Butts. In 1776 this was probably 'The Publick' held by William James, which became the **Malt Shovel** of 1839 owned and occupied by William Abraham. It appears that the **Malt Shovel** may have changed its name to the **Crown** in 1851, and from 1858 it was run by a shoemaker called Henry Gates who stayed there until 1870 when farmer George Pope served as the last licensee. By 1881 George Pope was an agricultural labourer still living at Lower Butts, but there was no mention of the **Crown**. West of Lower Butts lies the Butts that was occupied by Ernest Tummy at £8 a year in 1903. It was offered for sale as a 'superior cottage residence' with 'Sitting-room, Larder, Kitchen, Dairy, and 4 Bedrooms; Lean-to shed, Stable, Cider Mill-house with Mill and Press'.

The main route through Llangarron passes its attractive church, and crosses the river Garren to a former inn called the **Three Horse Shoes**. Now looking very forlorn, it was one of the 'Old Inns' of Llangarron with part of the premises dating from 1600. From the early 19th century John Wintle was the innkeeper, but before his death in 1838 he moved to Garronfield Cottage. He had been a member of a 'Friendly Society held at the Red Lion Westbury on Severn', but another member of the family called James Wintle was associated with the Llangarron Friendly Society which was held at the **Three Horse Shoes**.

In Llangarron and Llangrove four Friendly Societies were established between 1798 and 1853. The oldest was the

Sale of the Three Horseshoes in 1855

ALL THAT messuage or Inn in the Parish of Llangarren known as The Three Horse Shoes with the outbuildings cottage yard and gardens thereto adjoining and belonging

Sale of the Three Horseshoes in 1962

Llangarron Friendly Society which was later joined by the female branch, and the Independent Savings Bank and Lodge Union Society founded in the mid-19th century. All met at the **Three Horse Shoes**. The Llangrove Friendly Society started in 1842 and held their meetings at the **Smith's Arms**.

The rather run-down former Three Horseshoes in 2001

The 'Three Horse Shoes Public House, Blacksmiths Shop, Cottage Court and Garden' of 1839 was later run by Thomas and Mary Hardwick, before it was offered for sale in 1855 as a 'well-accustomed public-house and inn, called the Three Horse Shoes' when John Maxfield was the innkeeper. The premises also contained a large club room and a 'substantial stone-built dwelling-house with black-smiths shop and good garden'. Richard Davies followed in 1867 and had his license renewed in 1870 before 'John Tummey & Sons, farmers and innkeepers' were recorded at the inn from 1876 to 1902. The 1881 census records John Tummey aged 41 living at the Three Horse Shoes with his wife, Elizabeth, and their four children. There was also a female servant and a lodger working as an agricultural labourer. By 1922 Bessie Dew was the landlady, and in 1941 the pub was run by Albert Harris. The former pub is now used for selling second-hand doors, baths, gates etc, but it is rumoured that the bar and skittle alley still exist.

In 1977 the Women's Institute *History of Llangarron* described the **Three Horse Shoes**:

> This inn situated at the centre of the village was kept by Mr. and Mrs. Dew; it was the head-quarters of many village activities such as the darts and football teams and the Thrift Club. Mr. Dew suffered much ill health and after his death the Brewery Company decided to close down the 'pub' and the societies and clubs had to find other accommodation. While the erstwhile customers had to walk two miles to find companionship and slake their thirst—to the Royal Arms at Llangrove.

Although the name **Three Horse Shoes** seems an odd number for shoes that come in sets of four, it has been suggested that a sign of **Three Horse Shoes** indicates to unfortunate travellers that a blacksmith was readily available to replace a missing shoe. In former times the blacksmith was an important member of the community, the forerunner of the garage on the highway, when travel and transport was reliant on fit and well-shod horses.

INNS, BEER SHOPS, COTTAGES, AND LANDS.

		Occupiers.	A.	R.	P.	£.	s.	d.
6	Smithy	James Matthews				4	0	0
	The George Inn or Beer Shop, containing Six Bed Rooms, Parlour, Two Kitchens, Back Kitchen, Pantry, Cellar, with Shed, Piggery and Garden	W. Meadmore	0	1	15	18	0	0
87	Cottage and Garden	William Preece				4	10	0
	Cottage, Garden and Workshop	George Parry	0	1	21	10	0	0
	Cottage and Garden	John James				5	0	0
88	Cottage and Garden	James Clayton	0	0	19	6	0	0
89	The "Hostelrie" Inn, containing Six Bed Rooms, Ball Room, Landing and Water Closet, Two Parlours, Kitchen, Back Kitchen, Bar, with outdoor Larder and Loft over, Malt Room, Coachhouse, Stable for 6 Horses, Yard, Garden and Land							
80	The Ham Meadow	William Sillett	0	0	33	20	0	0
90	Cottage, known as the Antient "Croose," and Garden	James Clarke	0	0	18	4	0	0
91 & 92	Two Cottages and Gardens	James Davis, James Warr	0	2	20	12	12	0
93	Cottage, Stone and Tiled, containing Two Bed Rooms, Kitchen, Back Kitchen, with Blacksmith's Shop and Shoeing Shed	Cornelius Carter	0	2	5	10	0	0
	Cottage, containing three Bed Rooms, Kitchen, Back Kitchen, Pantry, Lumber Room, Laundry, Washhouse, Drying Ground, with Piggery and Garden	Thomas James				9	9	0
	Withey Bed	James Woolley		......		2	0	0
	TOTAL		A.2	1	11	£105	11	0

Sale of the George at Glewstone and Ye Hostelrie at Goodrich in 1869, part of the Goodrich Court estate

From Llangarron the road towards Ross crosses the A4137 Hereford to Whitchurch road and descends to Glewstone, a hamlet now in the parish of Marstow. From the minor crossroads a detour left leads along an ancient route leading to the **Red Lion** at Peterstow (Chapter 7) on the A49. It passes the

The George Inn at Glewstone is now a pair of cottages

sites of two beer houses that were open in 1838. One, at Coldwell, where a derelict building stands, and the other now lost in a cluster of modern houses. Both were replaced before 1869 by the **George Inn**, now a pair of cottages standing above the crossroads. It had been a 'Beer Shop, consisting of Six Bed Rooms, Parlour, Two Kitchens, Back Kitchen, Pantry, Cellar, with Shed, Piggery and Garden'

1967 advertisement for Glewstone Court Hotel

occupied by William Meadmore in 1869, with James Matthews at the adjoining Smithy in the same grounds. Although the smithy continued in use, the **George** had a short life as a pub.

From the crossroads the road towards Ross passes **Glewstone Court**, converted into a residential hotel around 1960. This gracious Regency house was built in the 1820s by Charles Ballinger on the site of an earlier building that was owned by the Guy's Hospital Estate. Around 1870 the high gabled wings and the former billiard room were added and further alterations were made during the 1930s. Its full history, researched and written by the author of this book, may be read whilst sipping a glass of wine in the comfortable bar.

CHAPTER SIXTEEN

Along by-roads to Pontrilas

Starting from Ross there are a choice of by-roads leading through the scenic countryside of the Welsh borders, where wayside inns were established in the villages and many beer houses sprung up in the scattered hamlets. Out of the 16 licensed houses mentioned in this chapter only four remain open at the beginning of the 21st century.

From Broad Oak, the Pontrilas road leaves the B4521 and leads to Garway Common, where the **Garway Moon** overlooks the cricket pitch. At present it is a pleasant, fully-licensed inn, but it originally started out as a beer and cider house. It was William Walters and his family who ran the beer house during the mid-19th century and called it the **Full Moon**, after being 'called or known by the name of the **Webbs**'. It was presumably named after a previous occupier called Henry Webb, although he is not recorded as a beer retailer.

It was still the **Full Moon** in 1881, and it was during the 1890s, when Reuben Edwin Pritchard and his wife Sarah were in charge of the inn, that it became known as the **Garway Inn**. In 1896 it was taken over by Charles and Alfred Watkins of the Hereford Imperial Brewery and was included in their sale two years later, eventually in 1948 to become part of the Cheltenhem and Hereford Breweries. Sometime between 1959 and 1985 the previous inn names were all combined to form the **Garway Moon**. The **Full Moon** was a popular inn sign, being comparatively easy to illustrate, and one at Morton near Southwell bears a poetic invitation:

> Step in my friends, and take a cup,
> It is not dark, for the moon is up,
> Sit down refresh, and pay your way,
> Then you will call another day.

245

Sale of the Garway Inn in 1898

The Garway Moon in 2001

Reports of drunkenness seem to have been very common in Garway in the 19th century. A George Williams was charged with being drunk at Garway in 1873 and fined 1s. with 11s. 6d. costs; two more villagers were fined on Licensing Day in 1875; Thomas Price was found 'worse for liquor' and would not leave the **Garway Inn** in 1894; and the following year Thomas Carrier was charged for refusing to leave the same inn, when in a 'drunken state'.

The road from Garway towards Pontrilas was turnpiked by the Ross, Abergavenny and Grosmont trust in 1833 and passes the **Black House** standing back from the road opposite the road leading to Garway Hill. There is enough evidence to suggest that this 16th-century cottage was used as a beer house in the mid-19th century when William Price, a shoemaker, was listed as a beer and cider retailer.

Garway is famed for its beautiful round church, founded by the Knights Templars in the 12th century, and its circular 14th-century dovecote. At the turning near the church is a row of houses, including one called the Old Vicarage. This was formerly the **Malthouse Inn** occupied by John Morgan in 1840. It became known as the **Malt Shovel** in 1857, and after closing as an inn was used as a vicarage in the late 19th century by Rev. Minos. He had a new vicarage built in 1900 so the old one was put up for auction when it was described as containing '2 Sitting Rooms, Kitchen, Back Kitchen and 5 Bedrooms with a large Garden, Stable and Piggery adjoining'.

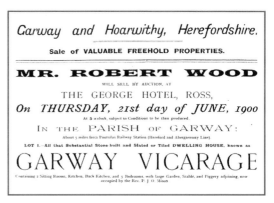

The Old Vicarage, formerly the Malthouse Inn

After leaving Garway the road closely follows the river Monnow, which forms the boundary between England and Wales, to Kentchurch. This is a large but sparsely populated parish where the Scudamores claim they have lived since 1086. In 1100 Corras, in Kentchurch, was held by Ralph Scudamore and the third Scudamore residence, Kentchurch Court, dates from the 14th century. Major alterations by Anthony Keck, John Nash and Thomas Tudor between 1773 and 1825 transformed the fortified manor into a country house. The seclusion of Kentchurch led to legendary tales associated with

Sign at the Bridge Inn, Kentchurch

Owain Glyndwr the Welsh freedom fighter, whose daughter, Alice, married John Scudamore, and Jack O'Kent a priest in league with the devil, who by tradition performed amazing feats.

One of Jack O'Kent's deeds is depicted on the sign outside the **Bridge Inn** in Kentchurch. Jack had promised to build a bridge overnight, but for this task the devil wanted the soul of the first person who crossed the bridge. The next day the bridge was completed, but Jack managed to outwit the devil by sending a dog chasing after a bone across the bridge. In 1851 when Daniel Powell was the victualler the sign read:

This bridge was built without a hammer or trowel,
Come in and take a glass with D. Powell.

Powell was followed as landlord at the **Bridge** by Richard Harris, his wife Caroline and their five children. He changed the lines to:

This bridge was built without hammer or addis
Come in and take a glass with R. Harris.

Throughout the 20th century the **Bridge Inn** has been run by a succession of publicans including John Garway, who served behind the bar during the 1920s, '30s and '40s. The **Bridge** remains a traditional pub, but with the addition of a modern restaurant that over-

The Bridge Inn, Kentchurch, 2001

looks the Monnow—an inn where fishing is promoted. From Kentchurch, the bridge leads across the Monnow into Wales, where up the hill was, until recently, an 'incredible little pub, a relic of bygone days' called the **Cupid** and, although 'over the border' deserves at least a small mention in this book. It was named after the Roman god of love, and when open was the place to drink and hear the local gossip. Sadly, the landlord Joe, well into his 80s, died in 2001 and the inn is now closed.

Not quite in the county, but a fond memory of the recent past—the Cupid

Continuing straight ahead from Kentchurch, the road climbs over a hill and drops into Pontrilas, still within Kentchurch parish. In 1858 Pontrilas was a 'hamlet, small village, and railway station ... distant from Kentchurch 2 miles north-west, on the Newport, Abergavenny and Hereford railway', Pontrilas was also the junction for the

Golden Valley line, a minor railway gem that meandered through Abbey Dore, Peterchurch and Dorstone, before dropping over the hill into the Wye valley at Hay-on-Wye. Never a profitable line, it opened in 1889 and finally closed in 1941. Following the arrival of the railway in 1853 Pontrilas grew rapidly into a laid-out village with a shop, timber merchants, a coal company, a chemical works and two inns. For almost a century Pontrilas had become an important place in the transport system of Herefordshire, but since then its station and inns have closed and even the main Hereford to Abergavenny road has been diverted around the village.

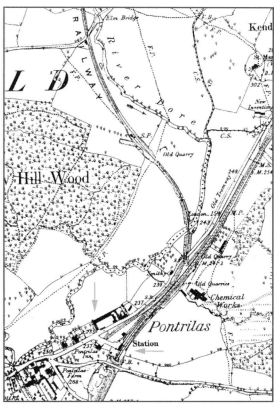

A section of the 1887 map showing the start of the Golden Valley line and the Pontrilas Inn (arrowed)

Due to pressures from the Temperance Movement in the late 19th century, Sunday closing of all public houses was adopted throughout Wales from 1881 until 1961. During this period the Herefordshire pubs on the Welsh Borders became frequented by Welshmen on the Sabbath. Pontrilas was easily accessible by road and rail from Wales, and charabancs of visiting Welshmen to the local pubs on a Sunday are well remembered.

There were two public houses in Pontrilas, each confusingly called the **Pontrilas Inn**, and by 1867 both were run by the same proprietor, Mr. William Jones. He changed the name of the larger inn to the **Scudamore Arms Hotel** and described it as 'a first-class hotel and private boarding house. It was formerly a baronial mansion, but is now fitted for the reception of gentlemen and families of position, with extensive rights of fishing in the River Monnow, one of the best trout streams in England'. Despite William's grand advertising and the expectancy of flocks of rail tourists, the trade was not there and the hotel closed around the mid-1870s.

1867 advertisement for the Scudamore Arms

The **Scudamore Arms Hotel** was housed in what had been Pontrilas Court, a gabled stone house of the early 17th century. In 1821 it was occupied by Sir George Shiffner, who put it up for sale as 'a very advantageous Property for Investment, being chiefly situated adjoining the turnpike road'. It was acquired by Colonel Lucas-Scudamore of Kentchurch Court and after his death it was placed on the market once again as 'A Tudor Manor House', described as 'modernised and containing four reception rooms and five principal and seven secondary bedrooms, complete offices; lighting and heating; stables and garage'. The whole estate comprised 'some 1,669 acres'. It obviously did not sell, as according to a directory entry for 1941, Pontrilas Court belonged to Mrs. Lucas-Scudamore and was the residence of Sir A.W. Keown-Boyd.

William Jones' other inn remained under the name of the **Pontrilas Inn** for many years, for it was a typical railway inn close to Pontrilas Station. At the beginning of the 20th

Pontrilas Court in the late 1920s

250

century this inn was run by the Davies family. However, to further confuse the story, in the 1920s the landlord, Mr. D. Davies, changed the name of this inn to the **Scudamore Arms**. In the 1940s William Henry Bishop, known as Harry, kept the **Scudamore Arms**. He was succeeded by his son Harold who was landlord until tragedy struck in December 1970. When Harold returned home after an evening function he saw flames, but before he realised what was happening, his inn was burnt down. Apparently he remarked to his companions 'sorry I can't offer you a drink tonight'. The *Hereford Times* reported:

> After a disastrous fire in the century-old Scudamore Arms at Pontrilas at midnight on Wednesday, customers had to go to nearby Ewyas Harold for a drink. The Pontrilas pub is the only one in the village.
> All that was left of the Scudamore Arms was the gutted shell. In the blaze Mr. Harold Bishop, owner of the house, lost all his personal possessions, his pet dog and most of the pub's stock was damaged.
> The fire was discovered at midnight by a passing motorist who telephoned the fire brigade. Mr. Bishop was not on the premises at the time and did not learn of the blaze until his return later in the night.
> The Ewyas Harold brigade was on the scene within six minutes and were followed by four other appliances—three from Hereford and one from Fownhope.
> Firemen fought the blaze nearly all night before bringing it under control. They left the scene at 9 a.m. on Thursday.
> Standing outside the blackened shell of his home, a distressed Mr. Bishop said he had offers from people in the district for accommodation. He did not yet know what he would do, but might stay with relatives.

The site of the inn was later redeveloped.

Throughout its life, the only direct competitor to the railway inn was the Pontrilas Coffee and Reading Room which was supervised by Miss Annie Powell in 1902. The only place where refreshments were available in Pontrilas during 2000 was at the garden centre.

Leaving Pontrilas, a minor road leading towards Orcop passes the former **Royal Oak Inn**, still in Kentchurch parish. This beer house, which was in the last cottage on the right, was run by Harriet Lewis during the 1870s and early '80s. A widow of 72 years at the time of the 1881 census, she ran the inn with help from her married daughter and her growing family. By 1902 Thomas James was the

The one-time Royal Oak at Kentchurch

innkeeper, and it appears that Daniel Vaughan was the last landlord at the **Royal Oak** before it closed during the First World War.

Nearby, at Llanithog, an extra parochial place with only a handful of inhabitants, John Nicholas was retailing cider from Llanithog Farm in 1851 before he became assistant overseer and road surveyor in 1858.

Continuing along the road towards Orcop, a left turning at Cross Lyde leads to Kilpeck, a small village with a fascinating past. The village dates from around 640 A.D. with the foundations of a Saxon church dedicated to St. Pedic. It was rebuilt in the 12th century by the Normans when they constructed the adjoining castle and laid out a small, defended village. Although the castle had been disused for some time and was finally destroyed during the Civil War, there are some scanty ruins. However, the church fortunately avoided destruction and, being in an isolated position, became almost forgotten until it was appreciated in 1810 as being a church that had been decorated in the style of the Herefordshire School of Sculpture. Since then its fascinating carved features have been carefully preserved and are much admired.

At Kilpeck the **Red Lion** survives as a wayside hostelry in a building that dates from the 17th century. A succession of landlords have certainly been serving refreshments to the community since the late 1880s. In 1881, John Johnson, his wife,

THE "RED LION" INN PUBLIC HOUSE,
Kilpeck.

Near St. Devereux Station on the Great Western Railway.

Brick and Slated Premises,

Comprising small Forecourt in front with Stable and Bake-house, Entrance Passage, Tap Room, Bar and Cellar, Larder, Parlour, Back Parlour and Two Bed Rooms, with Garden in the rear.

FREEHOLD. Let to Mr. George Powell at a Rent of **£19 : 10 : 0 per Annum.**

Sale of the Red Lion in 1898
by the Hereford Imperial Brewery

Eliza, and their three children were living at the inn. In the attractive bar a notice reads:

Ye Redde Lyonne Inne
Travellar, staye awhile thy feate,
And in thys Inne warme welcome meete,
Such fare as neede required thy wilt finde,
Wholesome and cheepe and to thy minde
Food served with courteous and quiet
(Goe elsewhere an thou lovest riot)

This awful rhyme continues, but of more interest are the old photographs displayed on the walls of the **Red Lion** and other Herefordshire scenes taken by Alfred Watkins. When he bought these prints, the landlord did not know that Charles and Alfred Watkins of the Hereford Imperial Brewery had purchased

Kilpeck's Red Lion in 2001

the **Red Lion** in 1890 from Mr. J. Johnson. By 1898 it became part of the Hereford and Tredegar Brewery, and in 1902 the **Red Lion** was run by George Powell, a carpenter and joiner. From at least 1913 and into the 1940s Alfred Batten was a long-term landlord at the **Red Lion**. In 1948 the 'messuage and public-house with the outbuildings, yard and garden thereto belonging known as the Red Lion Inn' was taken over by Cheltenham and Hereford Breweries Ltd.

In 1851 there was a **New Inn** at Marlas in Kilpeck. It was kept by the victualler, Edmund Lane, but no further record of this establishment has been traced.

Returning to the Pontrilas to Orcop road and continuing eastwards for a short distance brings the traveller to the Bagwyllydiart crossroads with the road to the right climbing up to the heights of Garway Hill, and that to the left having a similar climb to the slightly

The New Inn at Bagwyllydiart
Top : Otter hounds gathering
Bottom : The inn in 1967

Probably not a pub sign, but just a reminder of the Rising Sun

lower Orcop Hill. At the crossroads the former **New Inn** is on the right. It was occupied by William Meadmore in 1867 in competition to John Price a beer retailer and shopkeeper also at Bagwyllydiart. By 1881 Jane Smith, a 50-year-old widow, and her two young children were at the inn, followed by Mrs. Mary Ann Preece in 1891. The **New Inn** is just within Orcop parish, and was one of the many inns acquired by Alton Court Brewery. It managed to survive until after the Brewery sold it in 1962, but it has since been converted into a private house.

The small settlement at Garway Hill is in Orcop parish and standing in the shadow of the bracken clad slopes at 1,200 ft. above sea level is the former **Sun**, easily recognised by the present psychedelic sign, which probably dates to the 1970s when the adjoining cottage became a wholefood shop. The **Sun** had been a small beer house from about 1870 until around 1920 and was probably never very successful, Charles Morgan, the innkeeper in 1881, was also a general labourer, and was followed by John then Thomas Morgan. During its short life it became the **Rising Sun**, was acquired by the Watkins

Hereford Brewery, and was taken over by the Tredegar Brewery in 1898.

Almost opposite is a cottage which is still called the **Globe**, a reminder that this was an inn from about 1867 to the middle of the 20th century. In 1891 the 20-year-old Elizabeth Castree, who worked at the **Globe,** attempted to commit suicide by throwing herself into a tub of water, but was saved by her employer William Barrell. The **Globe** nearly lost its licence due to late night disturbances in 1871, and at the **Sun** a customer, Thomas Castree, was charged with assaulting another customer in 1894. He was given the choice of a 20s. fine or 14 days hard labour.

THE "RISING SUN" INN BEER HOUSE,
Garway Hill, Orcop,
About Five Miles from Pontrilas Railway Station.

A Stone and Slated House,

Containing Tap Room, Parlour, Kitchen, Wash-house, Three Bed Rooms, large piece of Garden ground behind fronting Road with stone-built Outhouse, Stable, Piggery and Dung-pit.

In the occupation of Mr. Thomas Morgan at a Rent of **£10 per Annum.**

A COTTAGE adjoining,

Containing General Shop, Back Kitchen with Oven, Kitchen, Parlour, Four Bed Rooms and small Yard.

Let to Mrs. Harriett Phillips, including part of the Garden, at **£6 per Annum.**

FREEHOLD.

Sale of the Rising Sun in 1898

The one-time Globe on Garway Hill

Returning to the Bagwylly-diart crossroads, the quiet road leads

The Lyons, a cider house at Orcop

through the centre of Orcop, described in 1912 as 'the remotest parish in Wormelow—itself perhaps the most secluded Hundred in the county. Off the main road, 6 miles from the nearest railway-station (Pontrilas), 9 from Ross, the nearest market and post town, $9^{1}/_{2}$ from Hereford, and 10 from Monmouth, it is no wonder that Orcop is popularly described

The 1821 sale of the Cross Keys at Orcop

as being 10 miles from anywhere. Its inaccessibility may possibly account for the kindliness of the inhabitants, if not for their healthy, handsome children'.

Before reaching Orcop Village Hall, a cottage on the left was a cider house called the **Lion Inn**, which was

The Cross Keys, now Church Cottage, in 1992

run by Mary Jones during the 1850s.

A right turn at the next crossroads leads to the church and to Church Cottage, a former public house called the **Cross Keys**, where the vicar formerly received his tithes. Its connection and close proximity to the church probably led to the pub's name, a popular sign

The Fountain Inn at Orcop in 1992

associated with Christianity. In 1821 the **Cross Keys** was occupied by Paul Meredith, and James Bevan appears to have served as the final victualler before the pub closed in the early 1850s. The cottage was later tenanted to John Barrell, a farmer, churchwarden and parish clerk before being completely refurbished in recent times.

Taking the opposite turn from the village crossroads, a gentle ascent leads to Orcop Hill where, thankfully, a popular pub is open and thriving. The **Fountain** is named after the spring of water that bursts out of the ground at the bottom of a grassy slope. The well, known as the copy well, was the only source of water available to the inhabitants of Orcop Hill until 1967 when mains water finally arrived. Previously the cottagers collected their water 'from the well to different homes each day in a variety of containers, buckets, tins, and even bottles'.

It appears that the **Fountain** replaced an earlier cider house in a dwelling adjoining the Baptist Chapel run by John Holly in 1841 and Edward Niblett in 1851. Edward was also a carpenter and shopkeeper, so needing more space moved to a larger premises opposite and established the present **Fountain** between 1851 and 1867. In 1894, when Henry Gazzard was in the midst of his long-term tenancy, the so-called 'beer-house keeper' was fined £2 for 'selling beer to be consumed in the highway'.

The Orcop Parish Council *Village Appraisal* of 1993 reported that the **Fountain** was 'very popular, with 75% of respondents indicating that they consider the **Fountain** is important to Orcop parish life and 25% taking the opposite view'. It was also noted in 1993 that: 'In any country area there is always an underlying fear that the village pub may close. When the time comes, one day, when the Fountain is put up for sale it seems the majority of Orcop people would be in favour of community ownership, as a way of stopping it being closed'. The three sisters who ran the **Fountain** so

The one-time Blue Boar, now Seabourne Cottage

The Seven Stars or Maltster's Arms which closed during the Great War

successfully in the late 1990s sold the inn to the new owners in 2001.

It has been suggested that Bramble Cottage at Orcop Hill, previously known as Seabourne Cottage was at one time the Blue Boar Inn, but so far no documentation has been found to verify this.

From Orcop Hill a narrow lane leads over Little Hill and after a sharp right-hand bend, at the junction of the road leading from Orcop, there is a white cottage that was known as the **Stars** in 1843. By 1851 it had become the **Seven Stars**, a beer and cider house run by James Whitehorn. His wife was called Hannah, and the couple's initials are on the datestone of the derelict blacksmith's forge. The inn's name was changed to the **Maltster's Arms** when James died, but was still kept by Hannah, with her son Thomas working in the forge. By 1890 Thomas had taken over the pub and was followed by Charles Allcroft who ceased serving beer soon after 1914 when the pub closed.

CHAPTER SEVENTEEN

North-west from Ross-on-Wye

Where the A49 Ross to Hereford road reaches Old Pike at Peterstow, the B4521 bears off westwards along a scenic route towards Abergavenny. This road follows a much altered course of a road that was turnpiked in 1772, and originally followed a maze of lanes to Crickhowell. By 1833 the local turnpike trust had clearly defined the road from Old Pike, through St. Owen's Cross, Tretire, Broad Oak and Skenfrith to Cross Ash, where it joined the turnpike road from Abergavenny.

St Owen's Cross in the 1920s.
The socket stone has symmetrical
hollows for kneeling

At St. Owen's Cross the Abergavenny road crosses a relatively modern route, the A4137, leading from the A49 near Pengethley to Old Forge in Goodrich. It was established as a turnpike road in 1819, and during its construction in Hentland parish the ancient earthwork at Gaer Cop was almost 'obliterated'. The remainder of the route cut through a tangled web of lanes and over a newly-built bridge and causeway across the Garron at Marstow before reaching Old Forge.

Until a few years ago a decorated sign marked the site

of St. Owen's Cross, which originally consisted of a mediaeval socket stone and shaft. Dominating the crossroads is the half-timbered **New Inn** built in the 17th century. Although of some considerable age, the inn was once new, and the name suggests the replacement of an earlier hostelry. There is some evidence to suggest that the 'New Inne at Crosse Owen' of 1540 stood slightly further west and was eventually replaced by the present building. A large two-storeyed barn, dating from the 17th century, once stood next to the inn, but in the motoring age it obscured the view, and after a serious accident involving Michael Foot MP in the early 1960s it was later demolished. The accident was reported in the *Hereford Times:*

> While heading back to London after a constituency weekend in Ebbw Vale, the Labour MP and his wife, Jill Craigie, decided to take a picturesque route through Herefordshire. At St. Owen's Cross, Jill failed to stop at the junction and a Lucozade lorry coming from the Hereford direction struck the side of the car. The couple were taken to the General Hospital, and in the biography *Michael Foot*, author Mervyn Jones relates how Foot, when lifted out of the ambulance, was able to say 'Mind you don't put me in a private ward'. Husband and wife were operated on during the night and Foot's life—his lungs had been pierced—was in the balance. He recovered consciousness after the operation just as a Salvation Army band in the street outside the hospital was playing 'Beulah Land, Sweet Beulah Land', a hymn that he had often heard in his Methodist boyhood. He knew the lines:
>
> *'I look away across the sea*
> *Where mansions are prepared for me'.*
>
> He was later to describe the experience: 'I thought for a few seconds, in my half-dream state, that the rendering was being given by a more celestial choir. Then the mist faded; someone arrived with a bed pan and I knew I was restored to the care of earthly angels'.
>
> After winning the battle Michael Foot was to declare: 'Hereford General Hospital is an institution devised by man; yet it came nearer to revealing supernatural powers than a confirmed rationalist like myself chooses to admit'.

During the latter half of the 20th century it became fashionable to change the common **New Inn** to something more trendier. For a short period in the 1980s the **New Inn** took on the name of **St. Owen's Cross**. This saint was alive in the mid-600s and became a monk then a bishop, and was canonised for his sanctity. The church in Hereford dedicated to St. Owen was destroyed during the Civil War, but the name survives in the parish and street name.

During the mid-19th century Ann and Francis Powell ran the **New Inn**, and in 1902

The New Inn in 1990

George Hyslop described his inn as the **New Inn Hotel**, a year before George Cooke moved in with his family. The Cookes kept pigs, cows, calves, poultry and a pony on the four acres of orchard and pasture. In the garden they built two greenhouses and planted wallflowers, forget-me-nots and geraniums which produced a 'blaze of colour most of the year round'. Whilst the Cookes were at the **New Inn** the Ross Harriers and the South Herefordshire Hunt met there at regular intervals, and at Christmas pigs were killed and salted, and poultry prepared and dressed for the festive season. Unfortunately under the Cookes occupancy the inn trade showed a consistent decline, so after 17 years they left in 1920 to purchase Old Court Farm at Lugwardine. George Cooke lived there until his death at the age of 100 years in 1960. Since then various landlords have kept the **New Inn** which is still open and thriving.

From the **New Inn** the Abergavenny road continues through Tretire, where no public houses have been recorded. This is hardly surprising as the population has always been quite small—in 1851 the total for the combined parish of Tretire with Michaelchurch was only 138. Beyond Tretire, the B4521 crosses the A466 at a rather nondescript crossroads. Turning right towards Hereford, the main road leads up the hill to St. Weonards, where a handsome 17th-century building, now the post office and village stores, was formerly the **Treago Arms**. The inn dates from at least 1795 and is named after the nearby Treago Castle, home of the Mynors family since the 14th century. The St. Weonards Friendly Society met at the **Treago Arms** from 1798 to 1839.

Now St. Weonards Post Office, this was once the Treago Arms

In 1875 the innkeeper James Jones gave evidence in court that Joseph Smith a labourer, was found drunk and abusive, and was reluctant to leave the inn. For this behaviour Smith was sentenced to three weeks 'hard labour', and it appears that the **Treago Arms** was closed shortly afterwards because of the 'riotous behaviour'. The property then became known as the Mount where Mrs. Elizabeth Williams ran a boarding house and a post office in 1941.

Returning to the Abergavenny road and on to Broad Oak, partly in Garway parish, a side road leads to a property now called Royal Elms, which is considered to have been the **Royal Standard**, a public house open in 1834. It became the property of Mrs. Ann South and, after a mortgage assignment of 1841, was purchased by Lord Southwell.

The **Broad Oak Inn** was built early in the 17th century with the porch added at a later date. Stories of the Civil War and ghostly horses are associated with the inn as told by Fred Bolt: 'Villagers have heard at night the sound of horses, on the road, and considering those quadruped are rare, can mean only one deduction—ghosts'. He continues that 'the nail-studded oak door, giving entrance to the lounge and bar, that many centuries have seen Cromwell's soldiers, local ploughmen, even the Protector himself, crossing the threshold'. Fred claims he saw 'a metal token, in shape reminiscent of the Boy Scout's badge, which we are told was left by Cromwell to show he had been there'. Discovered in a room named after Cromwell was 'a blocked-up space in the wall, used by a Cavalier, when the Ironsides were seeking for men'.

All this seems a bit far-fetched, but according to a more realistic source written by the Rev. John Webb in 1879, the nearest Civil War activities took place at Much Dewchurch during 1643 involving the Pye family at the Mynd. Similar to other large houses it 'came to be strengthened and were in process of time converted into garrisons'. Unfortunately for Sir Walter Pye, he 'lived to about the Restoration in poverty and obscurity'.

In 1840 Sarah Vaughan occupied the 'Broad Oak House Garden Fold etc'. She was followed by Henry Vaughan described as the victualler at the **Oak** in 1851, which became the **Broad Oak Inn** during his long stint at the pub. In 1881 John Powell and his family were living at the **Broad Oak**, but Henry Vaughan, an uncle, was the innkeeper and remained so until the 1890s when the Powells took over, and the Manor of Garway, Court Leet and Court Baron was held at the **Broad Oak** in

Broad Oak House—once the inn—in 2001

1891, and Furniture Sales in 1899. When Albert Okey was landlord in 1927 he applied for extended opening hours from 2.30 p.m. to 6 p.m. on Easter Monday. From 1916 he and other innkeepers were tenants of the Alton Court Brewery. The brewery sold the public house to West Country Breweries in 1962.

The country recollections of the past are remembered 'not so far back, lighted by night with lamps, settles, and one common bar, and visitors ... seldom'. It all dramatically changed under the supervision of Mr. and Mrs. Rudge in the 1960s and '70s who provided a 'modern public bar and lounge' and served 'meals and summer teas on the lawn'. In its final years it had become a comfortable and cosy pub renowned for its food. In 1982 the owners won the 'Dish of the Year' award for their 'Broad Oak Casserole', but after a change of ownership the **Broad Oak Inn** was closed. The present Broad Oak House was the former inn.

Beyond the crossroads at Broad Oak on a sharp bend in the road is a building that was once the **Southwell Arms**, a modest successor of

BROAD OAK, GARWAY,

HEREFORDSHIRE.

Particulars of Sale

OF

All that SMALL HOLDING

AND

BEERHOUSE,

CALLED

"The Southwell Arms,"

with useful buildings, orcharding and pasture lands containing

8a. - 2r. - 29p.

or thereabouts, which

MR. H. P. BARNSLEY

WILL OFFER FOR SALE BY AUCTION, AT

THE LAW SOCIETY'S HALL, EAST STREET, HEREFORD,

On WEDNESDAY, the 26th APRIL, 1922

at **3-30** o'clock in the Afternoon.

Subject to Conditions of Sale, including the Common Form Conditions of the Herefordshire Incorporated Law Society.

To view, apply on the Premises, and for further particulars to the AUCTIONEER, PALACE CHAMBERS, KING STREET, HEREFORD, or to

Messrs. E. L. WALLIS & SON,
Solicitors,
HEREFORD.

Sale of the Southwell Arms—a simple beerhouse—in 1922

the original inn a little further along the road. Despite being closed as a public house for many years it still bears the name. In 1873 James Morris, a shopkeeper and haulier applied for a beerhouse licence for the **Southwell Arms** which is also just in Garway parish. He had died before the 1881 census took place and his wife, Ellen, was the head of the household and keeper of the public house. It continued to be run by various members of the Morris family until 1922 when the 'Small Holding and Beerhouse' was sold to the Alton Court Brewery for £500. As there is no further mention of this beerhouse, it must have been closed by the brewery.

Further towards Skenfrith, the road passes a tall, elegant house. Now called Southwell Court, this was the original

The two Southwell Arms.
Top : now Southwell Court;
Bottom : the former beerhouse

Southwell Arms—a coaching inn established on the turnpike road some time before 1813. By 1840 William Dew was the victualler, and probably served as the last innkeeper before the **Southwell Arms** closed, to be replaced by the beerhouse of the same name. Both were named after Viscount Southwell who was Lord of the Manor during the 19th century.

On the opposite side of the road in the grounds of Darren Cottage is the overgrown foundations of a dwelling that is said to have been the **Darren** beer or cider house. A story exists that the pub's horse and dog were so friendly that they were inseparable, so when they died the animals shared the same burial place; their bones were discovered at a later date and left undisturbed. Beyond Darren Cottage the road

265

crosses the Monnow and passes into Monmouthshire, where the refurbished and extended **Bell** at Skenfrith, once belonging to Alton Court Brewery, serves the many visitors to Skenfrith castle and church.

The other high road leading north-westwards from Ross is the B4348, a road that eventually passes through the Golden Valley on its way to Hay-on-Wye. This road leaves the main A49 Ross to Hereford road at Llandinabo and bypasses Llanwarne on its way to Wormelow where it crosses the A466 Hereford to Monmouth road. Here the **Tump Inn** is still open and in the bar a notice informs the customers that the 'inn takes its name from the burial mound or tumulus that used to lie almost opposite' and continues that 'Men came to measure the tumulus which was sometimes 6 ft. or 9 ft. or sometimes even 12 ft. or 15 ft. Legend has it that in whatever measure you measure it in, the second time you would not find the same measurement'. By tradition, the tump was the burial place of Arthur's son Anir, but this did not stop it being removed in the 19th century for road widening.

The **Tump Inn**, which is in Much Birch parish, was built in 1778 by William Parrott, and, as indicated by the date stone, was opened in 1780. In 1812 the **Wormelow Tump Inn** was being used for auction sales, and in 1835 the victualler, John Mason, was made a Freeman of the City of Hereford. He was followed at the inn by Thomas then James Smith and either the 81-year-old James or his 29-year-old son of the same name saw the pub into the 20th century.

In 1933 the **Wormelow Tump Hotel** was offered for sale, but the highest bid of £2,700 did not reach the reserve so the property was withdrawn. In the sale particulars the **Tump** was described as a 'well-known and exceedingly popular house' which had been 'recently modernised throughout by the owner'. After this attempted sale it may have remained in the same family for Charles Smith was the landlord in 1941.

The Wormelow Tump Inn in 2001

WORMELOW

HEREFORDSHIRE

PARTICULARS of

A VALUABLE AND ATTRACTIVE MODERN

Freehold Fully Licensed Free House

KNOWN AS

"WORMELOW TUMP HOTEL"

On WEDNESDAY, MAY 10th, 1933.

Situate at WORMELOW, directly opposite Bryngwyn Mansion, on the main Hereford—Monmouth Road and at the cross roads to Allensmore and Ross, 7 Miles from Hereford and Ross, commanding an excellent trade and being a well-known and exceedingly popular house.

The Hotel adjoins the Kennels of the South Herefordshire Hunt and is also a listed R.A.C. house.

The Property, which has a Drive in for cars, is substantially built of Stone and has been recently modernised throughout by the owner.

The Rooms are all light and cheerful, the accommodation being conveniently arranged and comprising :—

ENTRANCE PASSAGE with Porch ;

BAR ;

LARGE SMOKE ROOM fitted with Register Grate and Picture Rail, with door giving access to SNUGGERY ;

LOUNGE, fitted with modern Register Grate ;

PRIVATE SITTING ROOM, fitted with Oak Mantelpiece, modern Register Grate and Hot-Water Boiler ;

SMALL TEA ROOM ;

KITCHEN, with Stove, Dresser, Glazed Sink and Drainer ;

STORE ROOM, with Concrete Floor ;

LARGE CLUB ROOM ;

FIVE EXCELLENT BEDROOMS and MODERN BATHROOM fitted with Bath, Lavatory Basin and W.C. ;

GOOD CELLARAGE with Concrete Floor and 2 Skid Ways.

There is a pleasant LAWN with Rustic Work and on the other side of the Property is a commodious Stone-built GARAGE with double Doors at both ends ; Urinal ; KITCHEN GARDEN, and an Excellent

PASTURE ORCHARD

well stocked with choice FRUIT TREES, and having a valuable BUILDING FRONTAGE of approximately 400 feet, the whole property extending to an area of

2 acres   1 rood   27 perches

(or thereabouts).

Solicitors :	Auctioneer :
Messrs. FREELAND & PASSEY,	H. P. BARNSLEY, F.A.I.
Athenæum Chambers,	Palace Chambers, King Street,
71, Temple Row, Birmingham.	Hereford.

Sale of the Wormelow Tump Inn in 1933

In Tump Lane, close to the inn, the Violette Szabo G.C. Museum opened at Cartref in 2000. Violette was the first woman to be awarded the George Cross for her dangerous work with the SOE (Special Operations Executive) during World War Two. She was captured and executed by the Germans in 1945, but had previously stayed at Cartref during her training. A six mile trail has been established by the Special Forces Association leading from the **Graftonbury Garden Hotel**, near Hereford. The trail leads through splendid countryside to the museum and the **Tump Inn**.

The B4348 Hay-on-Wye road continues from Wormelow to Much Dewchurch where the old **Black Swan** is in the middle of the village. The building dates from the 15th century, and originally formed part of

A cut-away of the Black Swan as it was c.1650

Sale of the Black Swan by the Alton Court Brewery

the Bishop of Gloucester's episcopal estate in Herefordshire. It was known as 'Dubberleys' and between 1704 and 1743 was 'converted into an Inn commonly called or known by the Name of the Swan' by Anthony Stephens.

Stories of the Civil War are traditionally associated with the **Black Swan**. During the war the Mynde estate in Much Dewchurch was owned by Sir Robert Pye, a leading Parliamentarian and politician. In 1642 the Mynde was seized and fortified by the Royalists. It was later abandoned and slighted, and at least two soldiers lost their lives as recorded in the parish registers. Francis Lee was 'a poor may[n]ed soldier' buried in 1644, and 'John A_____' was 'sore wounded' and was buried the following year.

Since the 19th century, innkeepers have carried out some research into the history of this interesting building. In 1835 Thomas Mason, probably related to John Mason at the **Wormelow Tump Inn,** was made a Freeman of Hereford. He was followed at the **Swan** by Allen Smith then William Sparks in 1851. Apart from acting as publican, William was also a tailor and draper. After the death of his first wife and daughter, he remarried and by 1861 his family had expanded to eight children all under the age of 13. In 1881 William and his wife Ann Elizabeth were left with only one child and a lodger at the inn.

The Alton Court Brewery purchased the **Black Swan** in 1902, and during their

The Black Swan early in the 20th century

269

ownership discovered early frescoes painted on the wooden bars of a window. This rare find was removed for safe-keeping in Hereford Museum before the *Woolhope Club* paid a visit to the **Black Swan** in 1927:

The earlier portion of the house, composed of timber framing with the exception of the chimney stack which is of stone, consists of an entrance passage running north and south with ceiling joists of the same pattern as others to be mentioned presently, and to the left of this passage entering it from the south is a room with the east and west walls formed of upright timbers and panels and an original doorway leading into it from the passage. Another original doorway in the north end of the west wall leads into another room with heavy moulded timber beams in the southern portion carrying the floor above and a large fireplace in the west wall, and to the south of this in the same wall was discovered the window opening with wooden bars mentioned above, which may possibly have belonged to an earlier building. A partition ran across this room from east to west, the timber joists of the ceiling being less elaborate than those in the adjoining portion. To the north of the chimney stack against the west wall is an annex which apparently contained a garderobe and the stairway to the upper rooms, but if so the latter has been reconstructed as a spiral stairway in the seventeenth century. There are two plain small slot windows for ventilation and light in this annex. The upper south room of this once gabled end portion has ceiling joists of the same pattern as the passage way downstairs, but these joists have all been turned upside down to obtain a better fixing surface for a plastered ceiling. In the seventeenth century the house was enlarged by building another gabled end to the east of the passage entrance, with a stone chimney stack, and rooms above and below, and a spiral staircase of stone in the lower part and timber above in the same relative position as at the other end of the house. At the same period a room was built between the two gabled wings which extend on the north side beyond the original fifteenth century central room, but are flush with this room on the south side. The roofs unfortunately have all been reconstructed possibly in the eighteenth century. It has been suggested that the house dates from the fifteenth century, but the plan and details might rather favour some time in the earlier part of the sixteenth century for its erection.

The inn is known affectionately by the locals as the **Dirty Duck** because of its sign, which the Rev. Moir explained in the *Woolhope Club Transactions* of 1963:

The heraldic swan was white, but the black swan was introduced as a fanciful variation, and it came as a surprise when an actual black swan was imported from Australia. The **Black Swan** at Much Dewchurch according to the manager Mr. John Bishop, started as a white swan or sitting swan, and was changed into a black swan in compliment to the owner of the Mynde, Mr. Symonds, who had visited Australia, the home of this bird. Ornithologists might complain that the beak is yellow instead of red.

The Black Swan sign in the 1960s

Within three miles of Much Dewchurch village, but still in the parish, is the **Tram Inn** at the level crossing of the B4348 with Hereford to Newport railway line. It is reputed to have been originally built in 1794, but it is more likely to have been erected at the same time as the Abergavenny to Hereford horsedrawn tramway which opened in 1829. In 1841 James Barnett occupied the 'Tram House, Malthouse, Gardens and Buildings'. After the tramway closed in 1853, the line was taken over by the Newport, Abergavenny, and Hereford Railway with Thomas Fisher at the **Tram House Commercial Inn**. He was in a good business situation to serve passengers using the Tram Inn Railway Station, and to sell coal delivered by rail. Apparently the **Tram Inn** was rebuilt in 1868 as a railway inn. In 1881 John Prosser, a coal agent, occupied the inn with his wife and three young children. He was still there in 1902 as 'subpostmaster, innkeeper, coal and lime merchant, and agent for

The Tram Inn in the early years of the 20th century

Hadfield's manures, post office, Tram Inn'. The inn appears to be open despite the station being closed for passengers in 1958.

Although the **Three Horse Shoes** is also in Much Dewchurch parish, it is on the western side of the Hereford to Abergavenny road and will therefore be included in yet another volume of Herefordshire pubs.

Sources & References

In the following lists the sources are given in date of publication order where appropriate.

GENERAL WORKS
The Torrington Diaries, Hon. J. Byng, 1781 – 87
Camden's Britannia, 1806 edn
The Book of Trades, 1811
Rural Rides, W. Cobbett, 1853 edn
Cider, Nat. Assoc. of Cider Makers, 1980
The Local Historian's Encyclopaedia, J. Richardson, 1981
Ripest Apples, R. Palmer, 1996
Victualler's Licences, J. Gibson & J. Hunter, 2000

THE COUNTY
Ross Guide, 1827
Excursion Down the Wye, C. Heath, 1828
Walks & Talks of an American Farmer, F. Olmsted, 1850
The Tourists Guide to the Wye, T. Smith, 1855
Handbook to Ross, G. Strong, 1863
Memorials of the Civil War, Rev. J. Webb, 1879
The Wye Tour, J.A. Stratford, 1896
Wye Valley*, 1905*
An Inventory of the Historical Monuments in Herefordshire, vol. I, SW, 1930; vol. II, E, 1931
Two Historic Parishes, F. Cape, 1930
Ross, A. Greer, c1930
Wye Valley Guide, 1930
Holidays at Hereford, 1930, 1931
Fownhope, E.F. Gange, 1950
Guy's Hospital Herefordshire Estates, 1961
The Buildings of England : Herefordshire, N. Pevsner, 1963
One Hundred Years, D. Prosser, 1975
Daughter of Wyedean, J. Stonham, 1978
A Good Plain Country Town, F. Druce, 1980
Weston & Lea, B. Cave, 1982
Old Industrial Sites in Wyedean, A. Cross, 1982
Lugwardine in the 19th Century, 1988
The Herefordshire Village Book, W.I., 1989
Kings Thorn Community Handbook, K. Compton edn, 1984
South Herefordshire Guide, 1987
The Palin Assignment, Rev. A. Ricketts, 1991
The History of Aston Ingham, M. Watson, 1991
The Folklore of Hereford, R. Palmer, 1992
The Old Roads of South Herefordshire, H. Hurley, 1992

Ancient Dean, B. Walters, 1992
Orcop, D. Coleman, 1992
Between the Wars, Linton History Soc., 1993
The Healing Wells of Herefordshire, J. Sant, 1994
The Wye Valley Walk, H. & J. Hurley, 1994
The Folklore of Gloucestershire, R. Palmer, 1994
Kings Caple in Archenfield, E. Taylor, 1997
The Story of Ross, P. Hughes & H. Hurley, 1999
Herefordshire Cider Route, Herefordshire. Council, 1999
Historical Aspects of Ross, Ross-on-Wye Civic Society, 2000
The History of Bill Mills, H. Hurley, 2001

JOURNALS & NEWSPAPERS ETC.
Transactions of the Woolhope Naturalists' Field Club, 1922 - 1995
Herefordshire Archaeology Newsletter, 1989
Ross Civic Society Newsletter, 1985, 1986
Hereford Record Office Friends Newsletter, 1997
Four in One, 1984
Wye Valley Countryside Service Newsletter, 1986
Wye Valley Journal, 1987
Herefordshire Field Name Surveys
Herefordshire Directories, 1794 - 1987
Hereford Journal
Hereford Times
Ross Gazette

INNS, TAVERNS & BREWERIES
Forest Steam Brewery Sale, 1923
Wintle's Brewery Sale, 1937
Arnold Perrett Sale, 1937
Your Local, Whitbread & Co., 1947
Hereford & Tredegar Brewery Sale, 1948
Drink, A. Simon, 1948
The Brewer's Art, B. Brown, 1949
A Taste of Ale, R. Palmer, 2000
The Old Inns of England, A. Richardson, 1952
Inns of Herefordshire, Bulmer's, 1959
200 Years of Brewing in the West Country, West Country Brewery, 1960
Stroud Brewery Sale, 1962
Alton Court Brewery Sale, 1962
British Inn Signs, E. Delderfield, 1965
The Inns & Friendly Societies of Monmouth, E. Davies & K. Kissack, 1981
100 Herefordshire Pubs, J. Hurley, 1984
Real Ale & Cider in Herefordshire, I. Wraight & M. Dyer, 1985
Pub Names, L. Dunkling & G. Wright, 1987
Brewing Industry, L. Richmond & A. Turton, 1990
Historic Inns and Taverns of the Welsh Marches, P. Davies, 1993
Paths & Pubs of the Wye Valley, H. & J. Hurley, 1998
The Pubs of Hereford City, R. Shoesmith, 1998
The Pubs of Leominster, Kington and north-west Herefordshire,
      R. Shoesmith and R. Barrett, 2000

Index of Inn Names

In the following index common names are used—others are cross-referenced. Adjectival descriptions are normally used except for 'new' and 'old'. To avoid confusion the parish or village is shown for country inns; in Ross the street is shown. Only the main entries are indexed.